THE ETHIOPIAN ECONOMY
1974–94

THE
ETHIOPIAN ECONOMY
1974–94

Ethiopia Tikdem and After

Göte Hansson

London and New York

First published 1995
by Routledge
11 New Fetter Lane, London EC4P 4EE

Simultaneously published in the USA and Canada
by Routledge
29 West 35th Street, New York, NY 10001

© 1995 Göte Hansson

Typeset in Times by
Solidus (Bristol) Limited
Printed and bound in Great Britain by
Mackays of Chatham PLC, Chatham, Kent

British Library Cataloguing in Publication Data
A catalogue record for this book is available from the British Library

Library of Congress Cataloguing in Publication Data
A catalogue record for this book has been requested

ISBN 0–415–13071–9

For Ethiopia with her 13 months of sunshine
and
for my dear wife Britt-Marie who is the sunshine of my life

CONTENTS

FIGURES

FIGURES

x

TABLES

PREFACE

This study of Ethiopia is based on information collected during my work on reports produced for the Swedish International Development Authority (SIDA) since 1989 (see the list of references). In 1988 I was asked to lead a research team at Lund University set up to follow and analyse economic development in some of the major recipient countries of Swedish aid. I took advantage of the privilege to look closer at a country that I have heard and read about since my early years in school. I have never regretted that choice.

Since 1988 I have made regular visits to Ethiopia, and during that time many interesting political and economic changes have been announced, tried, failed and, in some cases, successfully introduced and implemented. The present study tries to tell an economist's story of what took place in the Ethiopian economy during the 1970s and 1980s and of the reform process that has just been started with the objective of improving the overall situation for Ethiopia and its people. It is important to stress that the picture I give of this development is personal. It wants to communicate to the reader what I believe, from the point of view of my economic professional knowledge, are the most important man-made factors that led Ethiopia to a situation of deep economic crisis in the late 1980s and the beginning of the 1990s. The same is true of course for my choice of focus on what is now going on in the Ethiopian economy.

Writing a study like this as a foreigner means that one must rely more heavily than otherwise on others' analyses and descriptions. This is a weakness since the writer's degree of participation in the development of the society is naturally very limited. A lot of inherited values, knowledge, and cultural aspects that are of great importance for the development of a country are difficult if not impossible to obtain purely from written documents and interviews. On the other hand, it may be an advantage in some ways to have an outsider's view of what is going on. The reason is to be found in the same set of factors. It may be easier for a foreigner to take a neutral view when his or her own relations to the subject under analysis are not so deeply rooted.

In the present case, my reading of other researchers' analyses has been supplemented with several interviews and consultations with people working in Ethiopia. Thereby I hope to have overcome some of the disadvantages of not being a native. I take this opportunity to express my deep gratitude to all those, in ministries, political parties, and in the University of Addis Ababa who in various ways have provided me with material and other types of information of crucial importance for my research.

This study would not have been possible without moral, material, and financial support from the Planning Secretariat and the Office of Eastern and Western Africa at SIDA headquarters in Stockholm. In particular the officers handling the daily issues of aid to Ethiopia should be mentioned. The financial support from the Institute of Economic Research in the School of Economics and Management at Lund University is also gratefully acknowledged.

The most important people in building my network in Ethiopia and providing me with continuous information about the developments in Ethiopia have been Göran Engstrand, the economist at SIDA Addis Ababa during my first year of work with Ethiopia, and his successor Claes Norrlöf. I owe both the greatest gratitude. Claes Norrlöf has always been there to help me to fill gaps in information, provide professional comments on my reports and over the years has also developed into what I count as a friend. The latter also goes for other people at the SIDA office in Addis Ababa headed by Karl Gunnar Hagström up to mid-1994. I would also like to express my gratitude to the former Swedish Ambassador to Ethiopia, Birgitta Karlström-Dorph, who always showed great interest in my work and briefed me on the political situation during my visits, and to Eva-Carin Norrlöf who, besides making practical arrangements in relation to my visits, has shown great hospitality and made me feel welcome in Addis Ababa and in her and Claes' home for pleasant lunches and dinners.

Receiving moral support and open criticism from colleagues at the home department are privileges that I have benefited largely from in this work. In particular I would like to express my deep gratitude to associate professor Yves Bourdet who has read and commented on both this and previous studies that I have written about Ethiopia, to assistant professor Johan Torstensson who read and commented on the more analytical parts of the study, and to my doctoral student Hans Falck who has always been willing to assist me in my work and has read and commented on the complete draft of this study.

I would also like to express my gratitude to my colleagues at the Department of Political Science at Lund University, in particular professors Lars-Göran Stenelo and Christer Jönsson, associate professors Magnus Jerneck, Håkan Magnusson, and Torbjörn Vallinder who have provided general reading material in political science and through interesting discussions and joint lectures have tried to teach me about the political aspects of life. Hopefully some of the results from this learning can be seen in this study. I have also benefited from the generosity shown by the Department of Economics, Nottingham University and my colleagues in CREDIT for their hospitality during the weeks I spent there during my work on this study.

Finally, I would like to thank Mrs Patricia Wetterberg who has helped me with my English.

Of course, the above-mentioned people, all of whom I admire and thank for their friendship and help, have no responsibility for remaining errors. These are all due to my own shortcomings.

Göte Hansson
Lund, December 1994

1

INTRODUCTION

BACKGROUND

Ethiopia Tikdem (Ethiopia First) was the central slogan in the political rhetoric of Ethiopia during the period when the country was governed by socialist principles. It was also used by the president to end proclamations, such as announcements of new legislation, up to mid-1991 when the socialist government led by Mengistu Haile-Mariam was defeated. The slogan as such was first introduced in 1974 to mark the introduction of a new leadership and a new policy in Ethiopia following the revolution in that year. This completely urban-based revolution occurred as a reaction to the existing feudal society and in particular to Emperor Haile Selassie's life of luxury at a time when poverty and starvation were increasing among the masses. Haile Selassie and his government had not only created great inequalities but had also proved incapable or unwilling to combat poverty, in particular among those affected by the drought (see, for instance, Schwab 1985: 14ff, Goyder and Goyder 1988, Dawit Woldi Giorgis 1989: chapter 1, Clapham 1990: 32ff, Tiruneh 1993: chapter 2).

It is worth noting that *Ethiopia Tikdem* was in fact introduced by the new leadership, the Coordination Committee of the Armed Forces, Police and the Territorial Army (the Derg), on 4 July and published on 10 July 1974, i.e. before the actual overthrow of Haile Selassie on 12 September 1974 (Schwab 1985: 24f, Dawit Wolde Giorgis 1989: 14, Clapham 1990: 40, Tiruneh 1993: 66).

The essence of the new policy introduced under the motto *Ethiopia Tikdem* was that the common good should be paramount over other more special interests, such as the interests of the individual or of ethnic or regional groups. The famines in Ethiopia during the last decades of Haile Selassie's reign cost the lives of millions of Ethiopians (Goyder and Goyder 1988).

Initially, the *Ethiopia Tikdem* policy document did not contain any programme for changing the Ethiopian economic system. Instead, its thirteen sections dealt with such issues as

1

allegiance to the King and Crown, cabinet reform, the trial of the corrupt and inept officials, speedy implementation of the draft constitution, close collaboration with the cabinet, the continuation of humanitarian aid to the drought-affected people, foreign aid from friendly countries in general and expansion of tourism.

(Tiruneh 1993: 66)

An explicit objective was also to protect the unity of Ethiopia and to help the people to participate in the process of development. Furthermore, nationalism and equality were to be the governing principles, replacing the discrimination along national and religious lines that had been a major characteristic of Ethiopian society for so long (Tiruneh 1993: 66).

The second important policy statement of the new government came on 20 December 1974 when a declaration on Ethiopian socialism was presented and summarised in a ten-point programme. In this statement the slogan *Ethiopia Tikdem* was again central and emphasised prevention of the exploitation of the Ethiopian people, equality, government control, state ownership, self-reliance, and the indivisibility of Ethiopia's unity (*The Declaration on Economic Policy of Socialist Ethiopia* (DEP) 1975, Eshetu Chole and Makonnen Manyazewal 1992: 8).

Having adopted this ten-point programme, the Derg immediately started to implement its socialist ambitions and on 20 April 1976 a third important policy statement was released, *The National Democratic Revolutionary Programme of Ethiopia* (NDRPE) (Tiruneh 1993: 159f). This programme, which should be seen as a complement to the two previous ones, aimed at governing the process of transition to socialism (Schwab 1985: 34, Tiruneh 1993: 160). According to the announcement in the *Ethiopian Herald* on 21 April 1976 by the then leader of the Derg, Mengistu Haile-Mariam, the primary goals of the new policy were the 'elimination of feudalism, bureaucratic capitalism and imperialism' (quoted from Schwab 1985: 34).

It is clear that changing from a highly feudal aristocratic economy to a socialist country would meet with opposition from various political forces. In Ethiopia criticism came both from within the Derg and from outside, in particular from members of the Ethiopian People's Revolutionary Party (EPRP), the Confederation of Ethiopian Labour Unions (CELU), and the London-based Ethiopian Democratic Union (EDU) (Schwab 1985: 40f, Tiruneh 1993: chapter 5). However, the new Ethiopian leaders, and in particular Mengistu Haile-Mariam, were sincere in their desire to carry through the socialist-inspired programmes, and as a consequence, criticism was not accepted. Whenever opposition appeared it was combated efficiently, frequently through the execution of the opponents.

The process of eliminating opposition against the revolution and the ambitions contained in the *Ethiopia Tikdem* policy started in November 1974 when sixty aristocrats and Ethiopian notables were killed (Schwab 1985: 36).

Perhaps the most remarkable and clear demonstration that Mengistu was completely committed to the new strategy and would brook no opposition whatsoever, took place at a Derg meeting on 3 February 1977 when Mengistu, and his closest colleagues, executed seven other leading Derg members (Schwab 1985: 37, Clapham 1990: 56f, Tiruneh 1993: 190ff). In line with this attitude towards opposition, in May 1977 'five hundred students were rounded up and executed' (Schwab 1985: 40) and on 18 November 1977 Mengistu introduced a cleansing campaign called 'red terror' aiming at eliminating what was labelled the 'white terror' of EPRP.

The cleansing operations of the red terror cost the lives of thousands of urban Ethiopians and by early 1978 efficient open opposition had finally been eliminated (Schwab 1985: 40ff, Clapham 1990: 56f, Africa Watch 1991: chapter 6, Tiruneh 1993: 208–14 and 232ff).

For the Ethiopian economy, the reforms and policy measures introduced under the motto *Ethiopia Tikdem* had far-reaching implications. In the ten-point declaration on Ethiopian socialism in December 1974 it was clearly stated that the Derg aimed at a dramatic economic restructuring away from the imperial feudal-type of economic system which had prevailed under the Emperor Haile Selassie, to a socialist economic system where the resources crucial for economic development or for the provision of indispensable services were to be controlled or owned by the State (*The Declaration on Economic Policy of Socialist Ethiopia* 1975: 1). The ambitions of the Derg to reform the Ethiopian economy by introducing socialism were further developed in subsequent years, the first major reform being the land reform issued in April 1975 (Dessalegn Rahmato 1984, Kirsch *et al.* 1989: chapter 4, Clapham 1990: 41ff).

The Derg faced a number of problems in making the Ethiopian people act in accordance with the motto *Ethiopia Tikdem*. Even if open opposition could be stopped effectively by means of executions and imprisonments, people could not be forced to be committed and motivated beyond a certain limit. It soon became clear that the economic problems that were paramount in 1974, in particular for the poor sections of society, were increasing along with the implementation of the *Ethiopia Tikdem* policy and the escalating civil war. By mid-1991 the economy of Ethiopia and its people was in a state of deep crisis.

Eventually, after seventeen years of military rule, Marxist–Leninist socialism, growing economic problems, and an escalating civil war, the Ethiopian president Mengistu Haile-Mariam fled the country on 21 May 1991. One week later, on 28 May, after unsuccessful peace negotiations in London, the Ethiopian People's Revolutionary Democratic Front, EPRDF, took power by walking into a largely undefended Addis Ababa.

In the first week of July, the new leaders called for a National Conference on Peace and Democracy where the institutional framework for the immediate future of Ethiopia was discussed with representatives from the various liberation movements. It was decided that the United Nations Universal Declaration of Human Rights should be applied in Ethiopia and that a transitional government, consisting of a Council of Representatives and a Council of Ministers, should rule the country for the two coming years of transition. It was decided that this transitional period was to be terminated when there had been a democratic election of a new parliament and a new democratic government. The Eritrean people were to be given the right to decide whether they wanted their country to become a sovereign state or to continue to be a region within Ethiopia. After such a referendum on 23–25 April 1993, on 24 May Eritrea declared itself an independent sovereign state and four days later Eritrea became a member of the United Nations.

It is worth noting that the Council of Representatives, with eighty-seven representatives, consisted of members from various ethnic groups, regional movements, and political organisations. Thus, in a sense, in 1991 Ethiopia took a leap from being a one-party State led by one person, Mengistu Haile-Mariam, to becoming a multi-party State which had entered on the path towards democracy. The above-mentioned political change resulted in expectations for and introduction of quite far-reaching changes in the Ethiopian economic system.

As will be shown below, during the seventeen years of socialist rule, the Ethiopian economy degenerated from a highly problematic but relatively stable and balanced macroeconomic situation to an economy in deep distress. As in the former Soviet Union and Eastern Europe, economic realities led to the conclusion that changes to the economic system had to be introduced in Ethiopia. Economic reforms were also announced and, in varying degrees, implemented after November 1988. However, it should be noted that the reforms were not consistently developed and seriously implemented until the fall of the Mengistu government in 1991 and the concomitant abandonment of the motto *Ethiopia Tikdem.*

AIM OF THE STUDY

The transformation of Ethiopian society from imperial feudalism to socialism has been the subject of numerous studies, most of them by political scientists, historians, geographers, and sociologists. There have been comparatively few studies that have focused on and critically analysed the changes in the economic system and their effects on the overall economic performance in socialist Ethiopia. Recently, however, there has been an increase in the number of publications on the Ethiopian economy and its performance (*Ethiopian Journal of Economics*, Ottaway 1990, Griffin 1992, Mekonen Taddesse 1992, Berhanu Abegaz 1994). The aim of this study is to add to this literature by focusing on changes to the economic system and their respective effects on the Ethiopian economy during the period 1974–1994.

As political, social, and economic development go hand in hand and are mutually dependent on each other, this study will use the existing political and historical analyses of the transition from feudalism to socialism in Ethiopia as a basis for the analysis of economic policy and performance in post-revolutionary, socialist Ethiopia. In terms of policy we have already noted that there was a transformation of the economic system in Ethiopia from the ancient feudal economy to an economy based on socialist ideology and principles. In terms of economic performance the *Ethiopia Tikdem* period can be characterised as a time when the Ethiopian economy moved from a very problematic situation with low, but positive, growth rates and repeated severe famines, to a long-lasting economic crisis with negative growth rates and rapidly increasing imbalances in both fiscal and current accounts. Famines and an escalating civil war continued to cost not only rapidly increasing amounts of economic resources but also the lives of millions of people.

In seeking the causes of the deterioration of the Ethiopian economy, Clapham (1990: 186) states that

> any attempt to assign causes, or responsibility, for the decline in agricultural production per head which culminated in the catastrophe of 1984–85 is subject not only to a high level of emotive argument and political special pleading, but also to the impossibility of ascribing specific weights to any one of a cluster of interlocking environmental, social, economic and political variables.

This is naturally true since development, and thereby also lack of development, is not a function of just one single factor, but is the result of a complex interplay of numerous factors. In particular, this is so for the main period under analysis, 1974–1991. During this period Ethiopia suffered continuously from civil war and, like many less developed countries in the 1970s and 1980s, in particular those in sub-Saharan Africa, Ethiopia faced increased economic problems.

It is often claimed that the problems of less developed countries are the result of external factors such as increased oil prices, decreased demand and prices on the countries' export commodities and increasing international interest rates. However, the argument forwarded in this study is that even if the civil war demanded enormous resources and thus hampered the possibilities of economic growth and development, and even if international prices and interest rates have not always changed in favour of a country like Ethiopia, domestic policy measures played a central role in the negative process of development during the *Ethiopia Tikdem* period.

Economic growth and development is largely a function of the institutional framework of the country in question and an important part of this framework is the management of economic policy. In analysing the *Ethiopia Tikdem* period it is interesting to bear in mind the following rules for good economic policy management, thirteen of which were defined by Harberger in 1984,

5

with principle 14 added by Fischer in 1987 (here quoted from Dornbusch 1993: 15):

1   Avoid poor technicians in policymaking.
2   Keep budgets under adequate control.
3   Keep inflationary pressures under reasonable control.
4   Take advantage of international trade.
5   Keep in mind that some types and patterns of trade restrictions are far worse than others.
6   When import restrictions become excessive and reducing them is politically impossible, attack them indirectly by increasing export incentives.
7   Make tax systems simple to administer and (as far as possible) neutral and non-distorting.
8   Avoid excessive income tax rates.
9   Avoid excessive use of tax incentives to achieve particular objectives.
10 Use price and wage controls sparingly, if at all.
11 Remember that only rarely can a cogent rationale be found for quotas, licences and similar quantitative restrictions.
12 Take a technical rather than ideological view of the problems associated with public sector enterprises.
13 Make the borderlines between public and private sector activity clear and well defined.
14 Don't overvalue the exchange rate.

It will be apparent from the following analysis that Ethiopian economic policy during the *Ethiopia Tikdem* period conflicted with most, if not all, of these principles. To make our argument we will first use an economic, systemic frame of reference and point to a number of serious systemic problems and policy mistakes that characterised the period of socialist rule in Ethiopia. The result of this analysis will be the starting point for an analysis of the effects of these policy mistakes, with the help of a general equilibrium model for a dual economy.

Ethiopian production was dominated by the peasant sector, both during the Haile Selassie period and during the socialist period. The land reform of April 1975 introduced the possibility of stopping, at least after a transitional period, the low growth rates and regular famines that had cost millions of people their lives and that had contributed significantly to the revolution (Schwab 1985, Clapham 1990: chapter 2). However, the land reform was soon amended by a number of policy measures emphasising socialist modes of production that proved to be fatal to the potential positive growth and development effects of the initial policy.

To this was then added a failure to adjust to regime changes in the global economy. The year before the revolution in Ethiopia, the international monetary system, with fixed exchange rates with the US dollar as the reference currency, came to an end. However, as in most other less developed countries, this change was not followed by any decision to change the Ethiopian exchange rate policy.

It is our view that the changes to the economic system introduced during the *Ethiopia Tikdem* period, in particular the design of the incentives system, and the failure to undertake policy adjustments to meet changes in the international monetary regime, contributed heavily to the negative economic development that culminated in the economic crisis in early 1991, a crisis that weakened the strength of the military defence against the various liberation movements. Thus, we will argue that the economic policy of President Mengistu Haile-Mariam contributed greatly to his resignation and flight from Ethiopia on 21 May 1991 and to the eventual fall of the socialist government in June 1991.

PLAN OF THE STUDY

After this introductory chapter, Chapter 2 presents the analytical framework of the study. As mentioned above, an economic systems approach will be used combined with a theoretical analysis of the economic effects relating to the economic reforms and policy changes. Since Ethiopia is a typical dual economy with a dominating subsistence agricultural sector and a very small commercial sector, the model analysis will take place within a dual economy model framework. The analysis will be mainly verbal but will be based on a formal mathematical general equilibrium analysis, where the institutional or economic system aspects are integrated in the dual general equilibrium model. The verbal analysis and some illustrative analytical diagrams will make it possible to follow the analysis and understand the derivation of the conclusions made without having to go into the more complete formal model analysis.

Chapter 3 analyses the creation of the socialist Ethiopian economy. In addition, the chapter contains an economic system analysis of the changes introduced in order to satisfy the economic objectives in the adopted motto *Ethiopia Tikdem*.

Chapter 4 presents a theoretical general equilibrium analysis of the effects that could be expected to arise out of the changes and the concomitant economic policy measures that were introduced in order to support these changes. Then, Chapter 5 analyses the actual economic performance during the *Ethiopia Tikdem* period up to 1988. As in most less developed countries, reliable statistics are scarce. To make it possible to conduct an economic analysis, existing statistics are complemented with information collected and interviews made during regular research visits to Ethiopia during the period 1989–1994. Still, it is important to stress the problems in the quality of the statistics. During the autumn of 1994 the first series of data from thoroughly revised national income accounts from 1980/81 and onwards have been published. However, since the present study covers the period from 1974/75 and since the new series of national accounts is not complete yet, we will use the old series. Furthermore, since the major interest of this study is with the *development* of the economy during the socialist period and the implications of the recent economic reforms, the major focus will be with trends rather than with absolute levels. Thereby, we hope to overcome some of the problems of the reliability of the statistics.

Chapter 6 is devoted to a critical assessment of the economic reform programmes that were presented by the Mengistu government during its last years in power. In the same way, Chapter 7 contains a critical analysis of the economic policy programme that was presented by the transitional government in November 1991 and the recent implementation of this programme, including of the adoption of a Structural Adjustment Programme. The economic effects of the new policy are analysed in Chapter 8.

Finally, in Chapter 9 the conclusions of the study are summarised, both in relation to the economic system framework, the political changes under way, and in relation to the fourteen principles of good policy management quoted above. Lessons for the future are discussed, obstacles and potentials for economic growth and development are identified and some reflections and policy recommendations, both for Ethiopia and for those countries and organisations that assist Ethiopia in its development struggle are presented and related to the new political and economic strategy that eventually removed *Ethiopia Tikdem* as the motto of development.

2

ANALYTICAL FRAMEWORK

INTRODUCTION

This study focuses on changes in the Ethiopian economic system and the concomitant effects on economic performance. In the next section, in order to analyse the changes in the economic system, we define the concept of economic system and its various dimensions. The economic system approach is used as the basis for the analysis of the economic performance in Ethiopia from 1974 to the present. To get a better understanding of the economic forces that produce the performance a simple dual economy approach will be used. In the final section of this chapter these two approaches will be combined into an institutional dual economy approach, where in a mathematical general equilibrium type of model, we try to combine both the dual characteristics of the Ethiopian economy and the economic system changes that were introduced during the period 1974–1994.

AN ECONOMIC SYSTEMIC APPROACH

During recent years the debate on the importance of economic system factors in explaining differences in economic performance among countries has increased in intensity (see, for instance, Prybyla 1969, Koopmans and Montias 1971, Morris and Adelman 1989, Krueger 1990).

An economic system can be defined as the institutional (i.e. the legal and political) framework that determines how the scarce resources of the economy are used.[1] Thus, the economic system defines the way economic decisions are made. A topical issue is the question of how to design an economic system to achieve maximum efficiency, growth, and economic development. To present a more complete picture of the concept of economic system and to produce a frame for comparing economic systems of different countries and their evolution over time, Lindbeck has defined the main dimensions of economic systems shown in Figure 2.1 (Lindbeck 1973).

The first dimension, *decentralisation ↔ centralisation*, describes the level on which economic decision-making takes place. Are economic decisions made by a central authority, that is the government, regional or local

1 Decentralisation	$\longleftrightarrow$	Centralisation
2 Markets	$\longleftrightarrow$	Administrative processes
3 Private ownership	$\longleftrightarrow$	Collective ownership
4 Incentives	$\longleftrightarrow$	Orders
5 Competition	$\longleftrightarrow$	Non-competition
6 Internationalisation	$\longleftrightarrow$	Autarky

Figure 2.1 Main dimensions of economic systems

authorities, or are they made by individual economic actors, that is consumers, producers, capital owners, and employees? It is obvious that in the real world some economic decisions are taken on the central level, for instance decisions on the design of macroeconomic policy and the size of the public sector, while other types of decisions, such as on how to spend the major share of a household's income, are decentralised down to the household level. However, when it comes to activities such as investments, production, employment, and the division of consumption between public and private consumption, decisions are in most cases taken on the whole range of the *decentralisation* ↔ *centralisation* scale. It should be noted that as a rule, the higher the degree of centralisation the more information is needed at the central level for efficient decision-making and the higher will be the costs related to implementation and control. Finally, the more decentralised the decision-making, the more responsible and committed the individuals or organisations concerned tend to be.

The difference in the need for information and in the costs of control during implementation carry over also to the second dimension, describing whether *markets or administrative processes* are used as means in the allocation of resources. When markets are used, the income distribution, the prices, consumer preferences, and the production possibilities determine the allocation through the interaction of individual economic actors, while in a system with administrative processes, other, information-intensive, and thereby also more costly, processes have to be used to decide and co-ordinate the resource allocation.

The third dimension relates to the structure of *ownership*. As a rule, it is assumed that private ownership requires much less control for efficient long-run utilisation of capital and land than is the case when capital or land are publicly owned or are owned collectively by individuals in various types of co-operatives.

The fourth dimension, *incentives* ↔ *orders*, relates closely to the third and deals with the issue of how to make economic actors efficient. It is well-known that incentives tend to give the individual a feeling of being freer to act than is the case with orders. This, in turn, tends to increase the involvement, responsibility, and efficiency of individuals in their economic activities.

10

The fifth dimension, *competition* ↔ *non-competition*, also emphasises the efficiency aspect of economic activities. The higher the competition, the more efficient will be the individual actors, for instance producers. Lack of competition tends to lead to higher costs and, over time, to lower quality in production.

The final dimension, *internationalisation* ↔ *autarky*, is closely related to the issue of competition but relates also to the possibilities of increasing the total income of a country by opening up its economy to trade and foreign investment. Through internationalisation the degree of competition increases and foreign capital, raw material, and foreign technology are made available for the country.

From the above brief discussion of the various dimensions of a system it follows that an economy's flexibility and ability to adjust to external and internal shocks are heavily dependent on the characteristics of the economic system. The further to the left along the scales of the six dimensions in Figure 2.1, the more flexible the economy tends to be. Furthermore, there is a tendency for economic agents and organisations to be more committed and efficient in their performance when the economic system characteristics fall further to the left in Figure 2.1.

It is obvious that in the real world, we will not find economic systems that fall on the extreme left or right ends of the scale. Instead, existing economic systems fall somewhere in between these extremes for each and every dimension. This creates consistency problems that easily reduce the efficiency of the allocation of resources.

One of the most important consistency problems is related to the fact that the reliance on markets, instead of administrative process, in the co-ordination of economic activities requires a high degree of private ownership in the economy. For a well-functioning market economy well-defined and protected property rights are of crucial importance. Recent research has shown that the existence of proper institutions is a critical determinant of the nature and speed of development and that initial institutions have been found to be more important than resources, capital, technology, or demography in the process of economic development (North 1990, Adelman 1991, Oshima 1991, Hansson 1993d).

In subsequent chapters, the changes in the Ethiopian economic system during the period 1974–1994 will be analysed within this economic system framework. First, however, the second part of our analytical framework, focusing on the dual characteristics of the Ethiopian economy, will be presented. Then in the final section of this chapter, the two approaches will be combined into a mathematical institutional dual economy model.

A DUAL ECONOMY APPROACH

The Ethiopian economy can be characterised as a typical dual economy, in the sense that it has a dominating and highly traditional agricultural sector and only a minor commercialised industrial and service sector. Agriculture accounts for 40–45 per cent of GDP, 85 per cent of total exports, and employs some 85 per cent of the labour force.

The core problem in Ethiopia can be defined by referring to Ranis' words concerning dual economies:

> The heart of the development problem in the dual economy is thus the ability of the agricultural sector to yield sufficiently large agricultural surpluses and to preserve a sufficiently large part of such surpluses for productive investment in non-agriculture. Simultaneously, the non-agricultural sector, financed by this agricultural surplus plus the reinvestment of industrial profits, must grow fast enough to absorb the labor force being reallocated.
>
> (Ranis 1988: 82)

In order to analyse the economic policy measures, the economic development, and the actual situation in such a dual economy we need a model that captures the dual characteristics of the economy.

Dual models have been developed and used since the early 1950s when Arthur Lewis published his Manchester School article on labour surplus and economic development (Lewis 1954). By using a dual model that can be seen as a formalised, modified, and extended version of the model presented by Gustav Ranis (1988), we will analyse the Ethiopian socialist economic system and the economic performance during the years of *Ethiopia Tikdem* policy, but also make a critical assessment of the intended economic system changes that have been announced and introduced since the late 1980s.

Figure 2.2 describes the essence of the analytical model. For pedagogical reasons, in this figure we treat the agricultural sector in an aggregated form, comprising both peasant agriculture and non-peasant agriculture. Thus, the economy is assumed to consist of only two sectors: the agricultural sector (here identical to the peasant sector) and the non-agricultural. The labour force (= population or a constant share of the population for simplicity) and the employment in agriculture are measured along the horizontal left-hand axis (L, L_A), whereas the vertical downward axis (L, L_N) measures the same labour force and the employment outside agriculture. It is assumed that labour that cannot find employment in non-agricultural production will be employed in agriculture. The vertical upward axis measures the value of per capita agricultural consumption and production, whereas the horizontal right-hand axis measures the value of the non-agricultural per capita production and consumption. The relative price of agricultural goods and non-agricultural goods is measured in the upper right-hand quadrant and is here defined as the

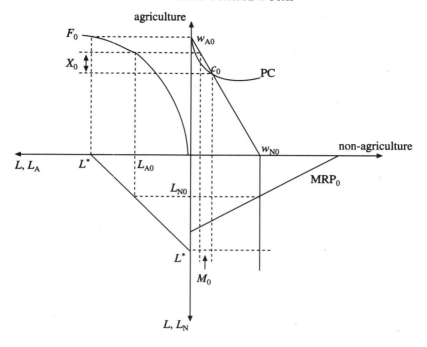

Figure 2.2 A dual economy model

terms of trade between the wage in terms of agricultural goods and the wage in terms of non-agricultural goods. For simplicity it is assumed that there is no wage differential between work in traditional agriculture and work in non-agriculture. The maximum agricultural per capita consumption (i.e. the per capita income measured in agricultural goods, w_A) is assumed to be given by the per capita production possibilities in agriculture (described by the F_0 curve in Figure 2.2) and is set equal to the maximum amount that can be produced per capita if the whole labour force, L^*, is allocated to the agricultural sector. We assume a non-negative relationship to exist between the labour input in agriculture and the per capita agricultural production. Furthermore, the per capita agricultural production is assumed to depend on the organisation of agricultural production, the technology, and the size of the cultivated land area.

The relative price between agricultural goods and non-agricultural goods (i.e. the relation between w_A and w_N) is assumed to be exogenously given by the domestic government or by the international market. Thus, the relative price line, or terms of trade line, can be interpreted as a budget line for the average citizen. It is assumed that as long as the agricultural sector is not commercialised, i.e. labour is not employed according to its marginal revenue

13

product, the wage level measured in non-agricultural goods is given by the wage level measured in agricultural goods, w_A, and the relative price of agricultural goods and non-agricultural goods.

The demand for labour in the non-agricultural sector is given by the marginal revenue product (MRP curve) in the lower right-hand quadrant.

To present the way the model works, assume that the per capita production possibilities in agriculture is given by the F_0 curve in Figure 2.2. Furthermore, assume that the typical worker (in agricultural or non-agricultural production) chooses to consume agricultural goods and non-agricultural goods according to the price–consumption curve, PC, a curve that describes the utility maximising consumption mix at various relative prices and a given income. Given the initial relative commodity price and per capita income, the representative worker will choose the consumption mix c_0.

Initially, the demand for labour in the non-agricultural sector is assumed to be given by MRP_0. At the wage w_{N0} this means that L_{N0} workers will be employed in the non-agricultural sector. Consequently, L_{A0} workers will be employed in agriculture. Given the per capita consumption mix c_0, this allocation of labour will produce a per capita agricultural surplus equal to X_0. This surplus will be exported.

Initially, the domestic price of agricultural goods relative to non-agricultural products is assumed to equal the international relative price. Then the agricultural exports give rise to a per capita import of non-agricultural goods equal to M_0 that can be invested in non-agricultural production. The producer surplus generated from the employment in non-agricultural production can also be reinvested in this sector. Thus, both the agricultural surplus and the profits from non-agricultural hiring of labour can be invested in non-agriculture and thereby increase both the value of the marginal productivity of labour and the demand for labour in non-agriculture, i.e. the MRP curve shifts outwards. Then, more workers can be employed in non-agriculture and the total production possibilities of the economy and thus the national income as well as the per capita income will grow, *ceteris paribus*. Thus, trade based on agricultural surplus production works as an engine of growth.

AN INSTITUTIONAL DUAL ECONOMY MODEL

For the analysis of the economic reforms and policy changes that have been introduced in Ethiopia since 1974 it is obvious that a two-sector model of the kind presented above is too simple for our purposes and merely sheds light on the major effects of various policy measures. Therefore, the diagrammatic dual economy approach will be developed further to incorporate the institutional aspects and economic system changes. The result of this combination is an institutional dual economy model that, in short, can be described as a mathematical four-sector general equilibrium model where institutional factors are also included, albeit in a very simple way.

In this extended model the agricultural sector is divided into two parts: one peasant or subsistence sector (S) and one non-peasant agricultural sector (C) which in the case of the pre-revolutionary, imperial, Ethiopia denotes the commercial agricultural sector and in the case of socialist Ethiopia denotes State farms and producer co-operatives.

Outside agriculture there are assumed to be two sectors: one governmental, public sector (G), comprising the defence and non-market service production for final consumption, and one non-agricultural market-oriented sector (M), comprising sectors like the market-oriented service sector, the manufacturing sector, and the extractive industry. In the following analysis we will use the term 'manufacturing sector' to describe the non-agricultural market-oriented sector.

In the rest of this chapter we give a more detailed presentation of the four-sector model that will be used in the analysis of the economic reforms and policies that were introduced between 1974 and 1994.

The production in peasant agriculture, non-peasant agriculture, manu-facturing, and the public sector are assumed to display constant returns to scale in the relevant factors of production and the production functions are assumed to be well-behaved with positive but falling marginal productivities. In the case of more than one factor of production, mutual complementarity is assumed between each pair of factors of production so that the marginal productivity of one factor increases when the use of another factor increases and vice versa.

The producers outside the peasant and the public sectors are assumed to be profit maximisers, i.e. to strive towards economic efficiency, given the institutional frame of the economy in terms of legislation and economic policy, and given the prices of their respective products.

The producers in the public sector are assumed to behave in a profit-maximising manner given the 'prices' set by the government in terms of allocated budget, and their defined tasks of operation.

Turning to the characteristics of the various sectors, the peasant sector is assumed to use labour (L) and land (R) in its production, whereas the non-peasant agricultural sector uses labour and land together with capital (K). The manufacturing sector uses labour and capital. The public sector, finally, is assumed to use labour and sector-specific capital (A), mainly in the form of military equipment.

In addition, the production in the economy is a function of the institutional characteristics of the economic system. Following Lindbeck (1973) and Figure 2.1, an economic system can be characterised by six institutional dimensions. These dimensions can all be applied for each sector of the economy. In the following, the institutional framework will be represented by the exogenous variable I that comprises the institutional framework for each sector, i.e. $I = I(I_S, I_C, I_G, I_M)$, where $I_j = I_j(i_1, i_2, \ldots, i_6)$ represents the six respective economic systemic dimensions for sector j, where $j = S, C, G,$ and M.

15

The variable I (and its internal components) is assumed to take the form of an index between 0 and 1 where 1 denotes a perfectly decentralised, market-based economic system where private ownership, incentives, and competition with both domestic and international producers determine the allocation of resources for the economy at large (or for the respective sector).

It is assumed that there is a positive relationship between the production in a sector and its respective institutional variable. Thus, S_{I_S}, C_{I_C}, G_{I_G}, and M_{I_M} (for short S_I, C_I, G_I, and M_I) are all assumed to be positive.

The wage level, or the per capita income, is assumed to be determined by the production possibilities in the peasant sector, which dominates the economy. The wage level, measured in agricultural goods, is assumed to be equal to a share α, where $0 < \alpha \leq 1$, of the maximum per capita agricultural production when all available labour, L^*, and all arable land, R^*, are used in the peasant sector.

Given this wage level, the profit-maximising producers in non-peasant production will employ labour up to the point where their respective marginal revenue product equals the per capita income (the wage level). The rest of the labour force will be employed in the peasant sector. This will be the case as long as this sector has not been commercialised but is rather to be classified as a subsistence sector.

Exports are assumed to come from agriculture and equal the part of agricultural produce that is not consumed domestically. The domestic consumption of agricultural goods is assumed to depend positively but to a decreasing degree on the per capita income. The exports of agricultural goods are exchanged for imports of capital goods and foreign-produced agricultural goods.

The stock of capital (K), except the sector-specific capital (A) in the governmental sector, is assumed to be allocated through a competitive market between the two non-governmental capital-using sectors. The stock of capital is assumed to consist of two parts, one foreign and one domestic. The foreign part of the stock of capital depends on the return to capital and the institutional characteristics of the manufacturing and non-peasant agriculture, $K_F(r, I_C, I_M)$. The institutional characteristics determine not only the interest of private foreign capital owners but also affect other countries' attitude towards Ethiopia and thus also the inflow of foreign aid, here treated as capital, to these two sectors.

The domestic part of the stock of capital is equal to the accumulated agricultural surplus and the accumulated producer surplus generated in the manufacturing sector. Changes in agricultural surplus are represented by changes in the per capita income. Furthermore, the producer surplus in manufacturing is assumed to be equal to the depreciation of the stock of capital. Thus, the change in the stock of capital will only depend on changes in the foreign part of the stock of capital and changes in per capita income. To summarise, the stock of capital $K = K(r, w, I_C, I_M)$.

16

The sector-specific capital (A) in the governmental sector is assumed to be exogenously determined by the Ethiopian government and by foreign military aid. The latter is in turn assumed to depend on the military ambitions and strategies of the Ethiopian government, here represented by the exogenous variable I_G.

Initially, the distribution of land between the two agricultural sectors is assumed to be given exogenously. Thus, the return to land will normally differ between the two sectors.

The prices of the output from the various sectors are assumed to be given exogenously by the international market or by the central planning authority. In the case of the governmental sector, the 'price' does not necessarily have to be the price that the consumers have to pay. The 'price' just works as a signal to the producers about the value that the politicians give one unit of output from the governmental sector. Governmental production is assumed to be financed through foreign aid, taxes and/or by selling the output at a positive price. However, for simplicity it is assumed that the output from the governmental sector can always be sold at the price set by the government. Consequently, we do not have to bother about the fiscal budget in our model world. The output from manufacturing is used as numeraire but initially, units of production from all sectors are defined so that all prices equal unity.

Given the above assumptions our institutional dual general equilibrium model can be mathematically described as follows:

Production functions:

$$S = S(L_S, R_S, I_S) \tag{1}$$

$$C = C(L_C, K_C, R_C, I_C) \tag{2}$$

$$G = G(L_G, A, I_G) \tag{3}$$

$$M = M(L_M, K_M, I_M) \tag{4}$$

Define $Z(L, R, I_S)$ as $S(L^*, R^*, I_S)$, where L^* and R^* denote the total available labour force and land, respectively. Then, the equilibrium conditions will be as follows:

$$w = \alpha Z(L, R, I_S)/L, \, 0 < \alpha \leq 1 \tag{5}$$

$$w = C_L(L_C, K_C, R_C, I_C) \tag{6}$$

$$w = M_L(L_M, K_M, I_M) \tag{7}$$

$$w = G_L(L_G, A, I_G) \tag{8}$$

$$r = C_K(L_C, K_C, R_C, I_C) \tag{9}$$

$$r = M_K(L_M, K_M, I_M) \tag{10}$$

$$v = [S(L_S, R_S, I_S) - \alpha Z(L, R, I_S)L_S/L]/R_S \tag{11}$$

$$q = C_R(L_C, K_C, R_C, I_C) \tag{12}$$

$$L^* = L_S + L_C + L_M + L_G \tag{13}$$

$$K = K_C + K_M \tag{14}$$

$$R_C^* = R_C \tag{15}$$

$$R_S^* = R_S \tag{16}$$

$$A = A(I_G) \tag{17}$$

$$K = K(r, w, I_C, I_M) \tag{18}$$

where w, r, v, and q represent factor returns for labour, capital, peasant land, and non-peasant land respectively. In the presentation of the analysis below we drop the * notation for total factor endowments.

In the following chapters, the various policy measures that have been introduced during the period under analysis will be represented as changes in the exogenous variables of the model, that is prices, institutional character-istics, and allocation of land between the two agricultural sectors.

To prepare for the analysis we derive the system of equations that will form the framework of our analysis. By substituting equation (18) into equation (14), substituting equations (13)–(17) into equations (5)–(12), and making a total differentiation of the resulting system we obtain the following system of equations:

$$dw = \alpha Z/L \, dp_S + Z/L \, d\alpha + \alpha[(Z_L - Z/L)dL + (Z_R dR + Z_I dI_S)]/L \tag{19}$$

$$dw = C_L dp_C + C_{LL} dL_C + C_{LK} dK_C + C_{LR} dR_C + C_{LI} dI_C \tag{20}$$

$$\begin{aligned} dw = {} & M_{LL} dL - M_{LL} dL_S - M_{LL} dL_C - M_{LL} dL_G + M_{LK} K_r dr \\ & + M_{LK} K_w dw + M_{LK} K_{I_C} dI_C - M_{LK} dK_C + (M_{LK} K_{I_M} + M_{LI}) dI_M \end{aligned} \tag{21}$$

$$dw = G_L dp_G + G_{LL} dL_G + (G_{LA} A_I + G_{LI}) dI_G \tag{22}$$

$$dr = C_K dp_C + C_{KL} dL_C + C_{KK} dK_C + C_{KR} dR_C + C_{KI} dI_C \tag{23}$$

$$\begin{aligned} dr = {} & M_{KL} dL - M_{KL} dL_S - M_{KL} dL_C - M_{KL} dL_G + M_{KK} K_r dr \\ & + M_{KK} K_w dw + M_{KK} K_{I_C} dI_C - M_{KK} dK_C + (M_{KK} K_{I_M} + M_{KI}) dI_M \end{aligned} \tag{24}$$

$$\begin{aligned} dv = {} & [S dp_S + S_L dL_S + S_I dI_S + (S_R - S/R_S) \, dR_S]/R_S \\ & - \{ZL_S(\alpha dp_S + d\alpha) + \alpha Z dL_S + \alpha L_S[(Z_L - Z/L)dL \\ & + Z_R dR - Z/R_S dR_S + Z_I dI_S]\}/(LR_S) \end{aligned} \tag{25}$$

$$dq = C_R dp_C + C_{RL} dL_C + C_{RK} dK_C + C_{RR} dR_C + C_{RI} dI_C \tag{26}$$

In the following analysis, in Chapters 4, 6, and 8, we will introduce changes in some of the variables in the model to capture the major characteristics of the changes in the Ethiopian economic system.

Chapter 4 analyses, within the above model, the expected economic effects of the changes that were introduced during the *Ethiopia Tikdem* period, i.e. the period when socialist political ideology and objectives governed policy-making in Ethiopia. Subsequently, after an assessment of the actual economic performance during the 1970s and 1980s, in Chapter 6, the model will be used to make a critical assessment of the attempted economic reforms that were presented by President Mengistu Haile-Mariam in November 1988 and March 1990. Finally, the reforms that the transitional government has developed and started to introduce in the early 1990s are analysed in Chapter 8.

One may question whether the analytical framework that has been described above is well-suited for analyses of the economic situation and development in a country like Ethiopia. Naturally, a model like this cannot capture all aspects and characteristics in a complex real world. In particular, one may question the role of prices in an economy where resource allocation is determined through administrative decisions rather than through the interplay of economic actors in markets. However, regardless of how prices are determined, economic actors are very sensitive to the costs and revenues of their activities and thus to prices. This is the case for the public sector also where the government allocates a certain budget for achieving the objectives that have been defined for the sector. When factor prices or factor productivities are changed, the decision-makers managing the public sector, as the ones managing non-public sector activities, will adjust to the new conditions, *ceteris paribus*. It should also be kept in mind that even for command economies, history provides ample evidence that incentives are of crucial importance. One frequent and serious, if not fatal, mistake in such economies has been that the role of economic incentives has been largely overlooked by the policymakers.

The objective of the model analysis in the following chapters is not to give a completely realistic description of the last twenty years of economic development in Ethiopia. The objective is rather to illustrate the economic forces that are set in motion when the economic system is changed or specific policy measures are introduced. Notwithstanding the limitations of simple formal models, like the one presented above, we think it is possible to make interesting analyses of the various policy phases in post-revolutionary Ethiopia. By using the six economic system dimensions in Figure 2.1 as a basis for our verbal description and institutional analysis, and for the formal model analysis, we hope to overcome some of the limitations of the purely formal model analysis. Through this set of analyses we think it is possible to generate useful conclusions that can be used as a basis for Ethiopian economic policymakers and foreign donors in their efforts to break the negative economic development trend and to combat Ethiopian poverty.

3

ETHIOPIA TIKDEM
The creation of the socialist economy

INTRODUCTION

This chapter analyses the changes in the Ethiopian economic system since the military revolution on 12 September 1974, when the Emperor Haile Selassie was overthrown, up to the end of the 1980s when the first signs of change towards a more market-oriented economic system appeared.

It is not an easy task to make a unique classification of existing economies according to the scheme in Figure 2.1. Notwithstanding these difficulties, this chapter tries to characterise and analyse the economic systemic development in post-revolution Ethiopia by means of the system framework presented in Chapter 2.

Policy objectives and intended programmes

On 27 June 1974, i.e. over two months before the overthrow of the Emperor, a group of 120 people, mainly from the major units of the army, formed the Co-ordinating Committee of the Armed Forces, Police and the Territorial Army, the Derg. Then, as mentioned in Chapter 1, in early July the same year this committee released a policy statement with the motto '*Ityopya tikdem*' (Ethiopia First) (Clapham 1990: 40, Tiruneh 1993: 86f). It is worth noting that this initial policy statement was not accompanied by any measures to change Ethiopia towards a socialist economy. On the contrary, on nationalisation, which is one of the most important issues when moving towards socialism, the Derg declared that, with the exception of the royal family and the aristocracy, no nationalisation of domestic or internationally owned property in Ethiopia was to take place (Tiruneh 1993: 86). Not surprisingly, this programme was heavily criticised by the Ethiopian left. Thus, some months after the overthrow of Haile Selassie, on 20 December 1974, the new government, the Derg, met the demands of the leftists and issued a ten-point programme in which Ethiopian socialism was emphasised.[1] The programme can be seen as an effort to combine nationalism with socialism under the slogan *Ethiopia Tikdem*. The points were as follows.

1 Ethiopia shall remain a united country without ethnic, religious, linguistic or cultural differences.

2 Ethiopia wishes to see the setting up of an economic, cultural and social community with Kenya, Sudan and Somalia.

3 The slogan *Ethiopia Tikdem* of the Ethiopian revolution is to be based on a specifically Ethiopian socialism (*hebrettesebawinet*).

4 Every regional administration and every village shall manage its own resources and be self-sufficient.

5 A great political party based on the revolutionary philosophy of *Ethiopia Tikdem* shall be constituted on a nationalist and socialist basis.

6 The entire economy shall be in the hands of the state. All assets existing in Ethiopia are by the rights the property of the Ethiopian people. Only a limited number of businesses will remain private if they are deemed to be of public utility.

7 The right to own land shall be restricted to those who work the land.

8 Industry will be managed by the state. Some private enterprises deemed to be of public utility will be left in private hands until the state considers it preferable to nationalise them.

9 The family, which will be the fundamental basis of Ethiopian society, will be protected against all foreign influences, vices and defects.

10 Ethiopia's existing foreign policy will be essentially maintained. The new regime will however endeavour to strengthen good-neighbourly relations with all neighbouring countries.

(Lefort 1983: 84)

From this programme it is obvious that the Derg had taken the leftists' criticism seriously. According to Tiruneh, the new policy could be seen as a compromise between the interests of the radical left, who wanted a more complete Marxist–Leninist programme to be introduced, and the existing 'interest groups and voices of moderation' (Tiruneh 1993: 88). However, Tiruneh also notes that 'the capitalist class, not to mention the landed gentry, did not have a vanguard organization to articulate its interests and its influence on the Derg remained minimal' (Tiruneh 1993: 88).

As a consequence, it was clear from the very outset that the new policy was to lead Ethiopia towards socialism or as Schwab describes it: '*Ethiopia Tikdem* also signified the attack on class stratification, tribal and ethnic differences, and on status being positioned on extracting capital from the abused labour of others within a feudal rubric' (Schwab 1985: 24). Furthermore, socialism in Ethiopia, according to the guidelines of 20 December 1974, 'was to be based on the alternation of property rights moving from a private to a collective system useful for economic progress' (Schwab

1981: 300). *The Declaration on Economic Policy of Socialist Ethiopia* in February 1975 (in the following called DEP) further developed the idea by stating that

> the elimination of poverty and the prevention of exploitation of the Ethiopian people can be achieved only when the Government as the representative of the people, and in the interest of the mass of Ethiopian workers and peasants, directly owns and controls the natural resources and key industrial, commercial and financial sectors of the economy.
>
> (DEP 1975: 3)

In line with this statement the declaration delineated and indicated the sectors and activities exclusively reserved for the State, activities where the State and private and public foreign capital could operate jointly, and finally, activities that were to be left to the private sector (DEP 1975: 10f, see also below). It was obvious that through these documents the Derg had the intention of taking control over the major parts of the Ethiopian economy.

Turning back to the 20 December declaration on Ethiopian socialism under the motto *Ethiopia Tikdem*, points 1, 2, 3, 4, 6, 7, and 8 are of particular interest for the present study. Even if point 1, about Ethiopian unity, does not explicitly deal with economics but rather with politics, it is of great economic importance. The reason is that it played an important role as the governing principle behind the Derg's attitude towards regional liberation movements, which in turn resulted in a rapidly growing share of the economic resources being devoted to the civil war. The war also affected economic policy. In particular, this was the case with the agricultural price policy, where low producer prices were important to hold back the defence expenditures.

As mentioned in Chapter 1, after the adoption of the ten-point programme under the motto *Ethiopia Tikdem*, the Derg immediately started to implement its socialist ambitions. On 20 April 1976, *The National Democratic Revolutionary Programme of Ethiopia* (NDRPE) was presented (see for instance Tiruneh 1993: 159f). The objective of this programme was to govern the process of transition to socialism in Ethiopia (Schwab 1985: 34, Tiruneh 1993: 160). According to an announcement by Mengistu in the *Ethiopian Herald*, 21 April 1976, the primary goals of the new policy were the 'elimination of feudalism, bureaucratic capitalism and imperialism' (quoted from Schwab 1985: 34). Tiruneh concludes that the NDRPE

> constituted a massive ideological shift on the part of the Derg, not for the first time either. 'Ethiopia First' of July 1974 could be described as the programme of a *coup d'état*; 'Ethiopian Socialism' of December 1974 as a programme of African socialism; and 'the NDRPE' of April 1976 as a programme of scientific socialism.
>
> (Tiruneh 1993: 163)

Finally, among the important policy documents and statements that governed the Ethiopian economy during the *Ethiopia Tikdem* period, some mention should also be made of the objectives of the *Ten-Year Perspective Plan* issued in 1984. Among the stated objectives of this plan we especially note the following:

- improving gradually the material and cultural well-being of the people;
- accelerating growth of the economy through the expansion of the country's productive capacity;
- conserving, exploring, and developing the natural resources of the country;
- expanding and strengthening socialist production relations;
- laying down the basis for the development of national science and technology capability;
- alleviating social and unemployment problems gradually;
- ensuring balanced and proportional development of all regions.

(quoted from Eshetu Chole and Makonnen
Manyazewal 1992:10)

In order to achieve these objectives special priority was to be given to agriculture, i.e. through co-operativisation of the peasants. Second priority was to be given to industry. Through the implementation of the plan the annual growth rate opted for was 6.5 per cent in real terms (Eshetu Chole and Makonnen Manyazewal 1992: 11). It is obvious that a programme of this magnitude demanded huge investments in the major sectors of the economy. Considering the magnitude of the economic problems at the time of the announcement of the plan, the necessary investments had to be financed largely through external resource mobilisation. According to Eshetu Chole and Makonnen Manyazewal (1992: 12) domestic savings were expected to cover 55.5 per cent of the planned investments. However, this was a highly optimistic estimate since it required an increase in gross domestic savings of around 24 per cent annually, or from 3.4 per cent of GDP in 1983/84 to 15.5 per cent in 1993/94. Even with this highly optimistic estimate, however, the need for foreign resources for investments was extremely high.

Actual economic policy measures

As a consequence of the above policy declarations and programmes of reform the following major economic measures and reforms towards socialism were actually introduced to satisfy the stated objectives:[2]

- Nationalisation of companies and urban land (started on 1 January 1975).
- Land reform (introduced on 4 March 1975).
- Collectivisation programme (mentioned as the main function of peasant

associations in the land reform proclamation 1975, and emphasised heavily in the ten-year plan 1984).

- Villagisation and resettlement programmes (villagisation was initiated during the Ethiopian–Somalian war, 1977–1978, extended in 1985 (Alemayehu Lirenso 1990: 136); resettlement schemes already took place on a small scale before the revolution but organised resettlements started when the Settlement Authority was established in 1976 (Pankhurst 1990: 120)).
- Distortionary domestic price incentives (closely related to nationalisation and collectivisation).
- Heavy controls of international trade and foreign exchange.

In the following sections we will analyse the content of these various points of changes within the economic system described in Figure 2.1. The expected impact of these various changes will be analysed in Chapter 4, while the economic performance that actually resulted from the changes will be presented and analysed in Chapter 5.

NATIONALISATION OF COMPANIES AND URBAN LAND

In short, nationalisation of companies and urban land moved the Ethiopian economy away from private to State ownership, i.e. a change along the third dimension in Figure 2.1. The nationalisation during the first years after the revolution in 1974 started on 1 January 1975 with the nationalisation of banks, insurance companies, and other financial institutions. One month later, on 3 February, seventy-two enterprises in the commercial and industrial sectors, inclusive of all major foreign-owned companies, were nationalised (Schwab 1985: 24f, Clapham 1990: 46, Tiruneh 1993: 89f). Some days later, on 7 February, the Derg released its declaration on the economic policy (DEP 1975) in which private ownership was condemned as responsible for the economic exploitation of the people. The following illustrates the Derg's hostile attitude towards private ownership:

> The basic cause of the economic exploitation of man by man is the private ownership of the means of production.... The elimination of exploitation through the public ownership and control of the major means of production is therefore one of the primary goals of Ethiopian Socialism.
>
> (DEP 1975: 4)

Thus, it was quite clear that the Derg saw no problems in nationalising whatever resources it found essential for economic development and the elimination of poverty (see also Clapham 1990: 46).

The *Government Ownership and Control of the Means of Production*

Proclamation that was issued in March 1975 followed the basic principles in the DEP and divided the enterprises in the Ethiopian economy into three groups (DEP 1975: 10f, Clapham 1990: 114f, Tiruneh 1993: 91f). The first group comprised business areas where the State should be the sole owner. This group included the financial sector (banks, insurance companies, and other financial institutions), the basic industries (petroleum companies, iron and steel companies), companies in textiles, drugs, tobacco, but also some small-scale manufactures such as leather goods and ceramics. The second group comprised activities where the State and foreign capital were to work together in joint ventures. The areas in this group, where foreign experts were needed, included mining, plastic manufacturing, and tourism. The third group, finally, covered business areas left to the private sector and comprised small-scale business and industry, domestic and foreign trade, and road transport.

Finally, on 26 July 1975 the government released the *Government Ownership of Urban Lands and Extra Houses Proclamation* by which urban land was nationalised as were all houses, except the one where the owner resided. Through the proclamation the urban inhabitants were allowed to form and join so-called *kebelles*, which were the urban dwellers' associations.[3]

As the nationalisation in 1975 took place without compensating the former owners, the declaration of 7 February (DEP 1975) made private investment an extremely risky business. The total number of private companies that were nationalised during the first two months of 1975 amounted to some 200.

Later on, the nationalisation and the introduction of other policy means aiming at State control over various parts of economic society, for instance wholesale trade, continued and by the end of the socialist period State ownership covered almost all large- and medium-scale manufacturing industries, mines, commercial farms, banks, insurance companies, transport companies (except road transports), wholesale trade, and a large part of the construction sector. To this should be added that all land was nationalised on 4 March 1975 (see the next section). More or less all the commercial farms were turned into State farms. Later on the government created new State farms by 'large-scale clearance of bush or forest in sparsely populated areas' (Clapham 1990: 179). Thus, nationalisation was far-reaching and covered the major share of non-peasant production even if a great number of small-scale industries and handicrafts were left in private hands throughout the entire *Ethiopia Tikdem* period. The *Census of Manufacturing Industries in Ethiopia, 1990*, shows that as much as 49.8 per cent of all industrial establishments were privately owned. However, these were on average very small and employed just 6.8 per cent of all industrial employees (see Table 7.2).

As a result of the extensive nationalisation, initially without compensation to the former owners and with the threat of further nationalisations whenever the government should find it preferable, Ethiopia experienced a severe loss of entrepreneurs, and thereby of private capital and know-how.

There are differing views about the magnitude and importance of the nationalisation outside the agricultural sector. Tiruneh concludes that, even if the estimates are very uncertain 'the size of the sub-sectors affected by the nationalisations was minimal when compared to the share of other sectors of the national economy' (Tiruneh 1993: 94) and that 'the desire [for the government] to be seen to be progressive in the eyes of the leftists and win them over to its side' appears to have been the major motive behind the introduction of the nationalisation policy (Tiruneh 1993: 96).

Even though it is true that, due to the peasant dominance, only a small part of the total Ethiopian economy was directly affected by the nationalisation of assets outside agriculture, and only a very small amount of foreign assets, less than US$30 million (estimates by Tiruneh 1993: 95), this should not lead us to conclude that the nationalisation policy was innocent. First, it is important to remember that the Ethiopian economy at the time of the revolution was a peasant-dominated rural economy with just a small modern commercialised sector (Pickett 1991: 187, Tiruneh 1993: 93). Thus, the number of people directly affected by the nationalisation must also be small. Secondly, it is often forgotten that one of the most important influences of policy changes and policy statements is due to the signals they send to various decision-makers in the society rather than the direct effects of the policy actions themselves. In the case of nationalisation in Ethiopia, it is obvious that the signals sent by the Derg in December 1974 and the first months of 1975 were signals of hostility towards private capital in general and foreign capital in particular. As a consequence, it was not surprising that the interest in making private investments in Ethiopia disappeared. In a typical agricultural-based economy that urgently needed to be diversified, this effect of the signalling contained in the 20 December policy statement was perhaps the severest one from the point of view of economic diversification and growth in Ethiopia.

In conclusion, referring to the six economic system dimensions listed in Figure 2.1, the nationalisation programmes that were introduced during the first years of the *Ethiopia Tikdem* period, in addition to the transfer of ownership to the State (dimension 3), also meant increased centralisation (dimension 1), less reliance on markets (dimension 2) and incentives (dimension 4), less competition (dimension 5), and less international openness (dimension 6) in the Ethiopian economy.

'LAND TO THE TILLER' – THE LAND REFORM

The land reform of 4 March 1975, announced in the *Rural Land Proclamation* (*Negarit Gazeta*, 1975, no. 31), and based on the slogan 'Land to the tiller', meant that all privately owned land was nationalised without compensating the former owners (Dessalegn Rahmato 1984: chapter 3, Schwab 1985: 26f, Goyder and Goyder 1988: 83, Clapham 1989: 10f, 1990: 46ff, Kidane Mengisteab 1990, Tiruneh 1993: 100f).

The reasons for changing the land tenure system were presented in the preamble of the *Rural Land Proclamation*. One reason was the concentration of power over rural land and thereby over the rural people:

Whereas, several thousand *gashas* [one *gasha* is approximately equal to 40 hectares] of land have been grabbed from the masses by an insignificant number of feudal lords and their families as a result of which the Ethiopian masses have been forced to live under conditions of serfdom.

(quoted from Lefort 1983: 89)

The land reform meant that only usufructuary land rights were given to the peasants and their families. Thus, it gave every person who wanted to cultivate land the right to access to land for him or her and his or her family (Dessalegn Rahmato 1984: 37f, Clapham 1990: 48). The land reform abolished all previous land tenure systems and the possibility of hiring labour in agriculture (Dessalegn Rahmato 1984: 38, Clapham 1990: 47f). In accordance with point 7 of the ten-point programme of Ethiopian socialism from 20 December 1974, the land reform emphasised owner-cultivation even if the land was the property of the State.

In order to carry out the reform, beginning on 14 January 1975, 50000–60000 secondary school and university students and teachers were sent out to the rural areas in a campaign, the National Development Through Co-operation and Enlightenment and Work Campaign, called *zemecha* (zematcha). Established in November 1974, this campaign had the objective of educating the rural population about the process of development (Dessalegn Rahmato 1984: 41f, Clapham 1990: 49f, Tiruneh 1993: 102, 171).

One objective of the land reform, and the *Ethiopia Tikdem* policy in general, was to improve the situation in the countryside. The intented results were presented in the Ethiopian press by comparing the situation under the *Ethiopia Tikdem* policy with the past feudal situation:

Feudalism		*Ethiopia Tikdem*	
exploitation	} lack of	liberation & struggle	} organiz-
illiteracy	} organiz-	education	} ation
lack of consciousness	} ation	consciousness	
under-production		production	
non-circulation		circulation	
injustice		justice	
lack of organization		associations and co-operatives	
foreign and absentee landlords		responsible local organizations	

(quoted from Lefort 1983: 93)

Peasant associations were organised with the aim of implementing the land reform (nationalisation) and to be responsible for the management of the distribution of land according to the new land tenure principles. The peasant associations covered around 800 hectares each. The individual farmers got usufructuary rights to up to 10 hectares per peasant family. As a rule, however, the allocated plots were of much smaller size, often around just 1 hectare. Considering that the peasants in large parts of the country had been suppressed by the land-owning class, the land reform was not only the most popular action taken by the Derg but was also a reform that could be expected to increase the efficiency in peasant agriculture.[4]

The land reform should be seen as a move towards a more decentralised peasant agriculture where individual peasants, and not the 'absent' landlords, make decisions about production. In particular, this was the case in the southern parts of the country while peasants in the northern provinces, where community land tenure and not traditional Ethiopian feudalism was the dominating land tenure system, were less affected (Cohen and Weintraub 1975: 30ff, Brüne 1990, Pausewang 1990a). Thus, in particular in the south, the reform was popular among the peasants but was naturally met by opposition from former Ahmara landlords. Those landlords who refused to adjust to the new policy were removed and executed (Schwab 1985: 27). There was also some opposition among the farmers in the northern parts who seemed to be quite pleased with the existing land tenure system. Also among the Afars, a nomadic group, there was some opposition to the reform which they saw as infringing their use of grazing lands (Schwab 1985: 26, Tiruneh 1993: 108).

The ultimate aim of the land reform was, according to Ståhl, to 'substitute the state for the landlords as the prime appropriate of agrarian surpluses' (Ståhl 1990: 20). Here it is worth noting that 40–60 per cent of the peasants were tenants, with great variation in this percentage between different parts of the country (Dessalegn Rahmato 1984: 22f). There are various opinions about the proportion of the produce that went to the landlords in the form of rent, but it seems reasonable to assume that the proportion fell somewhere between 30 and 50 per cent (Dessalegn Rahmato 1984: 25). It was an important improvement for former tenants and landless rural persons that they now were released from the tenure dependence on the landlords through the land reform principle of 'Land to the tiller'. The major economic potential of the land reform was in its effects on the incentives in the dominant peasant agricultural sector (dimension 4 in Figure 2.1), since it meant an increased economic freedom and increased renumeration for the individual peasants. The land reform could initially also be seen as strengthening the ties between the peasant and the land he or she cultivates. According to Dessalegn Rahmato (1984: 25), in the pre-revolutionary land tenure system 'the chief obstacle to improved production was the lack of security of tenure'.

It is also worth noting that at the time of the reform private commercial farms covered only some 1–2 per cent of the cultivated land in Ethiopia (Dessalegn Rahmato 1984: 21). As noted above, most of these farms were transformed into State farms. Only a small number of the large farms were transformed into peasant associations (Tiruneh 1993: 110). Therefore, the addition of cultivated land to peasant agriculture through the reform was quite limited. As the reform was based on the principle of 'Land to the tiller' and because this slogan was also linked to the right of the landless to be allocated land, the pressure on existing cultivated land increased. However, it should be noted that there was, and still is, quite a high proportion of arable land that lies idle in Ethiopia.

By the end of the 1980s, around 5.5 million peasant families had been grouped into peasant associations. After having fulfilled the initial objective of implementing the land reform, the peasant associations had the task of administering redistribution of land, and organising the rural population to promote rural development, for instance by stimulating and implementing various collectivisation policy programmes and measures.

In terms of economic system dimensions, the land reform can be classified as a change towards decentralisation of decision-making (dimension 1), reduced private ownership (dimension 3), and an increased role for incentives (dimension 4) and competition (dimension 5) through the distribution of usufructuary rights among individual peasants.

AGRICULTURAL COLLECTIVISATION

Collectivisation in Ethiopian agriculture consisted of the formation of two different parts: the service co-operatives and the producer co-operatives.

The service co-operatives were set up to supply their members with:

- crop marketing services;
- agricultural inputs (including fertilisers and improved seed);
- consumer goods;
- credit; and
- services like machinery, storage, and flour mills.

Furthermore, they were to promote the development of infrastructure, such as roads, clinics, and schools, and also to function as grain purchasers.

The service co-operatives, like peasant associations, were known to be relatively popular with the farmers, and membership of these became very common among the Ethiopian peasants. In 1986/87 more than 4.5 million peasant households, i.e. close to 80 per cent of all peasant households, were members of agricultural service co-operatives (Goyder and Goyder 1988: 83, IMF 1988: 27).

Besides the mainly economic objectives, the service co-operatives obviously also had political objectives. The service co-operatives were to:

- give an education in socialist philosophy and cooperative work in order to enhance the political consciousness of the peasantry
- provide political education, with a view to establish agricultural

29

producers cooperative societies by forming, promoting and con-
solidating mutual aid teams.

(Tegegne Teka 1988: 127)

Up to the first years of the 1990s the main economic function of most
service co-operatives was to supply the peasants with consumer goods. The
provision of health services, education, and grain mills were of course also
important roles but in practice the number of schools operated by these
co-operatives was very low; in 1986/87 there were 358 schools, i.e. one
school to twelve service co-operatives (IMF 1988: table IX). The situation
was no better in the case of health clinics. In 1986/87 there were 239 clinics
operated by service co-operatives (IMF 1988: table XII). This suggests that
the objectives of service co-operatives in providing social service have been
achieved only to a minor extent.

The political objective of agricultural service co-operatives to 'provide
political education, with a view to establish agricultural producers cooperative societies' was also less than successful.

Like the objectives of the service co-operatives, the objectives of the
agricultural producer co-operatives included both economic and political
aspects. According to Tegegne Teka, the objectives of the producer
co-operatives were:

- to bring to an end the capitalist exploitation and to see that it is not
  reinstated in the rural areas, and to do away with the exploitation of
  man by man.
- the use of modern agricultural technology to transform fragmented
  and small-sized farms to large-scale farming and to develop small-
  scale industry.
- by creating socialism in the rural areas, to safeguard the political,
  economic and social rights of the peasantry.
- to prepare the ground for national planning.

(Tegegne Teka 1988: 129)

The *Ten-Year Perspective Plan* issued in 1984 stated that agricultural
policy should transform agriculture to socialist modes of production. The
objective was that around 50 per cent of the total cultivated area in Ethiopia
should be farmed by producer co-operatives by the end of the plan period. At
the outset of the plan only 1.4 per cent of the cultivated area was under the
control of producer co-operatives (World Bank 1987b: 7). From having
comprised around 1.7 per cent of all peasant households in 1983/84, these
co-operatives in 1986/87 had increased their share to around 4 per cent of
peasant households. Obviously, the transformation of the agricultural sector
towards producer co-operatives was very slow compared to the scheduled
path. In terms of the ownership dimension (dimension 3) the collectivisation
programme did not change the Ethiopian economic system more than

marginally. This, however, does not mean that the government's emphasis on producer co-operatives did not have any effect on Ethiopian agricultural production. As will be argued below, the collectivisation programme had a severe negative impact on incentives (dimension 4) and production conditions in the peasant sector. Finally, the programme led to centralisation of decision-making (dimension 1) in the Ethiopian economy.

DISCRIMINATION AGAINST INDIVIDUAL PEASANTS

One inherent characteristic of the producer co-operativisation programme and the Ethiopian agricultural policy in general was the discrimination against peasants operating on an individual private basis. When a producer co-operative was formed (or when the number of members in the producer co-operative increased) the members of the co-operative had priority in the allocation of the best land as well as in access to irrigation facilities. This meant that superior land was transferred from individual or private peasants over to members of producer co-operatives. The private peasants concerned were allocated land of lower quality. This policy increased the great uncertainty about land security that existed already before the heavy emphasis on producer co-operatives. The uncertainty in land allocation meant that land conservation and other forms of improvements on the individual holdings became a highly risky investment for the private peasants. The uncertainties incorporated in the Ethiopian land tenure system during the socialist period can be expected to have had a determinate negative influence on the land use by private peasants and thereby on the overall agricultural performance.

In the allocation of inputs, such as fertilisers and capital equipment, priority (for instance through lower prices) was given to producer co-operatives over individual peasants. Other favourable incentives for producer co-operatives included such items as interest-free loans, lower land tax, and priority allocation of improved livestock and, compared to private peasants, disproportionate extension and co-operative staff support from the Ministry of Agriculture. An example of the consequences of the policy is that the use of improved seed and fertilisers continued to be low in Ethiopian peasant agriculture. According to the World Bank, only around 2 per cent of the farmers used improved seed during the second half of the 1980s (World Bank 1987a: 37, 1987b: 73). Another example can be taken from the credit market. Only 4 per cent of the official credit went directly to the peasant farmers, whereas the large-scale highly mechanised and thus capital-intensive State farms absorbed no less than 40 per cent (World Bank 1987b: 76, Kidane Mengisteab 1990: chapter 8).

State farms in particular, but also producer co-operatives, also obtained higher prices than private peasants on grain sold to the Agricultural Marketing Corporation (AMC) (producer co-operatives 4–5 birr per quintal, i.e. 10–20

31

per cent and State farms another 20 per cent higher prices) (World Bank 1987b: 45f). However, it should be noted that the producer co-operatives, like the State farms, were obliged to sell all their marketed grain to the AMC, whereas individual peasants were allowed to sell surplus over the AMC delivery quota in the open market. The open market prices were higher than the AMC prices. According to Eshetu Chole (1990: 95) the AMC farm gate prices on grain were less than 50 per cent of the open market prices. Thus, at least in theory, individual peasants who produced more than what was needed to fill the AMC quota obtained better prices for their surplus sales than producer co-operatives. However, for many peasants it was quite difficult to fill the quota delivery requirements, let alone produce a surplus (Dessalegn Rahmato 1984: 66, Befekadu Degefe and Tesfaye Tafesse 1990: 116).

The low prices did not only contribute to low agricultural production *per se* but also indirectly held back the use of fertilisers. Assume that it is necessary to achieve a benefit–cost ratio (cash output value compared to cash input value) of 2:1 from fertiliser use at recommended rates. Then, according to an estimate from the World Bank in 1987, the AMC farm gate prices for the three main cereals would have had to increase by at least around 60 per cent for wheat, by 26 per cent for maize, and by 34 per cent for teff to make it profitable for the farmers to use fertilisers for cash output production (World Bank 1987b: 49ff). If, on the other hand, the necessary benefit–cost ratio is 2.5:1 the price increases should amount to around 100 per cent for wheat, to 58 per cent for maize, and to nearly 68 per cent for teff (ibid.). From these estimates quite high price increases were needed to increase the use of fertilisers among Ethiopian peasants.

We have noted that there existed quite strong economic incentives for a peasant family to join the co-operative when a producer co-operative was set up in a peasant association. However, notwithstanding these favourable incentives the resistance towards joining producer co-operatives was strong. One reason may be that the co-operatives showed a poor performance compared to private individual peasants. It has been estimated that the 4 per cent of the peasants who had joined producer co-operatives up to 1987/88 contributed only around 2 per cent of the total agricultural output. One important, if not *the* most important, reason behind this poor performance was probably the lack of a direct link between an individual's work efforts and the private gains from these efforts.

As noted in the discussion about the various economic system dimensions in Chapter 2, the incentive system related to collective ownership is more complex and thus more difficult to make efficient than that related to individual ownership. There is no reason to expect that this is not the case also in peasant farming. By referring to the experience from the agricultural sector in Eastern European countries (during their socialist period), in 1987 the World Bank recommended the Ethiopian government to carefully consider that:

- cooperative democracy and autonomy, including the election of leaders, needs to be real rather than state imposed, otherwise the important advantage of member identification with the PC [producer co-operative] is lost;
- remuneration for both the PC and the members requires to be closely related to work input and output;
- PCs should be free to sell produce surplus to state 'quotas' on the open market;
- official producer prices should be frequently adjusted in response to changing economic forces;
- PCs should be free to decide which crops are grown and which other types of productive enterprise they might engage in;
- the size of the household plot should be such that individual families might have the incentive to produce above subsistence requirements for some commodities.

(World Bank 1987b: 54)

It is obvious that the situation in the Ethiopian producer co-operatives did not conform to these criteria. The negative effects on the ownership and incentives structure (dimensions 3 and 4) made the co-operativisation efforts unsuccessful. As will be seen in Chapter 6, by the end of the 1980s not only was the formation of new producer co-operatives very slow, but there were even producer co-operatives dismantled by their members.

VILLAGISATION AND RESETTLEMENT PROGRAMMES

The villagisation and resettlement programmes moved peasants from their old settlements to new sites. In the case of the villagisation programme that started on a national scale in December 1985, 35–40 per cent of the rural population were moved into villages.[5] Important official motives behind this programme were that it would be easier to improve social services such as health care and education. Furthermore, through the programme it would also be easier to increase the standards of living in terms of the accessibility of water and sanitation. However, other and perhaps even more important motives can be expected to have been at the centre of the efforts to achieve villagisation. One such motive was probably that by having the peasants in concentrated and controlled locations (villages) collection of taxes and quotas of agricultural produce by the AMC became more efficient. According to Cohen and Isaksson (1987: 2):

More importantly, the policy seems to be based on three assumptions rooted in the theories of Marx and Lenin:

(1) man is a social animal and the historical trend of rural people is toward village settlements;
(2) villagization is an essential step toward the formation of non-exploitative group farms that are the basis of agrarian socialism;
(3) revolutionary restructuring of the countryside requires strong political control at the grassroots, a control villagization well serves.

As will be made clear in Chapter 6, by the end of the 1980s, the government explicitly classified villagisation as a prerequisite for the establishment of producer co-operatives. One important reason behind this was probably, as mentioned by Cohen and Isaksson, that the government needed to increase access to the farmers and thereby make it easier to reach the peasants with information and political control. It also made recruitment of soldiers for the civil war easier.

The aim of the resettlement programmes, on the other hand, was to move people from one region or area to another in order to improve the balance between food potentials and population. The government presented it as a famine relief programme (Africa Watch 1991: 211ff, Oberai 1992).

Without going into details, it is clear that the objectives of the two types of programmes were not fulfilled. Social services were not created in line with villagisation, and producer co-operatives were not established to the degree that was intended. As for resettlement schemes, we note that there were also very doubtful consequences (Oberai 1992), partly as a result of the very high costs involved in resettling a family and the lack of adequate planning. Furthermore, both villagisation and the resettlement programme were implemented against the will of the peasants and the resettled. Therefore, violence was quite frequent in both programmes. The negative effects on peasants' incentives, plus the uncertainty and risks linked to these programmes counteracted, and may even have outweighed, the potentially positive effects on agricultural performance. In terms of the economic system dimensions, the villagisation and resettlement programmes can be classified as leading to increased centralisation (dimension 1).

FOREIGN ECONOMIC RELATIONS

By the motto *Ethiopia Tikdem* the new leadership showed its commitment to nationalism. Through the policy that followed they also clearly demonstrated hostility to private ownership in general and foreign capital owners in particular. As a result, foreign-owned capital was no longer invested in the country and foreign entrepreneurs left the country. Another factor that characterised the foreign economic relations of socialist Ethiopia is the continuation of the import substitution policy. This policy was introduced by the Haile Selassie regime in order to combat the trade deficit that had emerged since the 1950s as a consequence of falling export revenues and increasing import expenditures related to imports of finished products (Bulti Terfassa 1992: 142). Trade and exchange rate policy under the *Ethiopia Tikdem* period was characterised by the imposition of licences, quantitative restrictions, trade taxes and a centralised allocation of foreign exchange at an overvalued exchange rate. In the latter case one may well say that the Ethiopian government, for various reasons, neglected to have an active exchange rate policy during the entire socialist period, a period that started at more or less the same time as the collapse of the Bretton Woods system with fixed exchange rates.

It should be noted that exchange rate policy is a field of economic policy that is of the utmost importance to a country through its direct involvement by covering perhaps *the* most important price in open economies, the exchange rate. Even if Ethiopia moved towards autarky through her economic policy she was still heavily dependent on foreign trade and thus was very dependent on having a proper exchange rate policy. It is then remarkable, and we will come back to this in later chapters, that during the entire period of socialist rule, the Ethiopian currency, the birr, was pegged to the US dollar in a fixed and constant relationship: 2.07 birr = US$1.

This fixed exchange rate was not only a clear overvaluation of the Ethiopian birr (see the following chapters), the pegging to the US dollar was also inappropriate. The fixed relationship between the Ethiopian birr and the US dollar was probably due to the pre-1973 international monetary system, where the US dollar was the principal reserve currency whose value was defined and guaranteed in gold. However, since 1973, when the Bretton Woods monetary system with fixed exchange rates came to an end, there are no a priori motives for a country to relate its currency completely to the US dollar. In the case of Ethiopia, only a minor share of foreign trade during the *Ethiopia Tikdem* period was with the USA, whereas the trade with the EEC countries was much greater. Exports to the USA in the period from 1975 to 1990 varied between 8 and 33 per cent (on average 19 per cent) of the total Ethiopian exports. The corresponding variation of exports to the EEC countries was between 24 and 49 per cent (on average 37 per cent). On the import side the corresponding figures for imports from the USA were 4–19 per cent (on average 11 per cent) whereas the share of imports from the EEC countries varied between 32 and 46 per cent (on average 37 per cent) during the period considered. Thus, it is obvious that the pegging of the birr to the US dollar was inappropriate. The problems of the Ethiopian exchange rate policy will be more fully discussed in Chapters 6 and 8.

In terms of Figure 2.1, the development of Ethiopia's trade and exchange rate policy during the years of socialist rule can be characterised as a change towards the right along the *internationalisation* ↔ *autarky* dimension. The trade and exchange rate policy contributed to the depression of potential export production, both in agriculture and industry, and thereby undermined the potential for trade to work as an 'engine of growth' in Ethiopia.

Finally, in terms of foreign assistance to Ethiopia, the revolution also brought about important changes. The execution of sixty aristocrats and Ethiopian notables on 22 November 1974 aroused strong protests from the USA and Western Europe. An example of the tensions between the new Ethiopian government and the Western world is the following extract from the *Chicago Tribune*: 'if the old regime of Emperor Haile Selassie was corrupt, Ethiopia's ruling military council has shown after some months that the new regime is murderous beyond belief' (here quoted from Korn 1986: 12). The continuous violation of basic human rights in Ethiopia produced increasing political friction in Ethiopia's relations with Western countries in general and the USA in particular and by 1977, the USA, which for more than thirty years had been 'Ethiopia's main foreign friend and purveyor of economic and military assistance, was shorn of its presence and influence and its place was seized by the Soviet Union' (Korn 1986: 1, see also Korn 1986: chapter 2).

Although the Western countries did not leave Ethiopia altogether, the financial flows and assistance were kept on a low level. In contrast, the Soviet Union and its East European allies, together with other communist countries, increased their influence and activities in Ethiopia, in terms of economic institutional assistance and in military assistance. Because of the characteristics of the Eastern communist economic systems, the transition of foreign relations from West to East also strengthened the above-mentioned change in the Ethiopian economic system towards centralisation (dimension 1), administrative processes (dimension 2), collective ownership (dimension 3), orders (dimension 4), non-competition (dimension 5), and less economic openness towards the Western countries (dimension 6).

SUMMARY OF CHANGES TO THE ECONOMIC SYSTEM

In the previous sections it has been described how various programmes and reforms changed the Ethiopian economic system as a consequence of the 1974 revolution and the motto *Ethiopia Tikdem*. The dominance of the agricultural sector continued. Even if the land reform under the slogan 'Land to the tiller' was a change with important potential, it must be remembered that socialist ambitions soon outranged the potential positive effects of the land reform. The collectivisation efforts (dimensions 3 and 4), the villagisation and resettlement programmes (dimension 1), and the distortive domestic incentive system with the Agricultural Marketing Corporation's (AMC) monopoly in agricultural trading (dimensions 2 and 5), the heavy discrimination of individual private peasants and the government's emphasis on producer co-operatives and State farms in the allocation of resources (fertilisers, credit, and extension services) (dimensions 2 and 4) generally undermined the agricultural sector.[6] In particular, individual peasants suffered

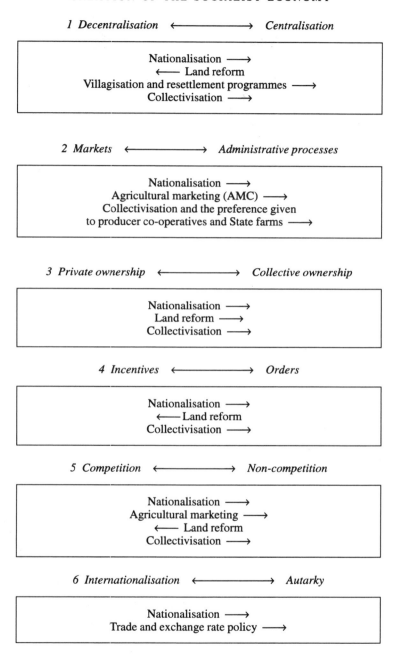

Figure 3.1 Ethiopia Tikdem – economic system changes

heavily from the distortive policy and the uncertainty in land tenure, despite the fact that the collectivisation efforts failed and only about 4 per cent, that is far below the targeted 50 per cent, of the peasants joined producer co-operatives.

In brief, in terms of the dimensions presented in Figure 2.1, the changes in the economic system that were introduced up to 1988 under the motto *Ethiopia Tikdem* can be summarised as shown in Figure 3.1.

Thus, by the end of the 1980s Ethiopia had an economic system with the following features:

- Highly centralised resource allocation.
- Administrative processes that dominated the allocation of resources of production, and where non-market prices on inputs and outputs were the rule. Furthermore, orders, not prices, dominated as the basis for industrial production and investments. Thus, Ethiopia could be classified as being close to a command economy. As a consequence parallel markets for consumer goods, and some inputs, flourished.
- Widespread State ownership in non-agriculture. In agriculture the State owned the land but private (individual) farmers dominated the use of it.
- Lack of incentives for individuals and companies, insecure land tenure for peasants, and an emphasis on State farms and producer co-operatives in agriculture.
- Lack of competition.
- Heavy trade and exchange rate controls with an overvalued exchange rate and a growing illegal trade both in goods and foreign exchange.

This classification, and Figure 3.1, indicate that after the overthrow of Haile Selassie the Derg, by implementing the content behind the slogan *Ethiopia Tikdem*, succeeded in transforming Ethiopia into a society with an economic system located way out on the right-hand side in relation to more or less all economic system dimensions.

Finally, in relation to the fourteen rules for good economic policy management (see Chapter 1), it is apparent that the design of the Ethiopian economic policy under the motto *Ethiopia Tikdem* conflicted with many of these rules. For instance, the price and tax policy, including trade and exchange rate policy, undermined the potential of using trade as an engine of growth (principles 4, 5, 6, 7, 8, 9, 10, 11, and 14). Furthermore, the borderlines between public and private sector activity were not particularly well-defined (principle 13) and the government took a clear ideological rather than a technical or economic efficiency view of the problems with public sector enterprises (principle 12). Finally, due to the emphasis on ideology it seems obvious that the *Ethiopia Tikdem* policy also conflicted with the first principle of good policy management, namely to avoid poor technicians in policymaking.

4

EXPECTED ECONOMIC EFFECTS OF THE *ETHIOPIA TIKDEM* PERIOD

INTRODUCTION

The previous chapter analysed how the Derg's policy under the motto *Ethiopia Tikdem* revolutionised the Ethiopian economic system in more or less all the dimensions listed in Figure 2.1. The changes led to an economic system quite different from a decentralised one where markets and private ownership govern the allocation of resources and where incentives, competition, and international openness are the major characteristics. What then could be expected to result from this type of systemic changes? In this chapter we will use the analytical dual general equilibrium model of Chapter 2 to obtain a better understanding of the economic consequences of the changes that characterised the *Ethiopia Tikdem* period. By doing this we also aim to prepare the reader for the following chapter's analysis of the *actual* economic performance during the *Ethiopia Tikdem* period.

It should be noted that the analysis of the expected effects of the economic systemic and policy changes in this chapter will be strictly theoretical and qualitative. First we will make a simple diagrammatical analysis of the expected economic effects followed by a more elaborated analysis of the economic system changes and the policy measures that were introduced during the socialist period.

The analysis will indicate how the system changes, together with other important factors in Ethiopia, such as the civil war and population growth, affected the structure of the economy up to 1987/88. In general, our model analysis will indicate that the *Ethiopia Tikdem* period was disadvantageous for the peasant sector, a fact that made it difficult for this sector to produce a surplus that through trade could be transformed into imports of investment goods.

A SIMPLE DUAL ECONOMY ANALYSIS

In terms of the diagrammatic analytical framework described in Figure 2.2 the major reforms and policy changes that were introduced during the *Ethiopia*

Tikdem period can be represented and analysed by dividing the policies into three categories: peasant policies, non-peasant domestic policies, and foreign economic policies.

Peasant policies

This category includes land reform, collectivisation, villagisation and resettlement policies, credit and tax policies, and the provision of extension services. The land reform included a significant potential for peasants by paving the way for increased decentralisation (dimension 1, see also Figure 3.1) and the role of incentives (dimension 4) and competition (dimension 5) in the economy. However, it is reasonable to assume that the other policy measures taken against individual peasants, that is the emphasis on villagisation, resettlement, and collectivisation programmes (implying changes in dimensions 1, 2, 3, 4, and 5) more than outweighed the initial potentials of this reform. Given this assumption, the per capita peasant production possibility curve shifts downwards as indicated in Figure 4.1. This negative shift reduces the per capita wage to w_{A1} in terms of peasant produce and to w_{N1} in terms of non-peasant produce. At this reduced wage level non-peasant employment will increase and peasant employment will decrease, *ceteris paribus*. As a

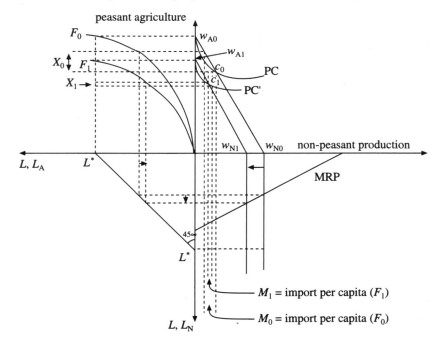

Figure 4.1 Effects of *Ethiopia Tikdem*: peasant policies

40

consequence, per capita exports from the peasant sector and thereby also per capita imports of non-peasant products will be reduced. Thus, the non-agricultural investments generated by the agricultural surplus will contract.

Non-peasant domestic policies

This category includes nationalisation of non-labour means of production and centralisation of non-peasant production with concomitant changes in the allocation of resources (see dimensions 1–5 in Figure 3.1) and a highly distortive price policy where the relative price on non-peasant products in terms of peasant products was increased by administrative decisions. In the diagrammatic model these policies all affect the marginal revenue product of non-peasant production, but in different ways and not all in the same direction.

Nationalisation should be expected to have a clear-cut negative effect on non-peasant production, due for example to loss of entrepreneurial skill and capital. Thus, the marginal revenue curve should be expected to shift inwards. On the other hand, the centrally, non-market determined prices (and allocation of inputs), included in the import substitution strategy, which were part of the *Ethiopia Tikdem* development strategy, meant that a higher relative value was placed on the output from non-peasant production. This might have out-weighed the negative productivity effect on the marginal revenue product mentioned above. In terms of Figure 2.2, the combined effect of the non-peasant domestic policies can be represented by an inward rotation of the relative price line and thus an outward shift of the MRP curve (see Figure 4.2). As a consequence, the peasant sector employment and production decrease, while we should expect a positive net effect on non-peasant employment and production. This results in lower per capita exports and imports. The implication of this is that imported non-peasant investments have to be reduced if the investments cannot be financed by other means, such as loans or foreign aid. Given the import substitution policy it is reasonable to assume that the surplus generated within the non-peasant sector will remain small until the non-peasant sectors protected by the policy reach international competitiveness. Therefore, this set of policies also tends to hamper growth in non-peasant activities even if in the short run the policies mean a stimulus for such activities.

Foreign economic policies

This category includes the trade and exchange rate policy during the *Ethiopia Tikdem* period. Severe restrictions on imports of non-peasant products, heavy taxation of agricultural exports, and a mismanaged exchange rate (that is a move towards autarky along dimension 6 in Figure 2.1) all meant a negative effect on the relative price of peasant produce. In terms of our diagrammatic

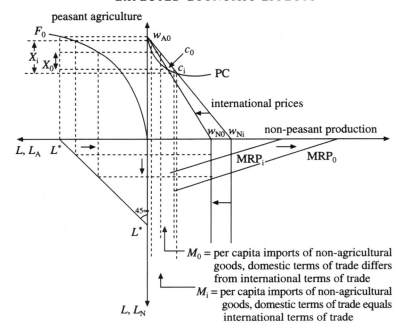

Figure 4.2 Effects of *Ethiopia Tikdem*: non-peasant domestic policies and foreign economic policies

analysis the effects of the foreign economic policy during the years of *Ethiopia Tikdem* can be represented in the same way as the net effects of the non-peasant domestic policies in Figure 4.2. In conclusion, the foreign economic policy can be expected to have strengthened negative effects on the peasant sector, thereby further reducing the potential for this dominating sector to contribute substantially to exports. To this should be added the fact that non-military foreign assistance was low and decreasing, due to the government's policy in general and the handling of security policy in particular. The latter included frequent violations of basic human rights, something that upset many donors and reduced their willingness to support Ethiopia. Thus, foreign aid did not increase to compensate fully for the deterioration of the peasant sector in the provision of imports of intermediate industrial goods and non-military capital equipment.

A GENERAL EQUILIBRIUM INSTITUTIONAL ANALYSIS

In this section we develop the analysis of the expected effects a little further by using the institutional four-sector dual economy model that was presented in Chapter 2. In terms of this model, the changes that followed the revolution in 1974 and the proclamation of the slogan *Ethiopia Tikdem*, together with population growth, can be represented as:

- deterioriation of the institutional conditions for commercial sectors $(dI_j < 0, j = C, M)$;
- deterioration of the institutional conditions for peasant agriculture $(dI_S < 0)$;
- collectivisation of peasant land $(dR_C = - dR_S > 0)$;
- land degradation and land erosion $(dR < 0)$;
- distorted prices through domestic resource allocation policy as well as trade and exchange rate policies $(dp_S < 0)$;
- population growth $(dL > 0)$; and
- demoralisation at the war front and in the public sector $(dI_G < 0)$ and concomitant increased government allocation to this sector $(dp_G > 0)$.

Deterioration of the institutional conditions for commercial sectors

In terms of the economic system analysis in Chapter 3, the deterioration of the institutional conditions for the commercial sectors mainly took the form of nationalisation and a threat of further nationalisation whenever the new socialist government should find it expedient. Besides the change in ownership structure, the nationalisation also meant centralisation, less reliance on markets, incentives and competition, and less international openness in economic relations.

The production function of the peasant sector has been assumed to be unaffected by the changes in the institutional conditions for commercial sectors. Thus, the wage level in the economy will not be affected by these changes. However, as can be seen in Tables 4.1 and 4.2, employment and the use of capital in non-peasant agriculture and manufacturing will clearly be affected and so will production in these sectors. This is not only a direct consequence of the institutional changes mentioned above but also an indirect consequence of these changes. The reason is that the institutional changes, according to our assumptions, affect the stock of capital. First, foreign-owned capital is expected to leave the country as a direct consequence of the nationalisation policy. Second, for the same reason and also because of the threat of further nationalisation, new foreign capital is expected to stop flowing into the country. Third, domestic private capital is also expected to flow out of the country, together with Ethiopian capitalists and entrepreneurs, as a direct consequence of actual and potential nationalisations. Finally, we may also expect a negative indirect effect since the new policy stimulates savings in kind, that is in non-productive non-capital goods, rather than in bank deposits, capital equipment, and real estate.

Since there was no effect on the wage level in our model world, employment and production in the public sector should be expected to remain

Table 4.1 Effects of institutional changes on manufacturing

$$dL_C/dI_M = (1/D)C_{LK}(M_{LL}M_{KI} - M_{LK}M_{LI}) < 0$$

$$dL_S/dI_M = (1/D)\{C[(M_{KK}M_{LI} - M_{LK}M_{KI})K_r - M_{LK}K_{IM} - M_{LI}] \\ - M_{LK}M_{LI}[(k_C - k_M)C_{LK} + C_{LR}R_C/L_C]/k_M \\ + M_{LK}M_{KI}[(k_M - k_C)C_{LK} - C_{LR}R_C/L_C]\} < 0, \text{ if } k_C \geq k_M$$

$$dL_G/dI_M = 0$$

$$dL_M/dI_M = -(1/D)\{C[(M_{KK}M_{LI} - M_{LK}M_{KI})K_r - M_{LK}K_{IM} - M_{LI}] \\ + M_{LK}C_{LL}(M_{KI} + M_{LI}/k_M)\} > 0$$

$$dK_C/dI_M = (1/D)C_{LL}(M_{LK}M_{LI} - M_{LL}M_{KI}) < 0$$

$$dK_M/dI_M = K_{IM} + (1/D)C_{LL}(M_{LL}M_{KI} - M_{LK}M_{LI}) > 0$$

$$dw/dI_M = 0$$

$$dr/dI_M = (1/D)C(M_{LK}M_{LI} - M_{LL}M_{KI}) > 0$$

where $C = C_{LL}C_{KK} - C_{KL}^2 > 0$, $D = -M_{LL}C > 0$, and $k_i = K_i/L_i$, $i = C, M$

Table 4.2 Effects of institutional changes on non-peasant agriculture

$$dL_C/dI_C = (1/D)M_{LL}(C_{KK}C_{LI} - C_{LK}C_{KI}) > 0$$

$$dL_S/dI_C = -(1/D)M_{LK}\{K_{IC}C + C_{LK}(k_M - k_C)(C_{LI}/k_C + C_{KI}) + k_M C_{KR}C_{LI}R_C/K_C \\ - C_{LR}C_{KI}R_C/L_C\}$$

$$dL_G/dI_C = 0$$

$$dL_M/dI_C = (1/D)M_{LK}\{K_{IC}C - C_{LK}(C_{LI} + k_C C_{KI}) - C_{LR}C_{KI}R_C/L_C\}$$

$$dK_C/dI_C = (1/D)M_{LL}(C_{LL}C_{KI} - C_{LK}C_{LI}) > 0$$

$$dK_M/dI_C = K_{IC} - (1/D)M_{LL}(C_{LL}C_{KI} - C_{LK}C_{LI})$$

$$dw/dI_C = dr/dI_C = 0$$

where $C = C_{LL}C_{KK} - C_{KL}^2 > 0$, $D = -M_{LL}C > 0$, and $k_i = K_i/L_i$, $i = C, M$

unaffected by the changes in the institutional conditions of the commercial sectors, *ceteris paribus*.

Turning to the two commercial sectors of production, manufacturing, and non-peasant agriculture, we note from Table 4.1 that deterioration in the institutional conditions for manufacturing, $dI_M < 0$, not only lead to a negative shift in the manufacturing production possibilities *per se* but will also lead to lower employment of both labour and capital in this sector. Thus, we should expect a determinate fall in manufacturing production. Since the wage level, as well as prices on commodities, is assumed to be unaffected by the institutional changes, initially there are no incentives for the non-peasant agricultural sector to increase its demand for labour and capital. At the initial price on capital the reduced demand for capital cannot be fully compensated for by increased activities in non-peasant agriculture. This means that the changes in institutional conditions for manufacturing production lead to a net reduction in the demand for capital, *ceteris paribus*. As a consequence there will be a downward pressure on the price on capital and a reduction of the total available stock of capital in the economy. The lower price on capital increases the use of capital in non-peasant agriculture. This increased use of capital leads to increased employment and production in this sector also.

The net effect on the distribution of labour between peasant and non-peasant activities depends on which is the more labour-intensive activity – manufacturing or non-peasant agriculture. Considering the quite high degree of mechanisation in State farms and the low use of capital in the dominating small-scale manufacturing and handicraft sector in Ethiopia, it is reasonable to assume that non-peasant agriculture is more capital-intensive than manufacturing, that is $k_C > k_M$ (Kidane Mengisteab 1990: 152–157).

When this is the case, that is when manufacturing is the more labour-intensive of the two, there will be a determinate fall in non-peasant employment and thus an increase in peasant employment.[1]

Turning to the effects of institutional changes in non-peasant agriculture, $dI_C < 0$, Table 4.2 shows that apart from leaving the wage unaffected such institutional changes do not affect the price on capital in our model world. Since manufacturing has been assumed to display constant returns to scale in labour and capital, the freed capital in non-peasant agriculture, after taking capital migration into consideration, can always be absorbed by the manufacturing sector at the initial manufacturing factor intensity and by the possibility of employing more labour at the initial wage level. It should be noted, however, that if the stock of capital is greatly reduced by the deterioration of the institutional conditions for non-peasant agriculture, that is if K_{IC} is high, the effect on the manufacturing sector may be reversed so that both non-peasant agricultural and manufacturing production fall. However, in countries like Ethiopia in the 1970s and 1980s, such an effect was more likely to arise as a consequence of the initial nationalisation of commercial farms, whereas the net effect on the capital availability following the system changes for non-peasant agriculture was probably much less pronounced. During this later period, the socialist objectives of the government were already clear to domestic and potential foreign capital owners, as well as to donors of non-military capital and equipment, who by then had adjusted to the policy of the government towards private ownership, in particular foreign ownership. Furthermore, because of the small size of the private stock of capital at the time of the revolution, the absolute change in the stock of capital as a result of the system changes was probably small. Thus, it seems reasonable to assume that manufacturing was positively affected by the deterioration of the institutional conditions for non-peasant agricultural production, *ceteris paribus*.

45

Finally, the net effect on peasant employment, as in the case of institutional changes in manufacturing, is dependent on a whole set of factors:

- the capital market supply response (the smaller this response, that is the lower K_{IC}, the weaker will be the tendency for a positive net effect on peasant employment);
- the relative capital intensities of the two capital-using sectors (the more capital-intensive non-peasant agriculture is compared to the manufacturing sector, the weaker will be the tendency for a positive effect on peasant employment when negative institutional changes are introduced in non-peasant agriculture);
- the land–labour ratio (R_C/L_C) and the complementarity of labour and land (C_{LR}) in non-peasant agriculture (the greater the land–labour ratio and the higher the complementarity between land and labour, the weaker the tendency for a positive effect on peasant employment), *ceteris paribus*.

In conclusion, our analysis shows that the deterioration of the institutional conditions for manufacturing or non-peasant agriculture can be expected to lead to reduced production in the sector for which institutional conditions have been changed, whereas we would expect a tendency for positive effects on the other sector. The wage level and consequently the public sector also, should be expected to remain unaffected by the changes. The net effect on peasant employment and production is indeterminate in principle. However, the stronger the deterioration of the institutional conditions for the labour-intensive sector, the stronger will be the tendency to a positive net effect on peasant employment and production.

Deterioration of the institutional conditions for peasant agriculture

The introduction of and emphasis on various collectivisation, villagisation, and resettlement programmes during the *Ethiopia Tikdem* period all had a direct impact on the production possibilities for the peasant sector. All in all, as we concluded in Chapter 3, it is reasonable to assume that these various programmes have outweighed the potential positive effects of the land reform. These programmes and the land reform meant a net deterioration of the institutional conditions for peasant agriculture. In our model these changes can be represented as $dI_S < 0$.

Due to the central role of the peasant sector in our model, in particular in the determination of the wage level, the deterioration of the institutional conditions for peasant agriculture leads directly to a reduction of the wage level in the economy. This means lower costs in the public sector and consequently increased employment and production in this part of the economy, *ceteris paribus*.

Table 4.3 Effects of institutional changes on peasant agriculture

$dL_C/dI_S = (1/D)\alpha Z_1 M_{LK}\{(k_C - k_M)C_{LK}/k_C - k_M C_{RK}R_C/K_C\}/L < 0$, if $k_M \geq k_C$

$dL_S/dI_S = -(1/D)\alpha Z_1\{2M_{LK}C_{LK} - M_{LL}C_{KK} - M_{KK}C_{LL} - C[M_{LL}/G_{LL} + 1$
$\quad - M_{LK}(K_w - K_r/k_M)]\}/L$

$dL_G/dI_S = -(1/D)\alpha Z_1 M_{LL}C/(LG_{LL}) < 0$

$dL_M/dI_S = -(1/D)\alpha Z_1\{C(1 - M_{LK}(K_w - K_r/k_M)) + M_{LK}[(k_C - k_M)C_{LK}$
$\quad + C_{LR}R_C/L_C]/k_M\}$

$dK_C/dI_S = (1/D)\alpha Z_1 M_{LK}\{(k_C - k_M)C_{LK} + C_{LR}R_C/L_C\}/L > 0$, if $k_C \geq k_M$

$dK_M/dI_S = (1/D)\alpha Z_1 M_{LK}\{(k_M - k_C)C_{LK} - C_{LR}R_C/L_C + C(K_w k_M - K_r)\}/L$

$dw/dI_S = -(1/D)\alpha Z_1 M_{LL}C/L > 0$

$dr/dI_S = -(1/D)\alpha Z_1 M_{LK}C/L < 0$

where $C = C_{LL}C_{KK} - C_{KL}^2 > 0$, $2M_{LK}C_{LK} - M_{LL}C_{KK} - M_{KK}C_{LL} < 0$,

$D = -M_{LL}C > 0$, and $k_i = K_i/L_i$, $i = C, M$

Turning to the effects on manufacturing and non-peasant agriculture, we note from Table 4.3 that these effects depend to a great extent on the difference in capital intensity between non-peasant agriculture and the manufacturing sector. The greater the difference in capital intensity and the higher the complementarity between labour and land in non-peasant agriculture (C_{LR}), the stronger will be the tendency towards a positive effect on the labour-intensive capital-using sector and a negative effect on the other capital-using sector. This is due to the change in the relative factor price (w/r decreases) that results from the negative institutional changes for peasant agriculture. As argued above, in the case of socialist Ethiopia it is reasonable to assume that $k_C > k_M$. Thus we should also expect a relatively strong tendency for the manufacturing sector to expand and for the non-peasant agriculture to contract, *ceteris paribus*. As a consequence rural–urban migration is expected to have increased when negative institutional changes were introduced in the peasant sector. Furthermore, provided that the capital supply response to the wage reduction is low and the capital supply response to the higher return to capital is high, peasant employment will fall. Thus, both agricultural sectors, and thereby also agricultural exports, tend to suffer from these changes.

In conclusion, according to our model analysis, the deterioration of the institutional conditions for peasant agriculture should be expected to have led to reduced wages and lower production in this sector, and thus to lower savings and agricultural exports. Furthermore, the public sector is expected to have expanded and there will also be a tendency towards expansion in the labour-intensive non-peasant sector.

Collectivisation of peasant land

The collectivisation programmes emphasised heavily between 1984 and 1990 meant not only a deterioration in the institutional conditions for peasants but also a transfer of land from individual private peasants to members of producer co-operatives. In our model analysis this transfer of peasant land can be represented by $dR_C = -dR_S > 0$.

Naturally, this transfer of land can be expected to have a direct negative impact on the peasant sector and a positive effect on producer co-operatives. When land is transferred from private peasants to members of producer co-operatives, the co-operative sector (part of sector C in our model world) increases its demand and use of capital and labour.

In the way the wage level has been assumed to be determined, it will be unaffected by the transfer of land. Thus, the public sector will also be unaffected.

The increased use of capital in the co-operative sector will come solely from the manufacturing sector and leave the price of capital as well as the total stock of non-military capital unaffected, *ceteris paribus*. The reason is that the manufacturing sector has been assumed to display constant returns to scale. Therefore, this sector will reduce its employment so that the initial factor intensity is unchanged. When manufacturing is more (less) labour intensive than the co-operative agricultural sector, the net effect on employment outside the peasant sector will be negative (positive).

In conclusion, the collectivisation programmes are expected to have had a directly negative effect on the peasant sector, whereas the co-operative sector can be expected to have been positively affected, *ceteris paribus*. The model analysis also suggests a negative effect on the manufacturing sector. The public sector, finally, can be expected to be unaffected by the collectivisation policies (Table 4.4).

Table 4.4 Effects of collectivisation of peasant land

$$dL_C/dR_C = (1/D)M_{LL}(C_{KK}C_{RL} - C_{LK}C_{RK}) > 0$$

$$dL_S/dR_C = -(1/D)M_{LK}(k_M - k_C)\{C_{LK}(C_{RK} + C_{RL}/k_C) + C_{RK}C_{RL}R_C/K_C\} \leq (\geq) 0$$
$$\text{if } k_C \leq (\geq) k_M$$

$$dL_G/dR_C = 0$$

$$dL_M/dR_C = (1/D)M_{LK}(C_{LL}C_{RK} - C_{LK}C_{RL}) < 0$$

$$dK_C/dR_C = (1/D)M_{LL}(C_{LL}C_{RK} - C_{LK}C_{RL}) > 0$$

$$dK_M/dR_C = -dK_C/dR_C < 0$$

$$dw/dR_C = dr/dR_C = 0$$

where $D = -M_{LL}\mathbf{C} > 0$, $\mathbf{C} = C_{LL}C_{KK} - C_{KL}^2 > 0$ and $k_i = K_i/L_i$, $i = C, M$

Land degradation and land erosion

The peasant policies, in particular during the 1984–1990 period of collectivisation, villagisation, and resettlement programmes, all meant insecure property rights for peasants. In addition, the civil war increased this insecurity and thus contributed to making investments in land risky. As a consequence land eroded in various ways due to the very limited incentives to preserve land and land quality. Therefore, to the above effects of the collectivisation programmes we should add the indirect effects of land degradation. In our analytical model this indirect effect of the *Ethiopia Tikdem* policy can be analysed by solving our model for $dR < 0$. This reduction of the available land is assumed to be distributed between the peasant sector (S) and the non-peasant agricultural sector (C) as follows: $dR_C = \beta dR$ and $dR_S = (1 - \beta)dR$, where $0 \leq \beta \leq 1$. Considering the relative size of the two agricultural sectors in Ethiopia it is reasonable to assume that β is low, in particular as we have noted that the peasant sector was subjected to negative discrimination compared with State farms and producer co-operatives in the distribution of fertilisers and extension services; that is, factors which can be expected to counteract land degradation.

It follows immediately from our assumption about wage determination that the wage level will decrease when land erodes. Due to the lower wage level, employment and production in the public sector (including defence) will increase at a given budget. Provided, as we have argued above, that manufacturing is labour intensive relative to non-peasant agriculture ($k_M < k_C$), that the capital supply response to the wage reduction is low and the capital supply response to the higher return to capital is high, peasant employment will fall along with the land degradation and land erosion, *ceteris paribus*. Furthermore, the lower wage gives rise to a tendency for the two capital-using sectors – manufacturing and non-peasant agriculture – to increase their employment and production. As a consequence of the increased profitability resulting from decreases in the cost of labour, more capital will be demanded and its price will increase, *ceteris paribus*.

The effects of the change in relative factor prices are indeterminate in principle. However, there is a tendency for the changes in factor prices arising from land degradation and land erosion to stimulate the labour-intensive sector and to lead to a contraction of the capital-intensive sector. The greater the difference in capital intensities ($k_C - k_M$) and the higher the complementarity between labour and land in non-peasant agriculture, the stronger will be the tendency for a positive effect on the labour-intensive capital-using sector and a negative effect on the other capital-using sector.

In non-peasant agriculture land degradation will have a direct negative effect that counteracts the positive effect coming from the lower wage. Thus, it reduces the positive effect when non-peasant agriculture is the relatively labour-intensive sector and strengthens the negative effect when non-peasant

Table 4.5 Effects of land degradation and land erosion

$dL_C/dR = (1/D)\{\alpha Z_R M_{LK}[(k_C - k_M)C_{LK}/k_C - k_M C_{RK} R_C/K_C]$
$\qquad + \beta L C_{RL} M_{LL}(C_{KK} - C_{LK})\}/L$

$dL_S/dR = (1/D)\{\alpha Z_R \{M_{LL} C_{KK} + M_{KK} C_{LL} - 2M_{LK} C_{LK} + C(M_{LL}/G_{LL} + 1$
$\qquad - M_{LK}(K_w - K_r/k_M))\}/L + \beta M_{LK}(k_C - k_M)[C_{LK}(C_{RL}/k_C + C_{RK})$
$\qquad + C_{RL} C_{RK} R_C/K_C]\}$

$dL_G/dR = -(1/D)\alpha Z_R M_{LL} C/(G_{LL} L) < 0$

$dL_M/dR = (1/D)\alpha Z_R M_{LK}\{C(K_w - K_r/k_M - 1) + C_{LK}(k_M - k_C)/k_C$
$\qquad - C_{LK}(k_M - k_C)^2/(k_C k_M) - C_{LR} R_C/(L_C/k_M)$
$\qquad + \beta L\{C_{RL} C_{LK}(M_{LL} - M_{LK}) + C_{RK} M_{LK}[(k_M - k_C)C_{LK} - C_{LR} R_C/L_C]\}\}/L$

$dK_C/dR = (1/D)\{\alpha Z_R M_{LK}[(k_C - k_M)C_{LK} + R_C C_{LR}/L_C] - \beta L M_{LL}(C_{LK} C_{RL}$
$\qquad - C_{LL} C_{RK})\}/L > 0 \text{ if } k_C \geq k_M$

$dK_M/dR = (1/D)\{\alpha Z_R M_{LK}[(k_M - k_C)C_{LK} - C_{LR} R_C/L_C + C(K_w k_M - K_r)]$
$\qquad + \beta L M_{LL}(C_{LK} C_{RL} - C_{LL} C_{RK})\}/L$

$dw/dR = -(1/D)\alpha Z_R M_{LL} C/L > 0$

$dr/dR = -(1/D)\alpha Z_R M_{LK} C/L < 0$

where $\mathbf{C} = C_{LL} C_{KK} - C_{KL}^2 > 0$, $M_{LL} C_{KK} + M_{KK} C_{LL} - 2M_{LK} C_{LK} > 0$,

$D = -M_{LL} \mathbf{C} > 0$, and $k_i = K_i/L_i$, $i = C, M$

---

agriculture is capital-intensive in comparison with the manufacturing sector.

In conclusion, provided that non-peasant agriculture is more capital-intensive than the manufacturing sector, land degradation and land erosion should be expected to lead to negative effects not only in peasant agriculture but in agriculture in general. Consequently, it can also be expected to lead to a reduction in agricultural exports and an expansion of non-agricultural activities, that is manufacturing and public sector activities, and thus to give rise to increased migration to urban areas (Table 4.5).

Distorted prices through domestic resource allocation policy and trade and exchange rate policies

Chapter 3 described how peasants were discriminated against in that they received lower prices for their produce as compared to producer co-operatives and State farms while at the same time paying higher prices for various non-labour inputs. The prices for grain that the peasants received from the Agricultural Marketing Corporation (AMC) were less than 50 per cent of the free market average prices (Eshetu Chole 1990: 95). As seen in Chapter 3, the peasants that had been tenants under the old feudal system (some 40–60 per cent of the peasants) were freed from the rents paid to the landlords (between

Table 4.6 Effects of price distortions

$$dL_C/dp_S = (1/D)\alpha Z M_{LK}\{(k_C - k_M)C_{LK}/k_C - k_M R_C C_{RK}/K_C\}/L < 0, \text{ if } k_M \geq k_C$$

$$dL_S/dp_S = (1/D)(-\alpha Z)\{2M_{LK}C_{LK} - M_{LL}C_{KK} - M_{KK}C_{LL} - C[M_{LL}/G_{LL} + 1 \\ - M_{LK}(K_w - K_r/k_M)]\}/L$$

$$dL_G/dp_S = -(1/D)\alpha Z M_{LL} C/(LG_{LL}) < 0$$

$$dL_M/dp_S = -(1/D)\alpha Z\{C(1 - M_{LK}K_w - M_{KK}K_r) + (k_C - k_M)M_{LK}(C_{LK} \\ + R_C C_{LR}/L_C)/k_M)\}$$

$$dK_C/dp_S = (1/D)\alpha Z M_{LK}\{(k_C - k_M)C_{LK} + R_C C_{LR}/L_C\}/L > 0, \text{ if } k_C \geq k_M$$

$$dK_M/dp_S = (1/D)\alpha Z M_{LK}\{(k_M - k_C)C_{LK} - R_C C_{LR}/L_C + C(K_w k_M - K_r)\}/L$$

$$dw/dp_S = -(1/D)\alpha Z M_{LL} C/L > 0$$

$$dr/dp_S = -(1/D)\alpha Z M_{LK} C/L < 0$$

where $C = C_{LL}C_{KK} - C_{KL}^2 > 0$, $2M_{LK}C_{LK} - M_{LL}C_{KK} - M_{KK}C_{LL} < 0$,

$D = -M_{LL}C > 0$, and $k_i = K_i/L_i$, $i = C, M$

30 and 50 per cent of their produce). Thus, for the average peasant, the unfavourable price policy seems to have more than outweighed this positive effect of the change in land tenure. To this should be added the overvalued exchange rate that meant artificially low prices on exports and high prices on imports when denominated in domestic currency.

It should be noted that, in terms of our analytical model, the elimination of rents, $d\alpha$, is equivalent to a price increase on peasant produce. Given the size of the rents under the old land tenure system and the taxation through the low AMC prices to the peasants, it is reasonable to assume that for the average peasant $d\alpha + dp_S < 0$.

In terms of our analytical model the elimination of the rents to landlords and the above price policies and exchange rate and trade policies can be represented by analysing the effects of $dp_S < 0$, which in this context should be interpreted as the net negative change in the per unit return in peasant production.

Comparing Tables 4.3 and 4.6 it can be seen that the policy changes analysed give rise to the same qualitative effects on the various sectors. A reduction in the price on peasant products means a lowering of the total potential value of peasant production, and thereby of the wage level in the economy. When the wage falls, the cost of labour in the public sector decreases. Thus, the policy makes it possible to expand employment and production in the public sector without increasing the total budget allocated to this sector.

For the two capital-using sectors – non-peasant agriculture and manufacturing – the capital intensities will have an important influence on how the respective sector is affected. When the wage level is reduced and prices on output from these two sectors are unchanged, both sectors will try to expand. Thus, they will demand both more labour and more capital. The reduction of the wage level that follows directly upon the changes in the price on peasant produce will be counteracted but not outweighed. The tendency to expand the activities in the capital-using sectors at a given stock of capital will give rise to an increase in the return to capital, *ceteris paribus*. This in turn will lead to an increase in the stock of capital, but this expansion will never be of such a magnitude that the return to capital will fall back to its initial level. Thus, there will be a determinate reduction in the relative factor price, *w/r*, and a tendency for a positive effect on the relatively labour-intensive sector and a negative effect on the capital-intensive sector. Thus, provided that there is a large difference in capital intensities between non-peasant agriculture and the manufacturing sector (that is provided a large $k_C - k_M$), we should expect manufacturing to increase and non-peasant agriculture to decrease.

In conclusion, the distorted and – for the peasant sector – unfavourable prices, that were central parts of the economic policies during the *Ethiopia Tikdem* period, should be expected to have led to a reduction of agricultural production, provided that non-peasant agriculture is more capital intensive than manufacturing, and also to an expansion of both the public sector and the manufacturing sector. Thus, given this assumption about relative factor intensities, the policy can be expected to have given rise to migration from rural to urban areas. Like the negative institutional changes for the peasant sector, the price, trade and exchange rate policies introduced by the Derg undermined the role of agriculture in generating export revenues.

Population growth

Up to now the size of the population, and thus the labour force, has been assumed to be constant. However, this is an unrealistic assumption in the case of Ethiopia where population growth was very high, at 2.5–3 per cent, during the 1970s and 1980s. How, then, can population growth be expected to have affected the economy?

From the way the wage level has been assumed to be determined, it follows directly that population growth leads to a lower wage, *ceteris paribus*. This change in wage level will give rise to higher returns to capital, increased production in the public sector, stimulation of production and employment in the labour-intensive non-peasant, non-public sector, and a contraction in production and employment in the other capital-using sector. The qualitative effects will thus be the same as the effects resulting from institutional changes for the peasant sector, the price, trade and exchange rate policies, and land erosion and land degradation – that is, an expansion of the public sector and

Table 4.7 Effects of population growth

$dL_C/dL = (1/D)\alpha(Z_L - Z/L)M_{LK}\{(k_C - k_M)C_{LK}/k_C - k_M C_{RK}R_C/K_C\}/L > 0$,
 if $k_M \geq k_C$

$dL_S/dL = (1/D)\{-M_{LL}L^2 C + \alpha L(Z_L - Z/L)[C[M_{LL}/G_{LL} + 1$
 $- M_{LK}(K_w - K_r/k_M) + M_{LL}C_{KK} + M_{KK}C_{LL} - 2M_{LK}C_{LK}]\}/L^2$

$dL_G/dL = -(1/D)\alpha(Z_L - Z/L)M_{LL}C/(G_{LL}L) > 0$

$dL_M/dL = (1/D)\{M_{LL}C - \alpha(Z_L - Z/L)[C(1 - M_{LK}(K_w - K_r/k_M))$
 $+ (k_C - k_M)C_{LK}M_{LK}/k_M + C_{LR}M_{LK}R_C/L_C)/k_M]/L\}$

$dK_C/dL = (1/D)\alpha(Z_L - Z/L)M_{LK}\{(k_C - k_M)C_{LK} + C_{LR}R_C/L_C\}/L < 0$, if $k_C \geq k_M$

$dK_M/dL = (1/D)\alpha(Z_L - Z/L)M_{LK}\{(k_M - k_C)C_{LK} - C_{LR}R_C/L_C + C(K_w k_M - K_r)\}/L$

$dw/dL = -(1/D)\alpha(Z_L - Z/L)M_{LL}C/L < 0$

$dr/dL = -(1/D)\alpha(Z_L - Z/L)M_{LK}C/L > 0$

where $C = C_{LL}C_{KK} - C_{KL}^2 > 0$, $M_{LL}C_{KK} + M_{KK}C_{LL} - 2M_{LK}C_{LK} > 0$,

$D = -M_{LL}C > 0$, and $k_i = K_i/L_i$, $i = C, M$

Note: $Z_L \leq Z/L$.

a tendency for manufacturing to increase and for peasant and non-peasant agriculture to decrease, provided that manufacturing is labour-intensive relative to non-peasant agriculture.

In conclusion, the population pressure should be expected to have strengthened the tendencies to reduce agricultural production and to increase manufacturing and public sector production. Thus, it should be expected to have increased rural–urban migration and undermined the role of agricultural exports in the process of economic growth (Table 4.7).

Demoralisation at the war front and in the public sector

During the whole *Ethiopia Tikdem* period there was an escalating civil war in Ethiopia. The central government, led by President Mengistu Haile-Mariam, faced growing military opposition and resistance, not only from the Eritrean liberation movements but also from other regional liberation groups within mainland Ethiopia. Besides incurring direct war costs this also affected the economy by increasing risks and transaction costs, such as costs for transportation (Azam *et al.* 1993). However, in this section we focus on the fact that the morale of the government troops was undermined through the way they were recruited and forced out to the front without any substantial training and with a steadily weaker military leadership. As the civil war continued to drag on and the various opposition groups became stronger, morale among the government troops became progressively lower. Within the

Table 4.8 Effects of demoralisation at the war front and in the public sector

---

$dL_S/dI_G = -(1/D)CM_{LL}(G_{LA}A_I + G_{LI})/G_{LL} < 0$

$dL_G/dI_G = (1/D)CM_{LL}(G_{LA}A_I + G_{LI})/G_{LL} > 0$

$dL_C/dI_G = dL_M/dI_G = dK_C/dI_G = dK_M/dI_G = dw/dI_G = dr/dI_G = 0$

where $C = C_{LL}C_{KK} - C_{KL}^2 > 0$, $D = -M_{LL}C > 0$

---

non-military public sector too there was a problem of motivation, due to the centralised way in which things were handled, leading to very limited, if not completely absent, possibilities for individual civil servants to take initiatives. This state of affairs, combined with the individual's fear of being classified as 'difficult' by superiors, led to increased alienation and demoralisation at various levels within large parts of the public sector.

In our model, the demoralisation in the public sector can be represented as $dI_G < 0$ (Table 4.8).

Due to the fact that the public sector does not compete for capital with manufacturing and non-peasant agriculture, the demoralisation at the front and in the public sector in general will only affect the distribution of labour between this sector and the peasant sector. If economic forces were allowed to work properly, the lower productivity within the public sector caused by the demoralisation within this sector would lead to reduced public sector employment. The freed labour would have to return to the peasant sector since the labour productivity in other non-peasant sectors would be unaffected by the changes within the public sector.

However, in a war economy, the success of the military sector is the overriding objective of the government. This was also the case in Ethiopia during this period. In such an economy one would expect the government to try to counteract the negative effects of demoralisation and to keep or even increase the level of defence by trying to get more military and arms support from abroad by pleasing donors or convincing them of the appropriateness of the military ambitions and strategies ($dI_G > 0$ so that A increases, thereby counteracting the effects of the demoralisation) and of course by allocating more domestically generated resources to this sector. In our model the

Table 4.9 Effects of budget increases on the public sector

$dL_S/dp_G = -(1/D)CM_{LL}G_L/G_{LL} < 0$

$dL_G/dp_G = (1/D)CM_{LL}G_L/G_{LL} > 0$

$dL_C/dp_G = dL_M/dp_G = dK_C/dp_G = dK_M/dp_G = dw/dp_G = dr/dp_G = 0$

where $C = C_{LL}C_{KK} - C_{KL}^2 > 0$, $D = -M_{LL}C > 0$

---

domestic resource mobilisation can be represented as an exogenous change in the price of public goods (defence), $dp_G > 0$. The effects of such a change are presented in Table 4.9 and are qualitatively opposite to the effects of demoralisation at the front and in the public sector as described above.

CONCLUSIONS

This chapter has complemented the analysis in Chapter 3 with a general equilibrium analysis of the expected economic effects of the *Ethiopia Tikdem* policy. In Chapter 3 it was concluded that this policy changed the Ethiopian economic system in ways that made it a highly centralised and inward-oriented system. Markets and incentives were replaced with administrative decisions, centralised planning and the use of orders to direct the economic actors. Collective or state ownership replaced private ownership in most sectors of the economy. These institutional changes have been concluded to lead to a deteriorating and less flexible economy. By means of our analytical dual institutional general equilibrium model we derived the expected effects on the economic structure. It was concluded that most changes worked against the peasant sector and thus led to decreasing wages and decreasing agricultural production and thereby also to less exports. The lower wage level made it possible to increase the public sector, mainly defence, even without increasing the costs of production.

Thus, assuming that defence was top priority for the military government, one may well conclude that the economic policy, at least in a short- and medium-term perspective was consistent, in particular as long as arms support and other types of assistance arrived from abroad (mainly from the former Soviet Union and Eastern Europe). However, as the war continued and soldiers were brutally recruited without any significant training and when the opposition groups became increasingly successful in the battlefield, there was clear demoralisation among the soldiers that reduced their efficiency even more. Therefore, in order to keep defence at a level which was acceptable, from the perspective of the central government, more resources had to be allocated to this sector, notwithstanding the lower direct per unit costs of soldiers. The lower wage level can be expected to have stimulated production in the labour-intensive non-peasant non-public sector also, even if these effects can be expected to have been counteracted by the negative institutional changes in this sector and the concomitant reduction of the stock of capital and thus the increased price of capital.

In general, our model analysis has led us to conclude that one should expect the *Ethiopia Tikdem* policy to have given rise to reduced agricultural activities and increased non-agricultural activities, in particular when manufacturing is labour intensive compared to non-peasant agriculture. As argued above, this seems to be quite a reasonable assumption considering the small-scale and non-mechanised character of large parts of the manufacturing and handicraft sector and the large-scale mechanised State farms in Ethiopia. Thus the policy should be expected to have led to increased rural–urban migration and also to have undermined the role of agricultural exports and thereby international trade to generate economic growth by providing imported capital goods and other inputs for the Ethiopian economy.

5

ECONOMIC PERFORMANCE OF THE *ETHIOPIA TIKDEM* PERIOD

INTRODUCTION

From Chapter 3 we learned that the objectives of the *Ethiopia Tikdem* period were extremely ambitious and that, in order to achieve these objectives, the Derg introduced far-reaching economic programmes and measures that drastically changed the Ethiopian economic system. Our economic system analysis and the general equilibrium analysis, however, both predicted increasing problems and a deterioration rather than an improvement in the economic situation.

Did the *actual* economic development in Ethiopia confirm these predictions? As will be shown in this chapter, the economic development in Ethiopia since the revolution in 1974 up to 1988, when the first signs of the government questioning their *Ethiopia Tikdem* policy can be identified, led to a situation even worse than the one leading up to the revolution.

LOW AND DECREASING REAL PER CAPITA INCOMES

During the period 1965–1973 the Ethiopian economy grew by an average of 3.9 per cent annually whereas the population growth was 2.6 per cent. Thus, on a national level there was an increase in per capita income. However, as noted earlier, this did not mean that the Ethiopian people attained improved standards of living. The distribution of income and wealth during the reign of Emperor Haile Selassie was extremely unequal: the vast majority of the population lived in poverty while the aristocracy were very prosperous. To change this situation was one of the explicit objectives of the new policy that was introduced under the motto *Ethiopia Tikdem*. However, as can be seen in Figure 5.1 and Table 5.1, the effects on the growth of per capita income that resulted from the *Ethiopia Tikdem* policy were discouraging and by the end of the 1980s Ethiopia was one of the poorest countries in the world.

In 1987 the GNP per capita was US$120–130, which was the lowest per capita income reported in the world (World Bank 1989: table 1), and less than

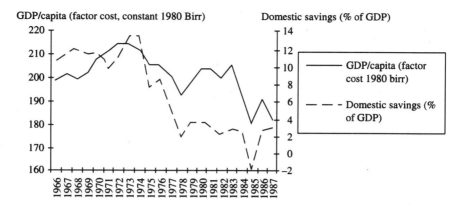

Figure 5.1 Development of GDP per capita and domestic savings, 1966–1987
Source: See Appendix A, Table A.1

Table 5.1 Growth of GDP, agriculture, and population, 1965–1987 (%)

	1965–1973	*1973–1980*	*1980–1987*
GDP, constant prices	3.9	1.6	0.9
	(5.9)	(2.5)	(0.5)
Agricultural production	2.1	0.6	–2.1
	(2.2)	(–0.3)	(1.3)
Population	2.6	2.8	2.4
	(2.6)	(2.8)	(3.1)

Note: Figures within parentheses denote growth rates for sub-Sarahan Africa
Source: World Bank 1989: tables 2 and 28, 1990: Statistical Annex tables 2.2 and 7.9, 1993: tables 2 and 26

half of the average per capita income for low-income economies and around one-third of the average per capita income for sub-Saharan Africa (Table 5.2). The low per capita income in Ethiopia by the end of the 1980s was the result of poor economic growth combined with high population growth. Looking at Table 5.1 we note that the average annual growth of GDP in Ethiopia from the mid-1960s up to 1987 was below the average of the sub-Saharan countries. This development is not surprising considering our previous description and analysis of the policy that followed the overthrow of Haile Selassie: nationalisation, heavy discrimination against agriculture in general and individual private peasants in particular, and the uncertainties in relation to land tenure as a consequence of the collectivisation, villagisation, and resettlement programmes. To this should be added the escalating civil war that

Table 5.2 GNP per capita, 1987 (US dollars)

Ethiopia	130
Low-income economies	290
Sub-Saharan Africa	330

Source: World Bank 1989: table 1

created great uncertainties and also demanded increasing resources during the whole *Ethiopia Tikdem* period.

In contrast to the low economic growth the population growth was quite high in Ethiopia. In 1987 the population was estimated at 44 million with an annual growth rate of around 2.5 per cent. Thus, during the *Ethiopia Tikdem* period population growth in Ethiopia was above the average for the developing countries and a bit below the average for sub-Saharan Africa.

The development of the agricultural production per capita was even worse. From the beginning of the 1970s there was a decrease in the per capita availability of locally produced cereal equivalents. In the 1980s up to the drought year 1984/85, when the availability was just 50 per cent of the 1970/71 level, the availability was never over 90 per cent. In the record year of 1982/83 the per capita availability reached 89 per cent of the 1970/71 level (World Bank 1987b: table 3.2).

SECTORAL DEVELOPMENT OF PRODUCTION

The low GDP growth rate was mainly due to poor performance in agriculture. The contribution to GDP from this sector decreased from 53 per cent in 1974/75 to 41 per cent in 1987/88. The emphasis on State farms and the privileges given to them in the allocation of resources resulted in a higher yield of major crops per acre for these farms than for individual private peasants. In 1986/87, the individual private peasant produced 10.9 quintals per hectare whereas the corresponding figure for state farms was 23.4 quintals per hectare (calculated from IMF 1988: table IX). However, this should not make us conclude that State farms were more efficient than peasant farms. On the contrary, if we look at the use of other inputs than land, it becomes clear that frequently State farms were quite inefficient production units. In the production of wheat in 1983/84, the State farms produced 1.35 tons per hectare resulting in an output value of 559 birr per hectare. However, the inputs that were used in this production amounted to 1838 birr per hectare. When calculating the social profits of wheat production (defined as the difference between the output value per hectare and the input costs per hectare, everything evaluated at the official exchange rate) the World Bank found that production in State farms resulted in a social loss of 646 birr per

59

hectare, while the same production in the peasant sector resulted in a social profit of 159 birr per hectare (World Bank 1987a: table 7.12). For maize production also, the yields per hectare were higher in State farm production (2.63 tons per hectare) than in peasant production (1.79 tons per hectare) but, on the other hand, the latter resulted in a social profit of 361 birr per hectare while the corresponding figure for State farms was a social loss of 279 birr (ibid.).

As described in Chapter 3, producer co-operatives, also, were favoured by the Mengistu government. However, notwithstanding the priority given to them, the producer co-operatives did not succeed in reaching a higher yield per acre than individual peasants. In fact, in 1986/87 the yield of major crops in producer co-operatives was even below the yield obtained by individual peasants at 10.3 quintals compared to 10.9 quintals (ibid.).

Compared to the growth rate in agriculture, growth rates for industry and services were higher, as was expected from our model analysis, and during the 1980s above the average for sub-Saharan countries. The growth of the services sector was mainly due to the ever-expanding defence expenditure during the socialist period, when keeping Ethiopia as a united country was one of the most important objectives. As a consequence, the contributions to GDP from industry and services increased (Table 5.3). In 1987/88 the contributions of these sectors were around 18 and 41 per cent, respectively.

The sectoral development described in Figure 5.2 conforms to the expected development derived from the institutional model analysis in the previous chapter, with a decreasing contribution from agriculture (peasant and non-peasant), a slightly increasing contribution coming from other commodity sectors (manufacturing in our model) and an increasing service sector (public sector in our model).

The poor development of the agricultural sector in the 1970s and 1980s is of course central for the overall economic development in Ethiopia. It should be noted that its share of GDP understates the importance of the sector. By the end of the 1980s around 80 per cent of the labour force was employed in agriculture and agricultural products made up 85 per cent of all export earnings (World Bank 1987b: iv).

Table 5.3 Average annual growth of production (%, constant prices)

	1965–1973	*1973–1980*	*1980–1987*
Agriculture	2.1 (2.2)	0.6 (–0.3)	–2.1 (1.3)
Industry	6.4 (13.8)	1.4 (4.3)	3.8 (–1.2)
Services etc.	6.6 (4.9)	3.3 (3.7)	3.5 (1.2)

Note: Figures for sub-Saharan Africa within parentheses
Source: World Bank 1989: table 2

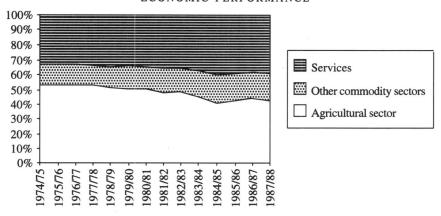

Figure 5.2 GDP by industrial origin, 1974/75–1987/88 (constant 1980/81 factor cost)
Source: See Appendix A, Table A.2

In the struggle towards self-sufficiency in food, it is important to remember the great potential of the Ethiopian agricultural sector (see e.g. World Bank 1987a: 13, 1987b: 11ff). The problem for the socialist government was how to increase the current area under cultivation and how to improve the performance of the agricultural sector. From Chapters 3 and 4 it is clear that the institutional changes aimed at transforming and collectivising agricultural production in Ethiopia during the 1970s and 1980s should be expected to have worsened rather than improved the situation. The process of socialisation, in terms of villagisation and resettlements, and the emphasis on producer co-operatives and State farms imposed great uncertainties and negative incentives on the individual peasants in their cultivation and preservation of land. As a result, the resource allocation both between agriculture and other sectors and between different types of producers within the agricultural sector, became distorted and highly inefficient.

However, it is important to note that less than 10 per cent of total food crop production came from State farms and producer co-operatives (World Bank 1987b: iv). Consequently, the poor performance in Ethiopian agriculture during the *Ethiopia Tikdem* period can only be explained by the poor performance of the State farms and the producer co-operatives to a limited extent. Instead, the major reasons behind it must be found in the way the individual peasant farms worked during these decades.

In Chapter 3 we argued that the major reasons for the low production of marketable agricultural products were the incentive system, the uncertain land tenure system, and the structure of prices and taxes. Delivery quotas and centrally determined agricultural prices far below the prices that would result from the free operation markets, combined with high taxation of cash sales,

61

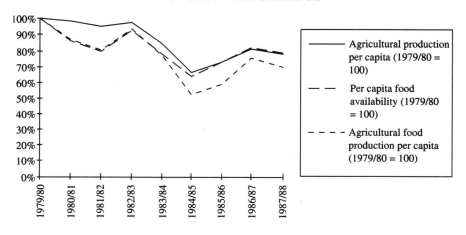

Figure 5.3 Agricultural production and food availability, 1979/80–1987/88
(volume, per capita, 1979/80 = 100)
Source: See Appendix A, Table A.3

meant that production in excess of the quotas was hardly profitable and thus held back increases of production. The result was that, as expected from our model analysis, the per capita agricultural production and food availability decreased. The rapidly falling per capita agricultural production resulted in increased imports of food to the country even during non-drought years. Notwithstanding these increased imports, by the end of the 1980s the per capita food availability (including cereal imports and exports of pulses) was around 20 per cent below the level at the end of the 1970s (Figure 5.3).

GROWING MACROECONOMIC IMBALANCES

The development of various expenditures as shares of GDP is described in Figure 5.4. This description of the structure of the expenditure side of the national account together with Figure 5.5 showing the developments of the resource gap and fiscal deficit confirms that the Ethiopian economy suffered from great and growing imbalances in the 1970s and 1980s. The resource gap (that is, exports minus imports of commodities and non-factor services) showed an increasing negative trend. By the end of the 1980s the resource gap amounted to around 12 per cent of GDP. This negative development was the result of the low growth in GDP, i.e. in domestic supply, and a relatively high growth of domestic demand, mainly for public spending and investments related to the civil war, whereas private consumption increased more or less in line with the domestic supply during the actual period.

The fast-growing public sector expenditure gave rise to a growing fiscal deficit. Figure 5.6 shows how the share going to capital expenditure increased

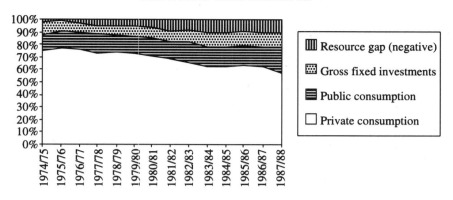

Figure 5.4 GDP by expenditure, 1974/75–1987/88 (current market prices)
Source: See Appendix A, Table A.4

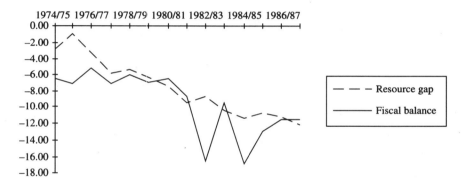

Figure 5.5 Resource gap and fiscal balance, 1974/75–1987/88 (% of GDP)
Source: See Appendix A, Table A.5

during the *Ethiopia Tikdem* period. In this way the government tried to compensate for the lower private investments that followed upon the change in policy and the nationalisations in 1975. Furthermore, Figure 5.7 shows that the industrial sector's share of central government capital expenditures increased during the 1980s, whereas the share going to agriculture fell drastically during the last years of the 1970s.

Going into a deeper analysis of the government current expenditure, Figure 5.8 reveals that general services and interest and charges on public debt both increased their respective shares of central government current expenditure between 1974/75 and 1987/88. These increases are closely related to the increased defence expenditure. According to a speech by President Mengistu

63

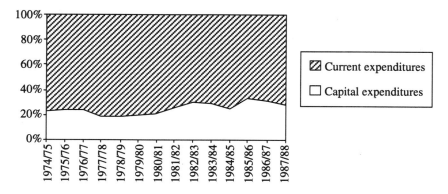

Figure 5.6 Distribution of central government expenditure, 1974/75–1987/88
Source: See Appendix A, Table A.6

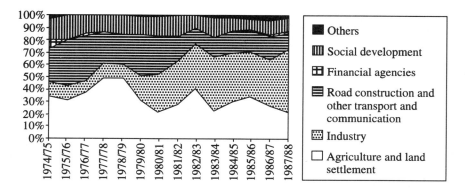

Figure 5.7 Composition of central government capital expenditure, 1974/75–1987/88
Source: See Appendix A, Table A.7

in November 1988 the defence budget had increased in nominal terms by 19 per cent annually since 1974 (*Ethiopian Herald* 1988: 4). In the fiscal years 1987 and 1988 this expenditure amounted to around 40 per cent of the total recurrent budget (World Bank 1994b). As a consequence, there was a decrease in the shares of public current expenditure going to economic services, social services, and pension payments.

Government revenues and grants increased as a share of GDP but not as much as public spending. Even if government revenues and grants increased rapidly in post-revolutionary Ethiopia, an increase in taxation in Ethiopia was very problematic owing to the poor performance in the various sectors of the economy, mainly in agriculture. This in turn resulted in a poor export performance and a low level of incomes relative to the subsistence needs of

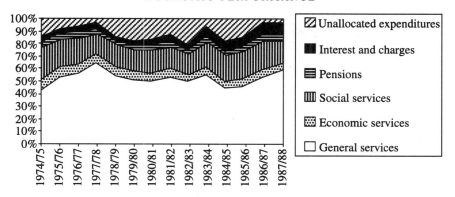

Figure 5.8 Composition of central government current expenditure, 1974/75–1987/88
Source: See Appendix A, Table A.8

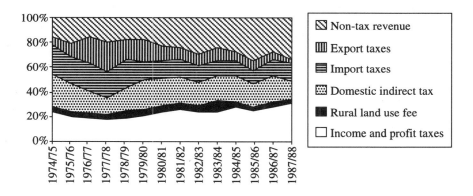

Figure 5.9 Central government revenues by source, 1974/75–1987/88
Source: See Appendix A, Table A.9

the population. As indicated by our model analysis in the previous chapter, the policy and system changes introduced during the *Ethiopia Tikdem* period tended to undermine the role of agricultural exports in the process of trade and economic development. In Figure 5.9 this is shown by the reduced contribution of export taxes to central government revenues (note that there was no trade liberalisation during this period). Instead the government had to increase its reliance on domestic borrowing and money creation as well as external borrowing, which, in its turn, not only fuelled inflation but also increased the expenditure on interest and charges as well.

Table 5.4 shows that the rate of investment in Ethiopia during the *Ethiopia Tikdem* period was very low and that domestic savings were even lower. Thus,

Table 5.4 Gross domestic investments and savings (% of GDP)

	1970		1980		1987	
	Invest-ments	*Savings*	*Invest-ments*	*Savings*	*Invest-ments*	*Savings*
Ethiopia	11	11	10	5	14	3
Low-income economies	21	20	25	25	28	26
Sub-Saharan Africa	17	16	20	22	16	13

Sources: World Bank 1992: table 9, 1989: table 4

since the revolution and up to the end of the 1980s there was a negative trend in the saving/investment relationship. Figure 5.1 showed the parallel and negative development of the GDP per capita and the domestic savings during the *Ethiopia Tikdem* period. This development is also in line with the results of the model analysis in Chapter 4 which suggested that, as a rule, the policy measures taken during the *Ethiopia Tikdem* period discouraged savings, and thus investments, by leading to lower real wages and incomes for the majority of the population. Furthermore, the nationalisation policy in 1975 and the concomitant explicit declaration that the government reserved the right to nationalise private property whenever it found it appropriate (see Chapter 3) meant that investments from abroad were discontinued (Figure 5.10).

As can be seen in Table 5.4, savings and investments in socialist Ethiopia were also very low from an international point of view. This is true in comparison both with the average for developing countries world-wide and with the average for sub-Saharan countries.

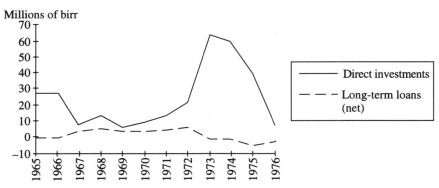

Figure 5.10 Foreign direct investments and long-term loans (net)
Source: See Appendix A, Table A.10

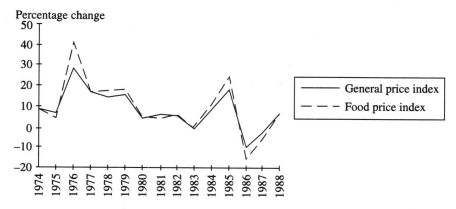

Figure 5.11 Rate of inflation, 1974–1988 (Addis Ababa retail price index)
Source: See Appendix A, Table A.11

INFLATION

As noted in Chapter 3, one important reason behind the low agricultural producer prices was that prices were to be kept down in order for the military to get food for soldiers at a lower cost, thereby containing government expenditure. Another objective was to keep down consumer prices for food for ordinary urban people. It is clear that keeping consumer prices down by imposing low producer prices is an inefficient line of policy. If low consumer prices is the objective, a subsidisation of the consumption, without taxing the producers through low prices, would be the best policy. The reason is that with this type of policy, domestic production will be higher and hence the gap between the true market prices and the official prices for price-controlled food products will be reduced, *ceteris paribus*. Furthermore, the demand for imports to fill the gap between demand and supply can be expected to be reduced also.

Looking at the food prices in Addis Ababa we note that notwithstanding the low producer prices and the fact that 43 per cent of the agricultural products were subject to price control (IMF 1988: 4), food prices have changed at least as much as prices in general (Figure 5.11). Therefore we can conclude that demand and supply also seem to have played an important role in the consumer food markets in socialist Ethiopia.

EXTERNAL ECONOMIC RELATIONS

In relation to the growing trade deficit, it is important to note that during the *Ethiopia Tikdem* period the need for imports (fuel, military equipment, and food for a rapidly growing population) increased. As a consequence the

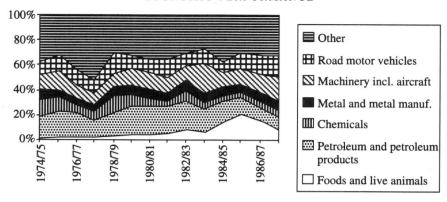

Figure 5.12 Import composition, 1974/75–1987/88
Source: See Appendix A, Table A.12

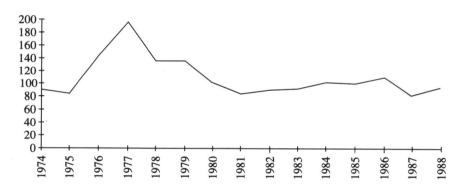

Figure 5.13 Net barter terms of trade, 1974–1988 (1980 = 100)
Source: See Appendix A, Table A.13

import volume increased by 90 per cent between 1978/79 and 1988 while the export volume increased by only around 40 per cent during the same period. To explain this development by the oil crises of the 1970s is not convincing, in view of the length of the period and the composition of Ethiopian imports (Figure 5.12). Furthermore, as is clear from Figure 5.13, the growing trade deficit cannot be explained by referring to the development of terms of trade.

Instead, the explanation can be found in the economic policy and the resulting poor economic performance. For instance, as can be seen in Figure 5.14, the exchange rate policy during the *Ethiopia Tikdem* period, with the fixed relationship between the Ethiopian birr and the US dollar, meant that from the revolution in 1974 up to 1985 the real effective exchange rate for Ethiopia increased with the appreciation of the US dollar at the same time as

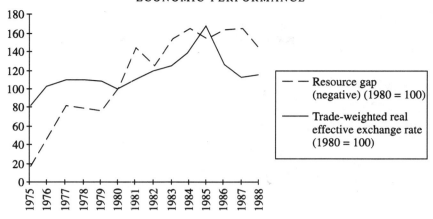

Figure 5.14 Real effective exchange rate and resource gap, 1975–1988
Source: See Appendix A, Table A.14

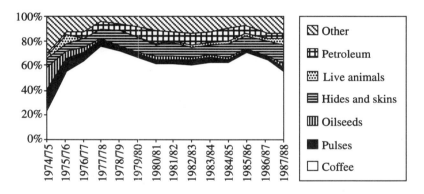

Figure 5.15 Export composition, 1974/75–1987/88
Source: See Appendix A, Table A.15

the resource gap increased. By the same reasoning, the real effective exchange rate decreased between 1985 and 1987 (but not enough to compensate for the development up to 1985) when the US dollar depreciated. Given the overall economic development in Ethiopia during the period up to 1987 it is clear that the development of the real effective exchange rate was quite inappropriate and clearly demonstrated the exchange rate misalignment during the *Ethiopia Tikdem* period.

Figure 5.15 shows that Ethiopian exports during the 1970s and 1980s were heavily concentrated. The dominating export commodity was coffee, which accounted for around 60 per cent of all export revenues from the mid-1970s onward, followed by hides and skins whose share of total export value varied

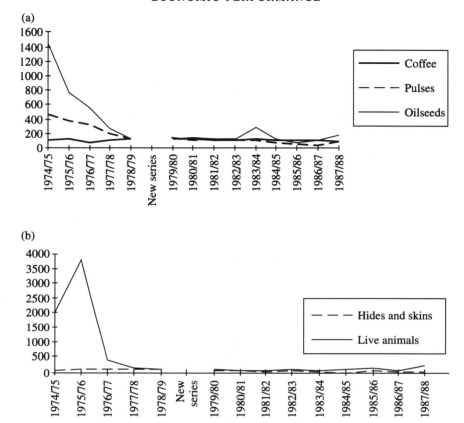

Figure 5.16 Per capita exports of major export commodities: (a) crops; (b) hides and skins and live animals, 1974/75–1987/88 (volume index, 1978/79 = 100 for 1974/75–1978/79; 1979/80 = 100 for 1979/80–1987/88)

Source: See Appendix A, Table A.16

between 8 and 16 per cent. By the end of the 1980s these two sets of commodities accounted for more than 75 per cent of total export revenues. On the export side pulses decreased in importance: from 10–15 per cent in the mid-1970s down to around 2 per cent by the end of the 1980s.

As was expected from our analysis of the domestic agricultural incentives system and the Ethiopian trade and exchange rate policy (in Chapters 3 and 4), during the *Ethiopia Tikdem* period per capita exports decreased dramatically, to one of the lowest levels in the world. In 1988 Ethiopia had the third lowest per capita export value (after Mozambique and Myamar) among the countries reported in the World Bank's *World Development Report 1990*; around one-fifth of the average for low-income countries and one-eighth of the average for sub-Saharan Africa. As shown in Figure 5.16 the per capita

70

export volume of Ethiopia's major export products, that is crops, hides and skins, and live animals, decreased drastically during the 1970s. The figure also clearly demonstrates that this fall was not reversed during the 1980s; on the contrary the per capita exports of coffee and pulses continued to decrease.

In relation to imports, during the *Ethiopia Tikdem* period the shares of raw materials and semi-finished goods in imports decreased, whereas the shares for capital and consumer goods increased. Among the capital goods imported, transport equipment and industrial goods dominated. It should be noted that to a large extent the imports were inputs to the civil war, e.g. fuel, trucks, weapons and ammunition, and not capital goods for investment in production. It is worth mentioning that the arms imports and military aid during the period 1978–1988 amounted to close on US$11 billion (constant 1988 dollars), which was more than all other imports during the same period (Eshetu Chole and Makonnen Manyazewal 1992: 27). It should also be noted that the value of Ethiopia's arms imports as a share of total exports increased quite drastically from an average of around 5 per cent during the period 1971–1974 up to an average of 175 per cent during 1980–1987 (the figures are calculated from Kidane Mengisteab 1990: table 8.10), which explains a large part of the deteriorating trade balance.

It should also be noted (see Figure 5.12) that imports of food and live animals made up a significant share of total imports. From 1976 up to 1983 imports of food and live animals varied between 4 and 8 per cent of the total import value. As a consequence of droughts in 1983 and 1985, however, these imports accounted for no less than 18 and 25 per cent of total imports, respectively. In per capita terms, food imports increased to compensate for the falling per capita domestic agricultural production. As a consequence the scope for imports of capital goods, inputs, and consumer goods did not expand as it would have done with an incentives system which was more conducive to economic efficiency.

Furthermore, because of the ongoing civil war and the frequent violations of human rights, but also because of the design of the economic system and policy, foreign assistance decreased from other countries apart from the former Soviet Union and other socialist and communist countries (whose support was mainly in the form of military aid and arms support). As a result, by the end of the 1980s, Ethiopia, with its large population and its very low per capita income, received very low per capita foreign assistance, also in comparison with many other less developed countries. Compared to other sub-Saharan African countries, Ethiopia received only around 70 per cent of the average per capita official development assistance (Table 5.5).

The increasing deficit in public finance, the low savings rate, in particular compared to the investment rate in the economy, together with the rising trade deficit and the low levels of foreign assistance, resulted in an increasingly problematic external debt situation (Table 5.6). The debt service ratio (debt expenditure, i.e. interest and amortisation, as a share of export revenues) did

Table 5.5 Official development assistance, 1988
(net disbursement)

	Per capita (dollars)	% of GNP
Ethiopia	20.5	17.4
Low-income countries	7.6	2.4
Sub-Saharan Africa	28.9	8.8

Source: World Bank 1990: table 20

Table 5.6 External debt

	1970/71	1980/81	1987/88
Total long-term debt:*			
Millions of dollars	169	701	2434
% of GNP	10	17	46

Note: *Disbursed and outstanding public and private debt
Sources: World Bank 1989: table 21, 1990: 4, 1993: tables 21
and 24, and Ministry of Finance for 1989/90

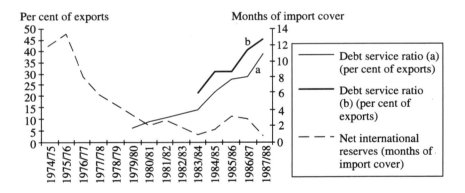

Figure 5.17 Debt service ratio and net international reserves, 1974/75–1987/88
Source: See Appendix A, Table A.17

increase from around 6 per cent to more than 45 per cent during the past decade (Figure 5.17). Thus, during the 1980s a major role for exports was to service public debt, rather than to contribute to economic growth through imports of investment goods and inputs for production. This in turn has made international reserves very scarce.

CONCLUSIONS

As concluded in Chapter 3, the design of Ethiopian economic policy under the motto *Ethiopian Tikdem* conflicted with most of the principles of good economic policy management. The economic performance during the *Ethiopia Tikdem* period underlines this criticism. For instance, the growth of the fiscal deficit clearly shows that the government has not succeeded in keeping the budget under adequate control (principle 2), the growing deficit in foreign trade shows that the government has not created a situation where advantage is taken of international trade (principles 4, 5, and 6), and finally the growth of foreign debt is a clear indication of the overvaluation of the Ethiopian exchange rate (principle 14).

Thus, as could be expected from both the conclusion about poor economic management and our theoretical model analysis in Chapter 4, by 1987/88 the Derg's economic policy had taken the country to a situation that can be characterised as even worse than the one at the outset of the new policy in 1974. This is so both in absolute terms and when compared with other low-income countries, including most sub-Saharan African countries. Thus, the Ethiopian per capita income ranked at the very bottom of the income scale, fiscal and foreign trade accounts had deteriorated greatly, and foreign debt had increased and now constituted a real problem for the country. Foreign assistance was very limited, especially in per capita terms, and far below the average for other sub-Saharan countries. Besides the economic system changes and the various policy measures that the Derg introduced, another important reason behind the severe economic crisis in Ethiopia was the ongoing and escalating civil war that demanded ever-growing resources and introduced great uncertainties for economic actors. As a result, in 1988, the Derg and President Mengistu Haile-Mariam were under heavy pressure, faced with a rapidly deteriorating situation on both the economic and the civil war fronts.

6

ETHIOPIA TIKDEM REVISED
President Mengistu's reform announcements

INTRODUCTION

As shown in the previous chapter, towards the end of the 1980s Ethiopia had run into a situation of deep economic crisis and was in great need of increased foreign assistance. At the same time the Mengistu government experienced increased criticism from other countries, including the Soviet Union. This chapter describes and analyses the reaction of the Ethiopian government to the deteriorating conditions in the country and to the external pressure for economic systemic and political changes. In November 1988 and March 1990 President Mengistu Haile-Mariam made two interesting economic reform announcements. The changes actually implemented were quite limited and the major characteristics of the *Ethiopia Tikdem* policy remained largely unaffected. This chapter presents and analyses some of the political–economic forces that paved the way for the fall of the Mengistu government and formed the political–economic environment of the new government that succeeded him.

Unlike other sub-Saharan African countries in a similar economic situation, Ethiopia had no agreement with the IMF and the World Bank to introduce any stabilisation or restructuring programme in the 1980s. This did not mean that Ethiopia was not given recommendations along similar lines to those incorporated in IMF and World Bank programmes. Thus in 1987, in a report on the economic situation in Ethiopia, the World Bank listed a set of recommendations, including adjustment of the exchange rate, liberalisation of markets, increasing procurement pricing for agricultural products, stimulation of the small-scale industries and introduction of an export action programme (World Bank 1987a: 11f). Thus, the recommendations had much in common with typical World Bank and IMF programmes.

The World Bank recommendations were closely related to several of the causes behind the poor economic performance identified and analysed in the previous chapters. In particular, meeting the recommendations would have meant a clear movement towards the left-hand side of the system dimensions of Figure 2.1. The economy would have moved away from centralism (dimension 1); markets, incentives, and prices (dimensions 2, 4, and 5) would have come to be more important in the process of resource allocation, and private ownership would have increased (dimension 3); and finally, the economy would have become more internationalised through the adoption and implementation of an export action programme and the adjustment of the exchange rate (dimension 6).

So why were these recommendations not introduced? The explanation can mainly be found in the fact that all the recommended changes were in deep conflict with the basic ideas behind the government's *Ethiopia Tikdem* policy. Therefore, as long as the government held on to this motto, it was unlikely that it would take serious and comprehensive steps to follow the IMF and World Bank recommendations. To this it should be added that, in the 1980s, the World Bank, and in particular the IMF programmes, were frequently criticised for their emphasis on short-run financial and macroeconomic problems, whereas growth and social welfare aspects were more or less neglected.[1] Pointing this out, Frances Stewart, for example, concluded that 'countries which undertook adjustment programmes [in the first half of the 1980s] often experienced rising poverty and malnutrition and weakening growth prospects, while in many cases the basic imbalances persisted' (Stewart 1987: 44). According to Stewart, the governments of the countries concerned should have been encouraged to devise their own adjustment packages (Stewart 1987: 43).

Given the above analysis of the economic situation in Ethiopia, the World Bank recommendations mentioned above, and the recommendation that governments should be encouraged to design their own programmes, it is interesting to analyse the policy response of the government led by President Mengistu Haile-Mariam.

One sign of the Derg's resistance to reforming their strategy of socialism, is the programme of the Workers' Party of Ethiopia that was issued in 1987. In this programme the following economic objectives were stated:

(1) to accelerate the growth of the productive forces so as to build a strong and internally self-sustaining national economy free from the influences of the capitalist market and division of labour;
(2) to expand, strengthen and ensure the dominance of socialist production relations with a view to creating a conducive environment for the growth of the productive forces, and to expand socialist economic organization and management in order to realize this;
(3) to accelerate, through (1) and (2), sustained growth of the standard of living and cultural well-being of the working people.
(quoted from Eshetu Chole and Makonnen Manyazewal 1992: 10)

Clearly the Ethiopian leaders refused to recognise that the *Ethiopia Tikdem* policy was leading the country towards ever-growing problems. The above-mentioned programme declared war on the capitalist system and expressed a devotion to the socialist modes of organising production. The programme is interesting and surprising since the Ethiopian economic system and policy, in particular its organisation of agricultural production (see below), had begun to come under severe criticism from the Soviet Union and its allies (Africa Watch 1991: 373, Tiruneh 1993: 350ff). One reason behind this criticism was that, according to Polyakov: 'By the time of the 1986 drought, the Ethiopian food problem had become the Kremlin's political headache' (Polyakov 1990: 81). Furthermore, it had become obvious to the Soviet leaders that if Ethiopia was to be able to pay her debts it was necessary to improve the performance of agriculture and that the only way to do this was through far-reaching reforms of the agricultural policy away from socialism and towards a greater role for individual private peasants. Here it is important to remember that in the Soviet Union President Gorbachev, from the mid-1980s, introduced both economic and political reforms that implied far-reaching changes to the system and a move away from the command economy. According to Tiruneh:

> during Mengistu's July 1988 visit to Moscow, Gorbachev told him that Soviet involvement in Ethiopia was a result of Brezhnev's years of stagnation from which the USSR had broken away and that the latter's unqualified economic and military commitment to Ethiopia could not continue much further. He told him that, for Soviet support to continue, the regime had to liberalize its political, agricultural and investment policies and to arrive at a non-military solution to the wars in Eritrea and Tigrai.
>
> Tiruneh (1993: 358)

Gorbachev's criticism and threat to discontinue the Soviet support to Ethiopia put Mengistu under heavy pressure. In 1989 the Ethiopian government presented a new Five-Year Plan, the main points of which were summarised in a speech at the Ninth Plenum of the Central Committee of the Workers' Party of Ethiopia in November 1988 where President Mengistu presented thirteen main resolutions that were passed by the Central Committee of the Workers' Party of Ethiopia (*Ethiopian Herald* 1988: 12 November). The next section presents a summary of the main content of these resolutions and should be read in the light not only of the problematic economic situation but also of the criticism that was delivered by Gorbachev some months earlier. The content of the resolutions is subsequently commented on from the perspective of the various dimensions of economic systems presented in Chapter 2. Thereafter, President Mengistu's follow-up reform announcement of 5 March 1990 is presented and analysed. The chapter concludes by discussing the realism of the revised *Ethiopia Tikdem* strategy and its potential to create a break in the negative economic trends that had characterised Ethiopia since the revolution.

THE NOVEMBER 1988 RESOLUTIONS

As a reaction to the poor economic performance during the first five years of the *Ten-Year Perspective Plan*, but also as a reaction to criticism from abroad, in November 1988 at the Ninth Regular Plenum of the Central Committee of the Workers' Party of Ethiopia (*Ethiopian Herald* 1988: 12 November) President Mengistu Haile-Mariam presented thirteen resolutions, most of which had a clear economic message. The official objective of the resolutions was to identify shortcomings in the Ethiopian economic system and development strategy and to introduce appropriate adjustment measures (Mengistu 1988: 9).

This section presents the content of the thirteen resolutions. In order to obtain a better understanding of the economic implications of the respective resolutions we shall also comment on them and how they would affect the various dimensions of the Ethiopian economic system.

Resolution one

Resolution one presented measures to defend 'the gains scored in the revolutionary process, to score new victories, to safeguard the people's security and the unity of the country'.

To meet these objectives it was concluded that:

> it is necessary to promote the process of transition towards an expanded form of accumulation by organising co-operatives in the agricultural, handicraft and service sectors and generally in the small-scale commodities sphere. . . .
>
> [T]here is no alternative to giving much priority to the struggle of organising the peasant into peasant producers' co-operatives to become self-reliant in food-grains by solving the problems of the agricultural sector. . . .
>
> The necessary support has to be given on the part of the government for bank loan services to the extent needed to hasten the growth of co-operatives. . . .
>
> The set of guidelines for organising associations has to be improved in such a way as to enable the associations to direct their progress systematically on the basis of experience and develop democratic methods of operation, proletarian discipline and greater hard work in line with planning and socialist emulation. . . .
>
> In keeping with villagization, the process of organising peasants' producers' co-operatives has to focus on surplus producing districts, later on non-surplus producing districts and ultimately on other areas. . . .
>
> Party members have to be deployed in rural areas in shifts for fixed periods so that by living with the working people, they will set an example

77

to them by supporting the activities aimed at changing their lives. . . .

Since the main objective of organizing co-operatives is, by transforming the small-scale sector into large-scale production stage, to speed up the country's economic growth, and particularly to create ample employment opportunity for the nation's nationalities, agricultural producers' co-operatives with the requisite level of development would be given appropriate assistance.

This resolution dealt mainly with the formation of co-operatives in general and agricultural producer co-operatives in particular. Thus, in terms of the economic system dimensions in Figure 2.1, this resolution meant a clear-cut change towards increased collective ownership (dimension 3). It also meant a unanimous change towards more centralised decision-making (dimension 1), and less reliance on markets (dimension 2) and competition (dimension 5).

Regarding the objective to establish various types of service co-operatives the resolution should not be criticised from the point of view of economic efficiency. As noted in Chapter 3, these co-operatives could certainly play an important role as suppliers both of various inputs and consumer goods and of various types of social services.

Producer co-operatives, on the other hand, as seen from the previous chapters, are of much more doubtful value. Productivity in such co-operatives had proved itself to be below that in individual peasant farming, notwithstanding the various types of favourable incentives. In May 1989, the Minister of Planning, Mersie Ejigu, in an interview with the author of this study, stressed that the government would be reluctant to grant permission for the establishment of new agricultural producer co-operatives. To underline this, the Minister stated that the government had turned down many requests from peasants to form producer co-operatives.

At first glance this could be seen as a positive line of policy in view of the overall objective of agricultural growth and economic development. However, in the resolution quoted above it is stressed that 'the process of organising peasants' producers' co-operatives has to focus on surplus producing districts'. Given this resolution, one cannot overlook the fact that the intended policy in 1988/89 clearly implied a risk of worsening, rather than improving, the situation in Ethiopian agriculture. By rejecting requests to establish producer co-operatives in non-surplus areas, where the productivity in agriculture and the potential of agricultural production were relatively low compared to the productivity and potentials in surplus regions, the average productivity of producer co-operatives would increase. The policy would thus tend to weaken the negative picture of the low productivity of producer co-operatives compared to the productivity of individual peasants. Thereby, the government also hoped to reduce the international criticism of the collectivisation policy.

Resolution two

Resolution two dealt with the strengthening of the villagisation programme. It was stressed that in order to 'create a sound basis for improvement in the production relationship under way in the rural areas and narrow the urban–rural relationship' it is important to:

- more properly coordinate villagization activities with the country's overall development strategy . . .;
- coordinate in a better way the provision of educational, health, commercial, flour mill, electric power and road services in the rural areas with the villagization scheme;
- provide village dwellers with adequate backyards and intensify work in home gardening afforestation so as to improve the livelihood of members and enhance the natural look of their surroundings;
- take appropriate measures to prevent the spread of urban social ills into newly established villages.

As the villagisation programme was designed and enforced by central decisions and had the explicit objective to co-ordinate the activities in the villages with the overall development strategy of Ethiopia, this resolution meant a clear move towards increased centralisation (dimension 1). It also implied increased reliance on administrative processes in the allocation of resources (dimension 2).

As noted in Chapter 3, much criticism can be directed at the villagisation programme. Under the programme people were forced to move from their old sites against their will, and peasants who had moved away from their land had to devote much time to walking and transporting people and agricultural inputs between the village where they lived and their land. Furthermore, peasants living away from their land were unable to protect their crops from attacks by monkeys and other animals at night.

However, from the perspective of economics and standards of living, the actions in resolution two were quite positive. By the end of the 1980s the social service dimension of the villagisation programme had not been given strong enough attention. For instance, the low sanitary standards in the villages, together with the low standards of social services and health conditions, paved the way for epidemic diseases that were less frequent in the traditional rural settlements. In short, the potential gains from villagisation easily turn into losses when the programme is not combined with the provision of various services in the villages. There is no doubt that in the case of Ethiopia, up to the end of the 1980s, the villagisation programme had not been efficient in providing improved living standards.

Resolution three

Resolution three stated that:

> The major aims of the next five-year plan are to attain self-sufficiency in food, improve and expand basic services to the people, ease the problem of unemployment, build the foreign exchange earning potential and broaden the scope of science and technology through strengthening socialist production relationship and speed up the pace of economic development. The realization of these objectives calls for the building of a stronger economy based on greater self-reliance and more rational use of domestic resources.

Among the various measures presented to attain these objectives, the following should be noted:

- Remove the constraints facing state farms and expand and strengthen them so as to produce in quality and in bulk raw materials needed for industry and the export market and to broaden the scope for job opportunities.
- Proceed with and intensify the resettlement programme in order to deal with harvest shortage by developing idle land, tackle the problems facing the totally unemployed or only partly unemployed in the urban or rural areas.
- To ensure the attainment of economic objectives, the budgetary allocation will give prominence as much as possible to high-yield, fast remunerative areas as well as to sectors with greater foreign exchange earning potential and projects which strengthen the interdependence of the economy.

In addition, the third resolution also dealt with the industrial sector. It was stressed that the heavy industries should be expanded to produce tools for the agricultural sector; that small-scale industries should be expanded to overcome the shortage of basic consumer goods; and that small-scale industrial zones should be established.

The objective of the resolution, namely to improve economic performance in Ethiopia, was to be realised by the introduction of measures that were to strengthen the socialist production relationship and produce an economy that would be self-sufficient in food production. Among the specific measures the emphasis on State farms and resettlements should be particularly noted.

As has been concluded in Chapter 5, State farms in socialist Ethiopia were very inefficient production units. There is no doubt that they gave very high yields per hectare compared to peasant farming. However, it is also clear that they used disproportionately high amounts of inputs. In total, the domestic resource cost of State farm production was high compared to that of peasant farming. Therefore, to make further investments and expand the State farms before these inefficiencies were eliminated was not a way to pave the road to economic growth but rather the opposite. Instead the emphasis should have been given to such actions that supported the last quoted points, namely to 'give prominence as much as possible to high-yield, fast remunerative areas as well as to sectors with greater foreign exchange earning potential and projects which strengthen the interdependence of the economy', provided that high yield and greater foreign exchange earning potentials are not interpreted in absolute terms but are closely analysed in terms of their net contributions after considering their input requirements.

From the point of view of economic system dimensions an implementation of the content of this resolution would have meant a move towards increased centralisation (dimension 1) and collective ownership (dimension 3) and thus a further reduction of the role of markets (dimension 2) in Ethiopian agriculture. The explicit emphasis on resettlements should also be seen as an intention by the government to increase centralisation.

Finally, it is fair to note that the third resolution also included an intention by the government to support small-scale industries in order to overcome the shortage of basic consumer goods. The availability of basic consumer goods is important, but often neglected by policymakers, as a source of incentives for producers and workers in both rural and urban areas. Thus, the resolution, at least implicitly, meant a move towards increasing the role of incentives in the economy (dimension 4). However, notwithstanding this positive component, it can be concluded that the third resolution indicated a negative change in relation to economic system aspects and economic efficiency.

Resolution four

Resolution four dealt with capital accumulation. According to this resolution, during the Five-Year Plan period:

- Measures will be taken to transform the small-scale commodity sector into expanded productive sector in order to build domestic capital accumulation as well as enhance the productivity of state development enterprises, control waste and pilfering in government and co-operative enterprises and also reduce state expenditure.
- a special strategy should be devised and put into practice that would raise the country's foreign exchange earnings by enhancing qualitative and quantitative commodity production for world market and in general encourage foreign trade.
- steps should be taken to develop the saving habits of the people . . .
- another source for boosting capital accumulation being the production of foreign economic relations [increase the efforts to obtain foreign loans and aid, amend the proclamation on joint ventures].

Like the three previous resolutions, the fourth resolution also implied a move towards more centralised resource allocation (dimension 1) and increased collective (State) ownership (dimension 3). It is worth mentioning, however, that in June 1989 the socialist Ethiopian government followed up both the fourth and the third resolutions and made decisions on a draft law concerning the development of small-scale industries, the participation of non-governmental bodies in the hotel industry, and the establishment of joint ventures (*Ethiopian Herald* 1989: 17 June). This decision can be seen as an attempt to increase the international openness (dimension 6) of the economy by inviting foreign investors. Without doubt these decisions could be seen as decisions in a positive direction from the point of view of economic efficiency. However, their resulting effects on investments were bleak if not insignificant.

If the resolution's explicit emphasis on transforming the small-scale commodity sector into an expanded productive sector is interpreted as a means to transform it into a large-scale sector it is very difficult to find any economic arguments for such a strategy in a country like Ethiopia with its abundance of unskilled labour and lack of capital. Policies aiming at such a transformation would clearly run into conflict with the underlying market forces that have their origin in the factor endowments of the Ethiopian economy. Thus, it would mean a move further away from market-based resource allocation towards greater reliance on administrative processes in the economy (dimension 2).

Furthermore, even if the resolution did explicitly mention the objective to raise the country's foreign exchange earnings, it did not mention the perhaps most important and, in the socialist Ethiopian context, also completely neglected policy area in this regard, namely the exchange rate policy.

Chapter 5 noted that, given the low incomes of the people in the 1980s, domestic capital accumulation through enhanced domestic private savings was a very difficult task. Therefore, to increase the savings among peasants required increased production in this sector which, as is clear from our analysis in Chapter 4, would require institutional changes and changes in the agricultural price policy (including trade and exchange rate policies) in order to increase the net cash sales returns for the peasants.

Finally, obtaining foreign loans and aid and stimulating joint ventures are alternative ways to boost domestic capital accumulation. However, at the time of the presentation of the resolution, the criticism from foreign countries against various aspects of the policy in socialist Ethiopia was an important and severe restriction on foreign resource mobilisation and so was the fear of nationalisation for the realisation of capital accumulation through joint ventures. Therefore, it was not surprising that the positive effects of the resolution on foreign resource mobilisation were quite limited.

Resolution five

Resolution five dealt with the appropriate economic management of the country. For instance it was stressed that during the next plan period:

- Central planning should be not only improved and strengthened to properly map out the social sector of the economy but also to cover the private sector in the indicative plan.
- Practice should be introduced to base salaries and promotions in accordance with the contributions to the growth of productivity by making payments to each commensurate with the work done; to employ lump sum systems in pertinent organizations based on appropriate working hours (norms) and organizational set ups, and generally to finalize studies on salary and incentive policies and to put them into effect as of the next plan period.

Like many of the preceding resolutions, this fifth resolution emphasised central planning and explicitly declared an objective to include and cover the private sector in the indicative plan. Thus, this resolution clearly pointed towards increased centralisation (dimension 1) and less reliance on markets and competition in the allocation of resources (dimensions 2 and 5).

To let the central planning system control the private sector more than it did at the time when the resolution was presented would clearly not increase productivity in the private sector but rather reduce it. Furthermore, the above intention to increase the capital accumulation through joint ventures between foreign private firms and Ethiopian firms was counteracted by the intention to increase central state control of the private sector.

The fifth resolution also declared an intention to increase the performance of State enterprises and co-operatives by making the returns to labour dependent on the efforts devoted to work. This was an issue raised by the World Bank in relation to the experiences from the then socialist Eastern European countries (World Bank 1987b: 54). However, this very market-oriented remuneration scheme was in conflict with the political ideology of socialism that was prevalent in socialist Ethiopia. Thus, by the end of the 1980s it seemed highly unlikely that an efficient system of this kind really could be introduced and implemented efficiently in Ethiopia by the Mengistu government. If introduced and implemented it would, however, have meant that incentives would have come to play a more central role (dimension 4).

From the above presentation and comments it is obvious that the fifth resolution contained conflicting elements in relation to the change to the system that it could bring about.

Resolutions six and seven

Resolutions six and seven dealt with science, technology, and education. In particular manpower training, including on-the-job training, was stressed. As these resolutions did not have any direct implications for the economic system, we do not comment on them in this study.

Resolution eight

Resolution eight dealt with the unemployment problem. It was stressed that:

- the selection of projects in every economic sector should focus on those areas which create job opportunities and to devise strategies that would better encourage generally labour intensive production technology.

The implications of this resolution for the economic system were also less obvious. Considering the unemployment problem in labour-abundant Ethiopia, the emphasis on labour-intensive technology in the eighth resolution can be interpreted as an intention to ascribe to market forces an increased role in the labour market (dimension 2). However, as noted above, in resolution four it was indicated that small-scale production should be transformed into large-scale production, which as a rule means that a more capital-intensive technology will be applied and thus less weight will be given to market forces. Consequently, there seemed to be an obvious contradiction between resolutions four and eight.

Resolution nine

Resolution nine dealt with the population issue and stated that 'demographic policy should be devised in conformity with the country's natural resources potential and development prospects'. Like resolutions six and seven this resolution did not have any implications for the economic system.

Resolution ten

Resolution ten dealt with the private sector of the economy and stated that:

- the role of the private economic sector is to continue during the transitional period ... to make the private sector contribute to the progress of the present economy, help alleviate prevailing social problems and make it contribute to the construction of socialist economy.

Furthermore, this resolution declared the objectives to:

- Create situations conducive for the peasantry to increase its produce, to conserve, develop and use local natural resources without impeding the rural social transformation and by proper land allocation to help the peasant increase its produce by developing confidence.
- Create legal conditions for individuals with adequate capital and management skills to participate without any capital limitations, privately, in partnership, concessional arrangements or joint ventures with the government in the fields of;
  - large scale agricultural development;
  - animal husbandry and animal by-products;
  - industry;
  - services.

This resolution is not easy to characterise in terms of the economic system dimensions presented in Chapter 2. From the previous chapters it is clear that the private or individual peasants were more efficient than the producer co-operatives and the State farms. Thus, from the point of view of economic efficiency, this resolution contained many positive points.

It is worth noting that in a report from 1985, a team of Soviet consultants attached to the National Committee of Central Planning, NCCP, of Socialist Ethiopia recommended that in order to bring about a rise in agricultural production it would be expedient to give 'due consideration to the possibility of establishing, in some zones of the country, private commercial farms specialized in growing exportable produce' (Considerations on the Economic Policy of Ethiopia for the Next Few Years 1985: 26). In the same report it was also stressed that intensified assistance should be given to the private agricultural sector by 'supplying it with labour tools, improved seeds, pedigree livestock, fertilizers, chemicals for combating plant pests and diseases' (ibid.: 28). However, notwithstanding that Soviet advisers gave these recommendations in 1985 there seems to be a contradiction between the present resolution and its emphasis on the importance of the private sector and resolution five, where the scope of central planning was extended to cover the private sector also, thereby reducing the role of private incentives. Thus, in 1988 it seems that the Ethiopian government wanted to keep and stress the Marxist–Leninist social economic system but could not afford to prohibit private enterprises in production and trade. However, these contradictory signals meant uncertainty about the future and thus it was not possible to take full advantage of the private sector potential. Furthermore, the risk of nationalisation of private enterprises and equipment naturally hampered the private sector activities, for instance the potential gains from joint ventures stressed in resolution four.

Even though, as noted above, it is far from easy to classify this tenth resolution into the economic system dimensions in Figure 2.1, it seems reasonable to characterise it as a slight move towards increased reliance on incentives (dimension 4) and private ownership (dimension 3).

Resolution eleven

Resolution eleven dealt with the role and efficiency of the Party, government, and mass organisations. These institutions and organisations were all to work to restructure the local political system and mobilise the whole working population in the economic sector.

Considering the central role that the Party and the government already had, the eleventh resolution did not mean a drastic change in policy even if it can be seen as a slight move towards even greater centralisation (dimension 1) and increased reliance on administrative processes (dimension 2) and orders (dimension 4).

Resolutions twelve and thirteen

Resolutions twelve and thirteen dealt with the question of peace and defence. In these two final resolutions it was stated that complete peace and tranquillity are necessary for improvement of the living conditions. For instance, in resolution thirteen it was stated that:

- Sanctity of the life, respect and pride all depend on the maintenance of the Motherland and based on the active participation of all citizens and every necessary support should be given for the construction and strengthening of our defence force which is the source of the country's and people's pride.

The implications of these final resolutions for the economic system are not obvious. However, considering the amounts of manpower and other resources allocated to the defence sector, and the fact that many of the system constraints and the poor performance of the Ethiopian economy could be attributed to the priority given to defence, the thirteenth resolution should also be read with the economic system and potential changes of this system in mind.

The important, and far from unexpected message of the thirteenth resolution was that the enormous and growing flow of resources to defence was to be continued and would thus further reduce the resources available for the productive sectors of the economy. Thereby, economic growth and development in Ethiopia would continue to be hampered by the emphasis on the security and defence of Ethiopian unity which was one of the corner-stones, if not *the* main cornerstone, of *Ethiopia Tikdem*. From the point of view of economic system dimensions this can be seen as a declaration of continued reliance on a centralised resource allocation system (dimension 1) based on administrative processes (dimension 2), and orders (dimension 4).

THE NOVEMBER 1988 RESOLUTIONS – A SERIOUS ATTEMPT TO CHANGE THE ECONOMIC SYSTEM?

An interesting issue is whether the November 1988 resolutions really could be seen as a serious attempt to change the economic system or if they were just presented to meet some of the growing international criticism against the Mengistu government and the *Ethiopia Tikdem* policy.

From the point of view of the economic system dimensions presented in Figure 2.1 the major tendencies implied by the various resolutions are summarised in Figure 6.1. As can be seen, all economic system dimensions would have been directly affected if the resolutions had been turned into policy actions.

Furthermore, Figure 6.1 reveals that, if implemented, most of the November 1988 resolutions would have moved the economic system towards increased centralisation, greater reliance on the administrative process in the allocation of resources and towards increased collective ownership. However, for most dimensions, the resolutions were internally inconsistent. In particular this was the case with the *incentives* ↔ *orders* dimension.

In terms of both the two-sector dual economy model and the more complete institutional dual general equilibrium model, the November 1988 resolutions can be described as negative changes in most variables. It is important to note that the few points that could be interpreted as indications of positive economic system changes were counteracted by the continued emphasis on defence and by the clear declarations about the continuation of the socialist and centralist development strategy. Thus, the effects that were derived in Chapter 4 should be expected to have been strengthened rather than weakened if the November 1988 resolutions had been turned into actual economic policy changes.

In conclusion, the November 1988 resolutions did not point forward to an improvement in the performance of the Ethiopian economy. Rather they pointed towards a strengthening of most of the negative tendencies and economic effects that followed upon the changes that had been introduced previously during the *Ethiopia Tikdem* period and that were analysed in Chapter 4.

Notwithstanding the above critical comments on the government's intentions in the field of economic policy, a personal discussion with the Minister of Planning, Mersie Ejigu on 15 May 1989, as well as the thirteen resolutions summarised above indicated that the government, by the end of the 1980s, was not only well aware of some of the domestic sources of the economic problems but also officially presented some appropriate policy measures to limit some of their negative effects.

According to the Minister of Planning, in May 1989 it was planned that the Five-Year Plan, to be issued later the same year, should include a number of

1 *Decentralisation* ←——————→ *Centralisation*

Resolution one (emphasis on producer co-operatives) ——→
Resolution two (emphasis on the villagisation programme) ——→
Resolution three (emphasis on State farms, the resettlement programme, and
    industry) ——→
Resolution four (emphasis on large-scale production) ——→
Resolution five (emphasis on central planning) ——→
Resolution eleven (mobilisation of the whole working population) ——→
Resolution thirteen (continued efforts to strengthen the defence) ——→

---

2 *Markets* ←——————→ *Administrative processes*

Resolution one (emphasis on producer co-operatives) ——→
Resolution two (emphasis on the villagisation programme) ——→
Resolution three (emphasis on State farms, the resettlement programme, and
    industry) ——→
Resolution four (emphasis on large-scale production) ——→
Resolution five (emphasis on central planning) ——→
←—— **Resolution eight** (emphasis on labour-intensive technology)
Resolution eleven (mobilisation of the whole working population) ——→
Resolution thirteen (continued efforts to strengthen the defence) ——→

---

3 *Private ownership* ←——————→ *Collective ownership*

Resolution one (emphasis on producer co-operatives) ——→
Resolution three (emphasis on State farms, the resettlement programme, and
    industry) ——→
Resolution four (emphasis on large-scale production) ——→
←—— **Resolution ten** (emphasis on the role of the private sector)

---

4 *Incentives* ←——————→ *Orders*

←—— **Resolution three** (stimulation of production of incentive goods)
←—— **Resolution five** (remuneration based on work done)
←—— **Resolution ten** (create incentives for the peasantry to increase its production
    and make more efficient use of natural resources)
Resolution eleven (mobilisation of the whole working population) ——→
Resolution thirteen (continued efforts to strengthen the defence) ——→

---

5 *Competition* ←——————→ *Non-competition*

Resolution one (emphasis on producer co-operatives) ——→
Resolution five (emphasis on central planning) ——→

(*continued on next page*)

6 *Internationalisation* ⟵————————⟶ *Autarky*

⟵—— **Resolution four** (emphasis on increasing export earnings, inviting joint
ventures, and improving foreign economic relations)

Figure 6.1 Ethiopia Tikdem revised – the November 1988 resolutions

positive changes in the economic policy in the coming years. In particular the
Minister emphasised changes in food policy (improved producer incentives
and increased emphasis on service co-operatives as opposed to producers'
co-operatives), investments, and exports (diversification in product lines
where the country can be expected to have a true comparative advantage, that
is a movement towards a more internationalised economy).

Given the statements in the programme of the Workers' Party of Ethiopia
from 1987 it is natural to ask whether the Ethiopian government really had
the intention to introduce these changes or whether the November 1988
resolutions and the points made by the Minister of Planning were just words
to please donors and increase the external resource mobilisation. This
question cannot be properly answered. However, as noted above, the
November 1988 resolutions clearly indicated that by the end of the 1980s the
socialist objectives summarised in the motto *Ethiopia Tikdem* were still at
the very heart of government policy and dominated the economic efficiency
objectives.

At first glance, this may seem consistent with Ethiopia's foreign political
economic relations. As noted in Chapter 3, Ethiopia's relations with the
Soviet Union and its allies, in terms of economic, advisory, and military
support, were of the utmost importance for the Mengistu government, who
had earlier broken off relations with the USA with the consequence that
support from the non-socialist world was less developed and uncertain. It
should also be noted that the contacts with these non-socialist countries
frequently included severe criticism and demands for policy changes without
clear promises of increased support in exchange. Thus, it is clear that the
Ethiopian leaders could not afford to do away with socialism and thereby risk
losing support from the Soviet Union, the Eastern European countries, and
North Korea as long as the civil war continued.

Things became much more complicated, however, partly because of the
changes in the economic system in the Soviet Union and its allies, which were
introduced during the second half of the 1980s. As mentioned above, in July
1988 Mengistu and his policy were subjected to severe criticism by
Gorbachev. At the same time opposition and liberation groups in Ethiopia
were making progress in their struggle against the central government. Thus,
the threat from Gorbachev to withdraw support if there were no changes in

the Ethiopian economic policy and in the civil war, made it important for Mengistu to present changes that could satisfy the Soviet leader. However, it is clear that Mengistu was not convinced that Gorbachev would succeed in his transformation programme in the Soviet Union. Tiruneh makes the following comment about Mengistu's reaction to Gorbachev's criticism:

> Mengistu's reaction was, apparently, to take comfort in the thought that Gorbachev was a revisionist and that the Soviet hard liners would overthrow him. Thus, Mengistu persisted in his old position by declaring that the reforms in the socialist countries did not have any bearing on Ethiopia's conditions.
>
> Tiruneh (1993: 358)

This may explain the inconsistency in the November 1988 resolutions. On the one hand, Mengistu tried to demonstrate to donors, including the World Bank and the International Monetary Fund, that changes towards less central planning and a more market-oriented economy were to be introduced in Ethiopia. By doing this, Mengistu hoped to reduce some of the basis of the criticism from Gorbachev. On the other hand, since Mengistu did not believe fully in the success of Gorbachev's policy reforms in the Soviet Union, he did not dare to present a plan for dismantling the socialist system altogether. Instead, he tried to keep the door open for new Soviet hard-line socialist or communist leaders in case such leaders should come to overthrow Gorbachev. Therefore, even though the November 1988 resolutions showed some positive signs of economic system reform they should not be classified as a serious attempt by the Mengistu government to change the Ethiopian economic system away from socialism.

THE MARCH 1990 ECONOMIC REFORM ANNOUNCEMENT

From the adoption of the resolutions in November 1988 up to March 1990, some minor steps were taken towards implementing the resolutions and introducing appropriate policy measures. However, these steps, mainly the *Joint Venture Proclamation* issued in June 1989, were far from satisfactory compared with the content of the resolutions.[2] Instead, the major impression one and a half years later was that the resolutions had not been followed by appropriate changes in the policy. For many observers, therefore, the 1988 resolutions were nothing but empty rhetoric.

Mengistu faced an increasing number of problems and the government's weakening grip on power that had began in 1987, or even earlier, continued (Tiruneh 1993: 344). As can be seen in Table 6.1 the economic situation continued to deteriorate. The debt service ratio (debt expenditure, i.e. interest and amortisation, as a share of export revenues) increased from around 6 per cent to around 45 per cent during the 1980s. Furthermore, by the end of the

Table 6.1 Some basic economic data for Ethiopia, 1988/89–1990/91

	1988/89	*1989/90*	*1990/91*
Annual sectoral growth (%) and sectoral composition (% of GDP at current factor cost) for some sectors			
GDP, constant 1980/81 factor cost	1.6 (100.0)	−1.4 (100.0)	−0.6 (100.0)
Agriculture	2.2 (38.7)	0.1 (39.1)	8.4 (44.3)
Manufacturing	1.7 (8.1)	−4.4 (7.8)	−26.8 (5.4)
Distribution services	2.0 (17.0)	−3.3 (16.7)	−9.2 (15.2)
Public administration and defence	3.5 (11.5)	−2.1 (11.4)	7.2 (12.3)
Social services	4.7 (4.3)	2.4 (4.5)	−5.0 (4.0)
External economic relations			
Exports (merchandise trade and non-factor services, % of GDP)	12.5	11.2	8.2
Imports (merchandise trade and non-factor services, % of GDP)	20.0	17.8	18.6
Resource gap (% of GDP)	−7.5	−6.6	−10.4
Debt service ratio (% of exports, accrual basis)	39.2	45.3	62.3
Import cover (reserve assets as week's imports 30 June)	4.4	1.3	4.7
Terms of trade (1983/84 = 100)	86.7	67.8	63.7
Real effective exchange rate (trade-weighted, annual average, February 1973 = 100)	121.8	123.0	131.7
Government finance			
Revenues and grants (% of GDP)	37.8	28.6	23.3
Expenditure (% of GDP)	46.6	45.2	36.3
Balance (including grants, % of GDP)	−8.8	−16.6	−13.0
Financing through the banking system (% of GDP)	3.3	10.2	8.9
Prices			
General retail price index, Addis Ababa (annual average, 1963 = 100)	501.8	527.7	637.8
Percentage change	9.4	5.2	20.9

Sources: National Bank of Ethiopia, Ministry of Finance, Ministry of Planning and Economic Development.

1980s the Ethiopian stock of international reserves was more or less completely depleted. In addition to the problematic economic situation the government forces faced increasing problems in the battlefield, notwithstanding the enormous resources allocated to defence under the motto 'everything to the warfront' (Mengistu 1988: 21f, Africa Watch 1991: 293). Despite these efforts and priorities, from 1988 Eritrean and Tigrain opposition groups made great progress in the battlefield (African Watch 1991: chapter 15, Tiruneh 1993: 345). In May 1989 a group of senior officers attempted, but failed to accomplish, a *coup d'état* against the Mengistu government, who responded with a number of executions of high-level officers. As a consequence the military strength of the government troops was significantly reduced.

The severe criticism by the donor community at large also continued, which made the prospects for increased foreign assistance bleak. To this we should add the declaration by Gorbachev that arms deliveries would not continue after March 1991 when the contract between the Soviet Union and Ethiopia expired (Africa Watch 1991: 373). Finally, Mengistu's belief that Gorbachev and the *glasnost* and *perestroika* policy would be disrupted proved in the event to be unfounded. The reform processes in the Soviet Union and Eastern Europe continued and the end of the 'cold war' between the USA and its allies on the one side and the Soviet Union and its allies on the other, reduced Mengistu's ability to attract support from the Soviet Union and its allies for global security reasons.

Even though there may have been expectations of some changes in the economic policy, it was a surprise when President Mengistu Haile-Mariam, at the Eleventh Regular Plenum of the Central Committee of the Workers' Party of Ethiopia on 5 March 1990, announced a far-reaching revision of the Ethiopian economic system. The stated objective was to create a mixed economy, in which, according to the adopted six-point resolution, economic actors and the market were to guide the allocation of resources.[3]

The major points in the new economic strategy can be summarised as follows:

- The Ethiopian economic strategy should be that of a mixed economy.
- The State enterprises, whose existence, according to the President, was motivated by the absence of a strong capitalist class, should be managed on the basis of competition, profitability, and productivity.
- The private sector should (from now on) be encouraged and strengthened in all ways.
- The land should continue to be owned by the State but the individual peasant's right to use a specific area of land should be indefinite in time and the peasant should be allowed to transfer land to legal heirs who also derive their livelihood from farming.
- Trees and other perennial plants grown on the land should be owned by the respective peasants.

- Individual peasants should be allowed to hire workers to work on their farms.
- It should be possible to dismantle producer co-operatives if this is the democratic will of the members.
- Private investors should be allowed to establish large modern farms.
- Private traders should be allowed to compete without any restrictions with the State-run trade enterprises in all sectors of the economy.
- The grain control stations and the quota system should cease to exist.
- The plans based on directives should be changed to a comprehensive indicative national plan that should reflect both the planning and marketing laws.

If this reform programme had been successfully completed, what would have been the effects on economic performance in Ethiopia? As noted above (and in Chapter 5), by the end of the 1980s the Ethiopian economy was an economy in deep distress. As in other less developed countries with severe economic problems, the basic economic problem was that of excess demand over the current capacity of domestic production, i.e. a growing negative resource balance. This type of problem can be solved or reduced by decreasing the demand and/or increasing the capacity of production.

As a rule, structural adjustment programmes and economic recovery programmes that have been introduced or recommended for countries with severe macroeconomic imbalances include four sets of measures: devaluation, deregulation of markets, trade liberalisation, and reduction of public spending.

Through the devaluation, the domestic demand will be reduced, *ceteris paribus*. In particular this is the case with the demand for imported commodities. This reduced import demand improves the economy's balance of payments and so, also, does the improved export production profitability, measured in domestic currency, that results from the devaluation.

Turning to the deregulation or liberalisation of the economy, this is included in the World Bank and IMF programmes in order to reduce distortions and improve the incentive system and thereby the efficiency, the production capacity, and thus the supply in the economy.

Finally, reduction in public spending is included in the programmes in order to curb the severe fiscal deficit that characterises many of the debt crisis countries.

How then did the 5 March reform programme compare with the typical World Bank/IMF programmes? In brief, the main focus of the Mengistu government's 1990 reform programme was on the deregulation of the domestic economy; reduction of public spending was less emphasised and trade liberalisation and exchange rate reforms were completely neglected.

Expected effects of the 5 March reform programme

The economic system changes that were announced in March 1990 are summarised in terms of the economic system dimensions in Figure 6.2. Clearly the reform announcement was quite far-reaching even if it was incomplete in several respects, in particular in relation to the *international* ↔ *autarky* dimension.

In terms of our two-sector dual economy model, the 5 March reform programme can be described by means of Figure 4.1, where now the per capita agricultural production curve will shift upwards and thus create increased possibilities for increased imports of capital goods and other inputs, i.e. fuels and fertilisers, and consumer goods. Thereby, it would be possible for the per capita agricultural production to expand even more and this can also be expected to be the case for the modern sector.

Turning to our more complete four-sector institutional dual economy model, the analysis in Chapter 4 of institutional changes for the peasant sector and collectivisation (Tables 4.3, 4.4, and 4.5, respectively) and of changes in the price of peasant produce (Table 4.6), can be repeated, however, now with all effects being reversed compared to the effects derived in Chapter 4. From these analyses it is clear that some of the negative effects that had been created by the *Ethiopia Tikdem* policy were to be counteracted by the March 1990 reform. In particular this applied to the situation of the peasants. However, this potential was partly counteracted by the continued efforts and resources devoted to the civil war and increased demoralisation among the soldiers during 1988 and 1989 (Africa Watch 1991: chapter 11, Tiruneh 1993: 351ff). Thus, the effects analysed and described in Tables 4.8 and 4.9 also apply to this period. To this should be added the continued very high population growth (for effects, see the analysis related to Table 4.7).

The incompleteness of the 1990 reform programme

Doubtless, the economic reform programme that was announced in March 1990 was far-reaching. Unlike the November 1988 resolutions, if the announced 5 March reform had been successfully implemented it would have meant an important step away from socialism and a clear potential for obtaining improvements in economic performance. We have noted that the March 1990 reform focused on deregulation. In comparison to World Bank and IMF programmes, the programme was lacking in reforms in important policy areas, in particular in relation to trade and exchange rate policies and in relation to public spending.

1 Decentralisation ⟵——————⟶ *Centralisation*

⟵—— Stated objective to change to a mixed economy
⟵—— The intention to replace central planning with indicative planning
⟵—— Introduction of the right to dismantle producer co-operatives
⟵—— Liberalisation of domestic trade

2 Markets ⟵——————⟶ *Administrative processes*

⟵—— The intention to replace central planning with indicative planning
⟵—— Introduction of the right to dismantle producer co-operatives
⟵—— Liberalisation of domestic trade
⟵—— Dismantling grain control stations and the grain quota system

3 Private ownership ⟵——————⟶ *Collective ownership*

⟵—— Emphasis on the private sector
⟵—— Introduction of the right to dismantle producer co-operatives
⟵—— Introduction of the right for private individuals to invest in large-scale farming
⟵—— Liberalisation of domestic trade

4 Incentives ⟵——————⟶ *Orders*

⟵—— Introduction of increased land user security for peasants
⟵—— Introduction of the right for peasants to transfer land to legal heirs who derive their living from farming
⟵—— Introduction of the right for private individuals to invest in large-scale farming
⟵—— Liberalisation of domestic trade
⟵—— Dismantling grain control stations and the grain quota system

5 Competition ⟵——————⟶ *Non-competition*

⟵—— State enterprises should be managed on the basis of productivity, competition, and profitability
⟵—— Liberalisation of domestic trade
⟵—— Dismantling grain control stations and the grain quota system

6 Internationalisation ⟵——————⟶ *Autarky*

No changes

Figure 6.2 Ethiopia Tikdem revised – the March 1990 reform programme

The need for an exchange rate reform

In 1990 the Ethiopian birr was heavily overvalued. Thus, as stressed repeatedly by economists, the World Bank, and the IMF, a devaluation was urgently needed. However, the reform programme did not contain any change in exchange rate policy. This is not to say that civil servants in the ministries were not well aware of the need for a devaluation. Interviews conducted in the various ministries in Addis Ababa in mid-March 1990 and February 1991 revealed a high awareness of the problem. It is a well-known fact that President Mengistu and his government were strongly opposed to a devaluation. However, according to our information, in early 1991 there was a governmental committee working on these issues in Addis Ababa, and the World Bank and the IMF continued their work in convincing the Ethiopian government to devalue their currency.

However, a devaluation of the Ethiopian birr was just one of two important changes that were needed in the Ethiopian exchange rate policy at the time of the 1990 reform announcement. As noted in Chapter 3, the birr was in a fixed relation to the US dollar. In the pre-1973 international monetary system with fixed exchange rates the US dollar was the currency against which the majority of currencies were fixed. However, in the current international monetary system there is no a priori reason for a country to peg its currency completely to the US dollar. Nevertheless, many less developed countries, of which Ethiopia was one, at the end of the 1980s continued to have their currency 100 per cent pegged to the US dollar even if there seldom existed a real economic reason for such a strong link.[4]

As noted in Chapter 3, Ethiopian foreign trade with the European Community, both on the export and the import side, was greater than the Ethiopian trade with the USA. The implication of this is that even if at first sight Ethiopia had a fixed exchange rate during the *Ethiopia Tikdem* period, this was definitely not the case in the commercial relations with her major trading partners, with the exception of the USA. In fact, the case was rather the opposite: Ethiopia had a system with very flexible exchange rates towards all her major trading partners but the USA. The relationship between the birr and the European currencies, for example, was determined by the relationship between the US dollar and these respective currencies. Therefore, when the US dollar appreciated due to an improvement in American economic performance or speculative movements, the Ethiopian birr appreciated as well. This took place independently of economic development in Ethiopia. Therefore, a revision of the exchange rate policy replacing the 100 per cent link to the US dollar with a more appropriate currency basket was urgently needed. An analysis of the Ethiopian trade situation at the end of the 1980s points to a heavy weight for the European currencies or the ECU in such a basket (see e.g. Chapter 3 and Hansson 1993c).

The need for trade liberalisation

As with the exchange rate policy, the March 1990 reform announcement did not include any trade liberalisation reform. This was a severe shortcoming since the lack of a trade policy reform, according to our view, was a threat to the whole idea of economic system reform. The reason is that the trade procedures, in particular the licensing and the rationing of foreign exchange, counteracted the positive efficiency and growth gains that were the main objectives of the reform. To achieve these gains it was important to let the market take care of the allocation as far as possible.

To allocate import licences and foreign exchange through administrative rather than market-oriented procedures requires an incredible amount of information. In the case of market allocation this information is provided automatically through the demands and supplies of the various economic actors. Even if in theory it is possible to simulate the market at the current exchange rate and trade policy, by selling the available licences and foreign currency in competition, i.e. through auctioning, such a procedure is less likely to work well in reality. Thus, to have a chance to break the negative economic trends, the March 1990 reform should have been accompanied by trade policy reforms.

Need for a reduction of public expenditure

As a rule, structural adjustment programmes have a fourth component – reduction of public expenditure. The March 1990 reform did not include any explicit measures in this respect, even if the pressure on State corporations for improved efficiency and profitability can be interpreted as a signal that State subsidies should be reduced. The lack of public expenditure reductions was probably due to the ongoing and escalating civil war that demanded ever-growing resources in order to defend Ethiopian unity.

CONCLUDING REMARKS

In this final section we will make some brief remarks on the realism of the announced March 1990 reform. Did the reform package have a potential to transform one of the most devoted socialist countries in Africa to a market-oriented mixed economy? We also discuss some of Mengistu's problems in convincing donors to increase their support. Finally we ask if Ethiopia after the March 1990 reform could be expected to continue being a socialist country or if it was to develop into a mixed economy, as was the official objective of the reforms, or if it was most likely that the conflicting interests and the incompleteness of the reform programme would just lead to chaos.

Was the March 1990 reform realistic?

By the end of the 1980s most observers were convinced that something had to be done to improve the performance of the Ethiopian economy. Nevertheless, the speech by President Mengistu on 5 March 1990 took most observers by surprise because of the far-reaching reform and the immediate implementation of some of its most vital parts. In particular, the changes regarding producer co-operatives and the complete and immediate liberalisation of the grain market were both surprising and promising. These measures were clear signals to the international community that important changes were under way in the Ethiopian economy.

A critical question in 1990 was whether the Mengistu government was really serious in its reform attempts or whether the reform was no more than rhetoric to please the World Bank, the IMF, and bilateral donors. It is of course impossible to answer this question. However, the author's visits to Ethiopia and meetings with a number of civil servants in March 1990 and in February 1991 revealed that the attempted changes in economic policy were greatly appreciated by civil servants.

This appreciation could also be found among people all over Addis Ababa where the most visible signs of communism and the 'old' system, like paintings of Lenin, Marx, and Engels, were removed more or less immediately. The same happened to the communist and socialist symbols at the various ministries. Overnight, these symbols were replaced and ministers and civil servants changed their communist type of suits to ordinary private dark suits.

Interviews performed by the author during February 1991, however, revealed that the optimism that existed in March 1990 had turned into doubts and pessimism among an increasing number of the advocates of the reform, even if, officially, the government still had a sincere intention to carry through the economic reform programme. The doubts and pessimism were due to the fact that the reform work slowed down significantly during the first months of 1991, when the civil war escalated. It was also due to the fact that donors and international organisations did not respond as hoped by significantly increasing their aid flows to Ethiopia. To this should be added the problems for Ethiopian trade that arose as a consequence of the Kuwait–Iraq crisis in early 1991.

Notwithstanding the slow implementation of the announced reform and the growing pessimism, in the first months of 1991 there were few who thought that the changes that had been introduced in the rural areas, and in agriculture in particular, could be reversed or stopped. Here it is important to note the international environment in which the Ethiopian reform was introduced.

Since the last years of the 1980s socialist economic systems all over the world had been subjected to severe criticism, and there had been changes towards a more market-oriented system in most former socialist countries. In the case of Ethiopia, however, it is important to note that very few proclamations concerning the reforms were presented during the first year after the March 1990 reform announcement. Thus, in early 1991, there was an obvious risk that the positive impact on agriculture during the first year of the reform would decrease over time, due to uncertainty about the future, even if it was considered unlikely that the incentive structure in agriculture would be forced back to the situation prior to 5 March 1990.

Another important question was whether there was enough competence in the country, that is in ministries and other organisations, to implement the reform efficiently? There was a general view that the competence of the Ethiopian civil servants was high compared to those in most developing countries and in sub-Saharan Africa developing countries in particular. Thus, there seemed to be a potential for an efficient implementation of the reforms, provided of course that the proclamations on the reforms become explicit and as clear-cut as possible, leaving the civil servants and other actors in no doubt about the content of the reforms.

The problems of convincing donors

From a humanitarian as well as an economic point of view, Ethiopia has for long been one of the most qualified nations for foreign aid. However, Ethiopia has not been among the major recipients of foreign assistance. In 1987 the net disbursements of official assistance from all sources amounted to US$14 per capita in Ethiopia. In 1991, the amount had increased to US$21 (World Bank 1989: table 18, *World Development Report* 1993: table 20, respectively). The average for sub-Saharan Africa was US$25 and US$33 for the two respective years. The relatively low level of foreign aid to Ethiopia was due to severe international criticism of the Ethiopian policy, both as regards the civil war and as regards the economic policy in general and the agricultural policy in particular.

It is obvious that the change in the economic system that was announced in March 1990 was a change that would have satisfied the demands from many donors and international organisations *if* it had been implemented efficiently. However, one year after the announcement of the reform, the flow of foreign aid had not increased as expected by the Ethiopian government. Many donors focused on the ongoing civil war and emphasised a peaceful solution as a pre-condition for increased aid flows.

As noted above, the Kuwait–Iraq crisis in early 1991 contributed to worsening Ethiopia's problems, particularly in carrying out foreign trade. The high oil prices at the beginning of the crisis worsened the shortage of foreign currency and petrol in Ethiopia. This in turn created shortages of fuel for transportation. As a consequence, the shortages of both domestically produced and imported goods increased and prices rose very rapidly, in particular in urban areas during the first months of 1991. Thus, the need for foreign assistance increased. Even if some of the donors, e.g. the EC and Canada, increased their aid flows there was still an urgent need for increased foreign assistance in general and foreign currency in particular. To make the situation even worse for Ethiopia, the Soviet Union and the other Eastern European countries were experiencing extensive and growing problems at home and after March 1991 the arms deliveries from the Soviet Union were to be discontinued (Africa Watch 1991: 373).

As we have already seen, President Mengistu had also turned down requests from President Gorbachev to introduce *perestroika* in Ethiopia. As a consequence of the problems in Eastern Europe, and the international pressure for change in Ethiopia, supported also by the allied Eastern European countries, there was a drastic reduction in the flow of non-food resources from these countries to Ethiopia. In 1989/90 the share of the fiscal deficit that was externally financed was down to 35 per cent from a high level of 86 per cent in 1987/88 (Eshetu Chole and Makonnen Manyazewal 1992: 19).

Ethiopia after the March 1990 reform – socialism, mixed economy, or chaos?

Given the situation in Ethiopia in 1990, one may ask if the reform of 5 March was complete enough to change the economic system from socialism to a system that can be classified as a mixed economy, and to bring about a long-term break in the negative Ethiopian economic development. The highly problematic economic situation in Ethiopia was the result of a number of factors, of which the civil war and the economic policy in force prior to 5 March 1990 were the two major ones. With the exception of public expenditure reduction and reforms of trade and exchange rate policy, the major defects in the economic system were tackled by the reform.

Without reforms in trade and exchange rate policies, central planning would continue to play a central role in the determination of investments, transports, and external trade activities, whereas the liberalisation of the domestic trade system could be expected to feed inflation. Notwithstanding the far-reaching March 1990 reform, the neglect of reforms in the field of foreign economic relations meant that there was still an obvious risk that the Ethiopian economy during the 1990s would be characterised by disorder or even chaos.

Looking aside from pure economics, the most severe threat to the Ethiopian economy at the end of 1990 and in early 1991 was the civil war. Due to failing leadership and increased demoralisation among the military after the *coup d'état* against the Mengistu government in May 1989, the Ethiopian army faced increasing problems. The enormous resources devoted to defence were a heavy and fatal burden to the Ethiopian economy and society at large. As long as the war continued, the investments in infra-structure in general and the transport system in particular were kept at a low level, which in turn reduced the possibility of an efficient allocation of resources and goods in the economy. Furthermore, the foreign aid flows could not be expected to increase more than marginally as long as the civil war continued.

Even if the 1990 reform programme was to be completed, without drastically increased foreign aid flows and without a sincere and far-reaching reform of the foreign trade regimes and foreign exchange rate policy the Ethiopian economy would continue to deteriorate. Considering the economic crisis in the early 1990s such a deterioration risked leading Ethiopia into a situation in which:

- the various regions would become even more isolated from each other than before;
- the peasants would concentrate on subsistence agriculture;
- urban areas would risk developing into chaos when inflation increased rapidly due to severe shortages of food and other necessities; and
- urban incomes would decrease as a consequence of increased unemployment that follows upon reductions in public non-military spendings and low or no private investments.

In such a scenario, the future of the Ethiopian economy still looked bleak. Furthermore, interviews in Ethiopia in early 1991 indicated that the Ethiopian government would hold back foreign trade liberalisation and exchange rate reforms until the World Bank were willing to go into serious discussions on a structural adjustment programme with heavy debt relief and favourable loans. But the World Bank demanded peace, or at least a move towards a peaceful solution of the Ethiopian internal conflicts, before giving financial support to a structural adjustment programme. It is important to note that the introduction of such a programme was also a very important basis for negotiations with bilateral donors on increased aid flows.

Finally, even though the March 1990 reform programme was quite far-reaching it is clear that the policymaking in Ethiopia would continue to be far from satisfying the fourteen principles of good policy management (see Chapter 1). In particular this was due to the complete absence of reforms in Ethiopian trade and exchange rate policy (principles 4, 5, 6, and 14).

7

ETHIOPIA TIKDEM FAREWELL
The Transitional Economic Policy

INTRODUCTION

Notwithstanding the content of the 5 March 1990 announcement and the immediate reforms, the flow of external resources did not increase as expected or hoped for by the Mengistu government. Instead, the criticism from the aid donors continued, in particular focusing on the ongoing civil war.

The result of the weak response from the donor community was that the implementation of the reform programme began to meet with internal opposition within the Ethiopian government. Thus, as noted in Chapter 6, the implementation in terms of introducing changes in policy and legislation, except for those in land tenure and agricultural marketing, became very slow and the economic situation continued to deteriorate.

One reason behind the slow changes was the increasing difficulties for the Mengistu government, both on the battlefield and in relation to economic conditions. On 21 May 1991, President Mengistu fled the country and one week later, on 28 May, after unsuccessful peace negotiations in London, the Ethiopian People's Revolutionary Democratic Front (EPRDF) took power by walking into a largely undefended Addis Ababa. In the first week of July the new leaders called for a National Conference on Peace and Democracy where the institutional framework for the immediate future of Ethiopia was discussed with representatives from the various liberation movements. It was decided that the United Nations Universal Declaration on Human Rights should be applied in Ethiopia. Furthermore, it was decided that a transitional government, consisting of a Council of Representatives and a Council of Ministers, should rule the country for the years of transition. The transitional period is to be terminated when there has been a democratic election of a new parliament and a resulting new government. Finally, the Eritrean people were given the right to decide whether they wanted their country to become a sovereign state or to remain a region within Ethiopia. On 24 May 1993, after a referendum, this resulted in Eritrea becoming an independent nation state.

When the tasks of the transitional government were defined in July 1991, little was said on the issue of economic reforms. However, this did not mean that there were to be no changes in the Ethiopian economic system during the transitional period. In August 1991, Prime Minister Tamrat Layne presented the preliminary economic policy intentions of the transitional government. The major objective during the transitional period, as presented in the policy document *Draft Economic Policy of Ethiopia During the Transition* (Draft Policy Paper 1991, in the following called the draft policy paper), was stated to be relief and rehabilitation. After a public debate, in which the public and various political, business, and other organisations were invited to give their views and suggestions for changes, decisions on *Ethiopia's Economic Policy During the Transition* (in the following called *The Transitional Economic Policy* (TEP)) were taken by the Council of Representatives in November 1991.

INTENDED CHANGES IN THE ECONOMIC SYSTEM
The changed role of the State

In socialist Ethiopia the State played a dominant role. In the 1990 reform announcement there were no explicit changes of the role of the State, with the exception of a change in the attitude to State enterprises. The transitional government, on the other hand, immediately started to question the role of the State, although the draft policy paper was rather confusing with regard to this issue. In particular the motives behind State involvement in economic activities were unclear.[1] In the TEP, however, the role of the State was much more clearly defined. There it was explicitly stated that 'it is evident that in the past state control over the entire economy was the major cause of economic decline' (TGE 1991: 17). Therefore, in transitional Ethiopia, the role of the State is to be as follows (TGE 1991: 17ff):

- To design economic policies and map out economic development strategies; to promulgate laws and regulations that foster economic development;
- To participate directly or through joint venture arrangements in activities that are considered essential and in which the private sector is not willing to participate;
- To design, implement and supervise the expansion of infrastructure, research and development, manpower training, etc. as a basis for economic expansion;
- To create enabling conditions that will encourage private capital participation and expansion and popular participation;
- To protect consumers and producers against price fluctuations and take regulatory measures to prevent shortages of basic commodities.
- To promote private investment. Therefore the State shall:
  (i) Create enabling conditions for the participation of both domestic and foreign private capital in various economic activities without any capital limitation;

(ii)   Remove all existing bureaucratic procedures and red-tape and introduce new laws and regulations and enforce them to enhance domestic and foreign private capital participation;

(iii) Provide incentives and encouragements to promote domestic capital participation; encourage a wider participation of private foreign capital.

(iv)   Provide special encouragements to communities participating in economic development free from state interference.

- To promote public involvement in development. Therefore:

(i)   Public involvement in discussions and implementation of the TEP should be encouraged and be free from state interference;

(ii)   Local administrative organs must be given the opportunity to play a greater role in the implementation of the economic policy as well as relief and rehabilitation programmes, not on the basis of compulsion but on a voluntary basis and in line with the interests of the public.

- To mobilize external resources;
- To involve national and regional administrative organs in economic management;
- To prepare macro-economic policies consistent with the new economic policy. Therefore, existing policies and laws must be revised and complemented by new policies and laws e.g.

(i)   policies, laws and regulations regarding money supply, credit and interests, taxes and investment that encourage private sector participation and facilitate and encourage the efficient operation of existing establishments;

(ii)   a new labour law that promotes productivity and efficiency and that protects the rights of the workers;

(iii) a population policy which ensures a balance between rates of population and economic growth;

(iv)   a technology policy to ensure the development of all sectors as a basis for sustained growth.

From this list, it can be concluded that the intentions announced by the former president, Mengistu Haile-Mariam, in his speech on 5 March 1990, i.e. that the Ethiopian economic strategy would be that of a mixed economy where the private sector would be encouraged and strengthened in all ways, were to be continued and strengthened by the transitional government. The TEP went far beyond the 1990 reform announcement not just by declaring that there was to be a change over to a mixed economy but by clearly defining the role that the State should play in a non-socialist economic system without creating consistency problems. In particular, the last point in the list above dealing with legislation should be noted. The importance of revising institutions and legislation has often been overlooked in economic reform or structural adjustment programmes but this is of the utmost importance if a change from socialism over to a market-oriented economy with private enterprises is to be successful. Furthermore, in the TEP the role of the State in relation to private capital was clarified, both compared to what was the case in the 1990 reform announcement and in the draft policy paper on the economic policy during the transitional period.

If implemented successfully, the changes in the role of the State will move the economy towards a higher degree of decentralised decision-making (dimension 1 in Figure 2.1), private ownership (dimension 3) and a resource allocation based on market prices, incentives, and competition rather than on administrative processes, orders, and non-competition (dimensions 2, 4, and 5).

After having concluded that the TEP meant a far-reaching reform of the role of the State in the Ethiopian economy, let us now turn to the implications of the TEP for some specific sectors.

Changes for agriculture

The transitional government, like the Mengistu government, emphasises the importance of a land tenure reform. Agriculture, since it is by far the most important sector of the economy, is the sector from which Ethiopia must take its point of departure for growth and development. The productivity of the agricultural sector must be improved so that a growing agricultural surplus can be produced in order to reduce the need for food imports, but also in order to produce an exportable surplus and thus make agriculture produce the 'fuel' for Ethiopian trade to work as an engine of growth, industrialisation, and development.

Among the factors that have led to the poor economic performance in Ethiopia the various forms of discrimination against individual peasants needed special attention. This was already started by the Mengistu government, which in March 1990 stopped the drive for collectivisation, allowed for the dismantling of producer co-operatives (today no producer co-operatives remain), and liberalised the grain trade. However, there are still important uncertainties about the land tenure system, in particular regarding the property rights defining the operational framework of peasant farming in the long run. In the reform programme of 5 March 1990, it was stated that the land should be owned by the State.

The issue of land ownership is so controversial that in the TEP any changes were postponed until the end of the transitional period (TGE 1991: 21). As noted in Chapter 3, one problem in imperial as well as in socialist Ethiopia was the frequent redistributions of land, which made long-term investments in land conservation, fertilising, and planting of perennial crops risky activities, with the individual peasant bearing the whole risk. Already the March 1990 reform announcement dealt with this issue, and besides the guarantee given for indefinite user rights, it was declared that trees and other perennial plants grown on the land would be owned by the respective peasants.

Both in the draft policy paper and the definitive TEP the transitional government declared that it would continue the initiatives taken by the Mengistu regime in March 1990. In the TEP it was stated that the individual peasant's right to use a specific plot would be indefinite in time and could be transferred to his or her legal heirs who also derive their livelihood from farming.

As regards other incentives, the TEP set out to eliminate the special contributions imposed by the Mengistu government on the agricultural sector. The farmers shall, accordingly, be liable or accountable only for payment of normal taxes. Furthermore, the policy introduced in March 1990 on agricultural marketing that allowed agricultural producers to sell their produce in the free market, will also be continued by the transitional government.

The supplies of extension services, fertilisers, improved seeds, and farm implements were all concentrated heavily on State farms and producer co-operatives during the Mengistu regime. In the TEP it was declared that a major part of the budget and manpower would be allocated by the State to agriculture in order to rehabilitate and develop peasant agriculture (TGE 1991: 22). The support to peasant agriculture will take the form of, for example, an expansion of the rural roads and an increased availability of improved seeds, fertilisers, and agricultural experts in peasant agriculture.

It goes without saying that the policy reorientation regarding peasant agriculture will have important positive effects on the performance of this dominating sector of the Ethiopian economy and will strengthen the tendency to economic system change in relation to ownership, incentives, and resource allocation in general. That peasants are responsive to changes in the conditions related to their production can be seen in the reactions that followed upon the March 1990 reforms of peasant agriculture. One year after the speech by the president, peasants had increased the cultivated area by 12–20 per cent and agricultural production was estimated to have increased by between 5 and 7 per cent.[2]

However, Ethiopian agriculture is not only peasant agriculture. In imperial Ethiopia, commercial farms played an important role. In socialist Ethiopia these farms were turned into State farms, and later on there was also an expansion of the State farms, in some cases by means of forced labour.

In the 1990 reform announcement, President Mengistu declared that private investors should be allowed to establish modern large farms. The importance of making private investors enter into agriculture was underlined and strengthened in the transitional government's policy documents, according to which private commercial farming would not only be permitted but would be promoted and encouraged with no capital limit set on investments. Thus, in the TEP the role of State farms was largely reduced. However, it was stated that: 'When necessary, the state may operate those state farms that are strategic to the economy jointly with domestic or foreign private capital' (TGE 1991: 26).

Finally, in terms of agricultural policy it is interesting to note that the highly debated, resisted, criticised, and costly villagisation programmes and forced resettlement schemes that were introduced by the Mengistu regime were not to be continued during the transitional period (TGE 1991: 23f). This should be seen as a positive change towards a more decentralised economic system.

Changes for industry and services

With regard to non-agricultural sectors, the draft policy paper and the TEP were both much more explicit and detailed than the economic reform announcement of 5 March 1990. In the latter, there were rather general statements on State enterprises and private sector encouragement. There was also a paragraph giving private traders the right (after registration) to compete without any restrictions with the State-run enterprises in all sectors of the economy. In the grain trade this change was implemented immediately.

The draft policy paper and the TEP, on the other hand, went into explicit detail in relation to the above-mentioned areas of policy. This does not automatically mean, however, that from the point of efficiency and growth potential the draft policy paper was superior to the 1990 reform announcement. In fact the draft policy paper contained a number of confusing and contradictory statements, in particular regarding the role of the State in the Ethiopian industry and service sectors. As noted in the section on the role of the State, adjustments were made in the TEP which eliminate most of these weaknesses.

The March 1990 announcement was quite clear in stating that private companies would be allowed to compete with State companies in all fields of economic activity without any restrictions. However, between March 1990 and May 1991 very little implementation of this policy was seen.

According to the TEP, a very limited number of establishments essential for the development of the economy would continue to be either public or jointly owned by the State and private capital owners. Furthermore, according to the above list on the role of the State, the State would also be active as the sole or joint owner in establishments in which the private sector is not willing to participate.

It is interesting to note also that, according to both the draft policy paper and the TEP, the remaining establishments under State or joint State–private ownership are to have full autonomy and be governed by a board where the workers are to have one-third of the votes (TGE 1991: 28). The governing criterion for these enterprises should be profitability. Furthermore, it was stated that during the transitional period, the focus would be on attaining full capacity utilisation, higher efficiency and profitability. It is important to note the obvious risk of inconsistency in aiming at all these objectives. In a country like Ethiopia, where investments have been determined through administrative processes, profitability is likely to be maximised at a level of production that falls below full capacity utilisation. From an efficiency point of view, in a market-oriented economy with profitability as the governing management criterion, it is important to define clearly the role of managers and the management boards. It is likewise important to make a clear distinction between this role and the role of workers and their representatives. Thus, the proposed one-third of the votes to the workers can be expected to be a barrier to making State enterprises profitable and efficient.

Like the 1990 announcement on economic reforms, in the TEP the transitional government assigned to private capital a central role in industrial development. However, as far as the relationship between domestic and foreign capital is concerned, the TEP contained a problem by stating: 'Domestic investors should always receive preferential treatment unless it is established that a given activity is beyond their capacity' (TGE 1991: 29f). This type of statement may easily be construed as a continuation of the unfriendly attitude to foreign capital and entrepreneurs during the *Ethiopia Tikdem* period (see Chapter 3) and does not help in stimulating the greatly needed net flow of private capital into Ethiopia.

A crucial sector for economic recovery in Ethiopia is the transport sector. In the 1990 reform announcement the transport sector was not explicitly dealt with. However, in the draft policy paper and the TEP, the transport sector was given due attention. This sector, also, would be opened up for private capital. Since, according to the transitional government, in 1991 there was not enough capacity in the private sector to run air, sea, and rail transports, such operations, with the exception of medium-sized air and rail operations, would be under public control during the transitional period (TGE 1991: 37). Regardless of this, for the operation of these services, profitability and thereby efficiency, should be the governing principle (TGE 1991: 39).

For road transport, the road transport administration, transport corporations, and companies would be dissolved. Instead, private capital is to be encouraged to play a major role (TGE 1991: 39f). Thus, government road transport companies would be sold or turned into joint ventures and the government would promote the formation of private transport associations.

Furthermore, government regulation of road transport is in the future to be carried out through the Road Transport Authority. It is interesting to note that existing controls on private-sector transport are to be removed. However, it is also stated in the draft policy paper that a new freight tariff structure 'is a must' and the TEP declares that a new tariff structure will be issued. In negotiations with the World Bank on an Emergency Recovery and Reconstruction Project, in February 1992 the transitional government agreed to raise the freight tariffs immediately by 70 per cent and to remove them before the end of 1992.

One of the points of the 1990 economic reform programme that was implemented immediately was the reform of domestic trade, dismantling the AMC monopoly and dissolving the grain control stations. The transitional government declared that it would continue this policy. Accordingly, the State monopoly in wholesale trade would be broken up and this trade left to the private sector. According to the TEP, the future role of the State in wholesale trading would be to 'pave the way for domestic private capital to play the dominant role in wholesale trade' and to issue laws and policies to regulate private sector activities in the sector (TGE 1991: 30). Furthermore, it was stated that the only case calling for State trading in wholesale trade would be when there is a need to stabilise prices on basic consumer goods (TGE 1991: 31). In the case of retail trade it was clearly declared that this should be left completely to the private sector and that the government is to perform only its regulatory functions. Thus, in the field of domestic trade, the intentions of the transitional government, if implemented successfully, meant a very drastic and, from the point of view of economic efficiency, a very positive change.

According to the draft policy paper foreign trade is to be left to the private sector. However, the draft policy paper also stated that 'Although the private sector will play a major role in foreign trade, the Government may also engage itself in the imports and exports of major commodities such as petroleum and coffee' (Draft Policy Paper 1991: 6). No explicit reason was given for this intervention into foreign trade activities and it is difficult to see any economic or efficiency reasons why, in an economy such as that aimed at by the transitional government, the State should be involved as a trader in foreign trade. In the TEP it was stated that 'the state will end its monopoly over foreign trade, and instead, limit its control to areas that cut across sectors, in consideration of the problems that may be encountered if left to private capital' (TGE 1991: 32). Even if this looks like a step towards a policy more in line with the overall objectives of the TEP, the precise meaning of this statement was far from clear when the TEP was presented.

In contemporary Ethiopia financial institutions, i.e. banks and insurance companies, are not very well suited to play the important role that the intended economic system demands from it. Notwithstanding this fact, in the 1990 reform the financial institutions were completely neglected. In the draft policy paper, it was stated that the financial institutions are to continue to be under public control and State ownership during the transitional period. No explicit motives for this view were given. Like other companies in the economy, the financial institutions are to be given greater autonomy to design their operations in accordance with the profitability criterion. In the public debate on the draft policy paper there were demands for letting private banks and insurance companies operate in Ethiopia. This would increase efficiency in the allocation of capital, provided that proper legislation that gives protection to the customers of the financial institutions is also introduced. However, no change in the government's attitude on the ownership issue in relation to financial institutions was presented in the TEP.

In conclusion, the intended changes for industry and services would lead to an economic system change towards decentralisation, increased reliance on markets, private ownership, incentives, and competition. Even though there still remained some uncertainties in relation to the role of the private sector in foreign trade, the sixth dimension, *internationalisation ↔ autarky*, could also be expected to be positively affected by the announced policy changes for industry and services.

Changes in foreign trade and exchange rate policy

In economic reform and structural adjustment programmes, as a rule, changes in foreign trade and exchange rate policy are crucial components. However, as seen in Chapter 6, in the March 1990 reform programme these issues were completely neglected. The policy documents presented by the transitional government, on the other hand, announced clear and positive changes in both trade and exchange rate policies. In order to promote exporters, quantitative restrictions would be replaced with tariffs (TGE 1991: 32f). This is a positive change, not only in relation to exports but also for the overall allocation of resources in the economy. Furthermore, it was stated that bureaucracy related to foreign trade was to be minimised and investments in export-oriented activities to be stimulated. Thus, in the field of foreign trade, the TEP meant a clear-cut positive reorientation.

Furthermore, the TEP stated that 'the state will ensure prudent utilisation and allocation of foreign exchange' (TGE 1991: 33). Therefore, all exporters are to deliver all their foreign exchange earnings to the State in exchange for local currency, some of which, after approval by the State, can be exchanged back into foreign currency for business expansion.

The above procedure is understandable in a country that has long been governed not by markets but by various regulations and administrative procedures and where, at the time of making the statement, the trade deficit has long been a real and growing problem; international reserves were more or less completely depleted, while debt and the need for foreign exchange to service this debt grew very fast. However, in spite of this acute economic situation, the suggested procedure of foreign exchange allocation could easily return the economy to central planning. Of course there are types of government needs that should be given priority but when it comes to allocation within the private sector and also between the major share of public sector activities and the private sector activities, there are no efficiency gains to be made from such central allocation procedures.

Furthermore, it should be noted that foreign exchange that has been obtained in other ways than official exports could be used freely for imports (the Ethiopian system of franco valuta). Naturally, this possibility meant an important incentive for illegal trade. It is a well-known fact in Ethiopia that in 1991/92 there was a considerable illegal trade (for example smuggling of coffee out of the country to Kenya); some estimates pointed to illegal exports amounting to as much as 40–45 per cent of the official exports. This in turn not only took away foreign exchange from control and allocation by the State but also reduced the tax basis of the country.

It was noted above that there had been an exchange rate misalignment in Ethiopia. From the very beginning the transitional government was clearly aware of this. Unlike the Mengistu government the transitional government declared that corrective measures should be taken (TGE 1991: 35). However, regarding when and how to make the adjustment, it was stated in the draft policy paper that in the short run,

> devaluation is bound to result in inflationary pressures, aggravate problems of unemployment and lead to further decline in output, thereby endangering the processes of peace and democratization.... Therefore, unless devaluation is handled carefully and introduced on a phased basis, based on progress in economic recovery, it is bound to have adverse consequences on the economy.
>
> (Draft Policy Paper 1991: 7)

The same view was presented in the TEP where it was concluded that 'exchange rate adjustment should be a gradual process to be undertaken in tandem with improvements in the performance of the economy' (TGE 1991: 36).

The above views were not discussed at length but interviews conducted in ministries during October/November 1991 and January 1992 identified the high import contents of inputs into domestic industry as one major reason behind the fear that a devaluation would give rise to increased inflation and unemployment.

Balancing the State budget

Finally, with regard to the important issue of improving the State budget balance, which is generally a central component in much criticism of economic reform or structural adjustment programmes, the transitional government went beyond the former Mengistu government by announcing a tax reform. Although no details were presented, it was declared that 'the state should take urgent measures for achieving fiscal balance' (TGE 1991: 36). Besides the reduction of military expenditure, no major reductions in public spending can be foreseen. On the contrary, the government declared that, during the transitional period, it must take action and use resources to reconstruct regions and infrastructure devastated by the war and to rehabilitate soldiers. Thus, during the transitional period Ethiopia would have to continue to rely on external sources to fill her fiscal gap.

Summary

Both the draft policy paper and the TEP can be seen as a continuation and further development of the reform process initiated by the Mengistu government (see Chapter 6). During the autumn of 1991 there was a debate on the issue of whether the economic draft policy paper should be seen as a step forward or backwards compared to the reform programme announced by President Mengistu in March 1990.

In Table 7.1 the transitional government's economic policy papers are compared to the March 1990 reform announcement. The points of comparison selected are those that are normally included in structural adjustment programmes initiated by the World Bank.

From the above analysis of the content of the policy documents produced by the transitional government and the summary in Table 7.1 we conclude that the transitional government's intentions, both as expressed in the draft policy paper and in particular as expressed in the TEP, went far beyond the intentions of the Mengistu government. The content of the TEP was close to the content of a traditional structural adjustment programme, notwithstanding the critical remarks made above on some specific issues. In particular the hesitance to introduce an exchange rate reform during the transitional period can be taken to be a severe weakness.

In terms of Figure 2.1, the transitional government's policy intentions, if translated into real policy, would mean a movement towards the left-hand side of the scale for more or less all economic system dimensions. Decision-making would be decentralised and markets, rather than administrative processes, would determine the allocation of resources in an economy where private ownership would increase in industry, trading, and agriculture, the exception being the ownership of land. Incentives, like prices, would increase in importance in the Ethiopian economy where profitability and competitiveness would be some of the major characteristics. However, even though there were intentions to liberalise foreign trade, the problems related to foreign exchange policies and foreign exchange allocation were far from solved.

Table 7.1 A comparison of economic reform announcements in Ethiopia

	The March 1990 reform announcement	The transitional government's economic reform intentions	
		Draft policy paper	TEP
Privatisation	x	x	x
Liberalisation of product markets	x	x	x
Liberalisation of factor markets	x	x	x
Trade liberalisation			x
Devaluation		x	x
Expenditure reductions			x

IMPLEMENTATION OF THE TRANSITIONAL ECONOMIC POLICY

We have concluded that the transitional government's intentions in relation to changes in the economic system and policy were far-reaching. So what changes have actually been introduced since the presentation of the Transitional Economic Policy programme in November 1991?

Market liberalisations

During the first years of the transitional period substantial liberalisation of both factor and commodity markets occurred. Price controls were eliminated for all goods except for petroleum and petroleum products, pharmaceuticals and sugar for household consumption, the road transport monopoly was eliminated, and a new labour code introduced. This code regulates worker–employer relations, for example allowing the employer to lay off workers when the demand for the firms' goods or services falls. This proclamation also guarantees workers and employers the right to form trade unions and employers' associations, respectively. Furthermore, it explicitly prohibits child labour employment (below 14 years of age) and labour market discrimination of women.

Another set of changes that can be expected to have a positive impact on the functioning of the Ethiopian economy is the upward adjustment and reformed structure of private interest rates, resulting in positive and largely non-discriminatory real interest rates, and the reformed income tax structure implying that the maximum marginal tax rate has been adjusted downwards, e.g. for incomes of employment the maximum marginal tax rate has been reduced to 50 per cent.

Furthermore, public enterprises were categorised according to their future ownership status. The public sector proclamation implied not only privatisation of State-owned enterprises but also a reorientation of the organisation of remaining State-owned enterprises to make them more efficient, competitive and thus more profitable. The nine State corporations that dominated the Ethiopian industry were dissolved and their rights and obligations were transferred to ninety-seven new public-owned enterprises. Furthermore, a hard budget constraint was imposed on parastatals and the monopoly power of the official distribution and trade corporations eliminated. To stimulate private domestic and foreign investments, a new investment code was released and a privatisation agency set up. The commercial code is under review with the objective to support the new intended market-oriented economic system. Finally, the financial sector (banking and insurance business) was liberalised in order to stimulate investments in the private sector. Thus, we can conclude that the various market liberalisation measures introduced by the transitional government meant positive changes along all economic system dimensions.

Trade and exchange rate policy

One important set of changes in Ethiopian policy aimed at improving the macroeconomic situation concerns foreign economic relations, i.e. trade and exchange rate policies.

As noted several times in this study the Ethiopian birr was heavily overvalued during the *Ethiopia Tikdem* period. Thus, a devaluation was needed urgently. Early on the transitional government declared that 'the exchange rate of the Birr compared to the US dollar is unrealistically overvalued' (TGE 1991: 35). However, many politicians, economists, and other observers were afraid that a devaluation would produce severe inflation and social problems (Inter-Africa Group 1992). In the TEP it was stated that: 'any major change in the exchange rate of the Birr without economic recovery and growth is likely to exacerbate problems of inflation, unemployment and economic decline' (TGE 1991: 33f). For this reason, the World Bank and the IMF together with bilateral donors were prepared to contribute with resources to reduce the social problems that were expected to arise due to the implementation of the economic reforms and in particular the devaluation of the Ethiopian currency.

After nearly twenty years of exchange rate misalignment, on 30 September 1992, the Ethiopian birr was devalued from 2.07 birr to 5.00 birr per US dollar effective by the 1 October 1992. The allocation of foreign exchange to the private sector was improved, both through the normal allocation process of the National Bank of Ethiopia, the implementation of the Emergency Reconstruction and Rehabilitation Programme, and through the introduction of foreign exchange auctioning in May 1993. The auctioning takes place every second week and is open to all licensed importers for imports of goods not included in the negative list. Besides allocating foreign exchange the auctions also set the price on foreign exchange for private banking transactions between the auctions. The marginal rate, that is the lowest exchange rate at the auctioning, applies to all such transactions until the next auction.

So far, the Ethiopian foreign exchange auctions have worked quite well and the exchange rate stabilised quite rapidly as shown in Figure 7.1. The figure also shows that the spread in successful bids has narrowed. In June 1984 the rate was stabilised around 6–6.2 birr per US dollar. As a consequence of the new exchange rate regime the parallel market exchange rate premium decreased from 250–300 per cent in 1990 (the parallel market rate was around 7.5 birr per US dollar whereas the official rate was 2.07 birr per US dollar up to the devaluation in October 1992) to around 50 per cent in May 1993 and around 10 per cent in August 1994. Furthermore, it should be noted that around 45 per cent of the foreign currency that was sold at the first thirty-four auctions went to the private sector.

According to the plans, the negative list, comprising 102 items at the outset, was to be progressively narrowed, so that it will finally comprise just

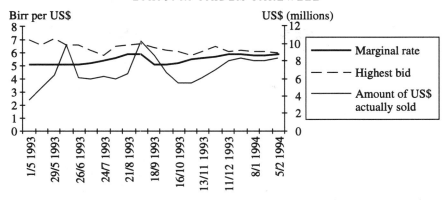

Figure 7.1 The first year of foreign exchange auctioning in Ethiopia
Source: See Appendix B, Table B.1

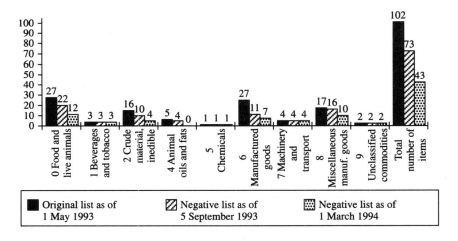

Figure 7.2 Development of the composition and the number of items on the National
Bank's negative list, May 1993–1 March 1994
Source: See Appendix B, Table B.2

those items whose import would be harmful to national security, public health, the environment, etc. (unpublished memo from IMF, Addis Ababa). In accordance with the plans, during the first year the negative list has been reduced from the initial 102 items to forty-three by 1 March 1994 (Figure 7.2).[3]

Other sections of Ethiopian foreign trade policy, including the system of franco valuta imports, have also been liberalised. A trade policy reform has been introduced with a significant reduction of import duties from 230 to 80 per cent, elimination of specific tariffs and export taxes (except for coffee), and the introduction and implementation of a new sales- and excise-tax system with equal treatment of domestically produced and imported goods. Thus, we can conclude that in relation to both trade and exchange rate policies the transitional government has made important improvements that underline the government's commitment to the reform announcement that was made in November 1991 (TGE 1991).

Summary of changes to the economic system

In terms of economic system dimensions, the major economic reforms that the transitional government of Ethiopia introduced up to June 1994 are summarised in Figure 7.3.

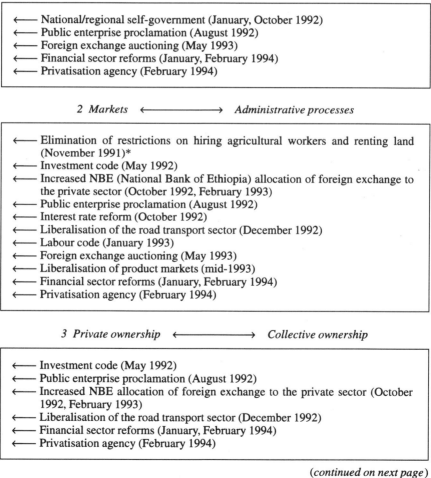

1 Decentralisation ←——————→ *Centralisation*

←—— National/regional self-government (January, October 1992)
←—— Public enterprise proclamation (August 1992)
←—— Foreign exchange auctioning (May 1993)
←—— Financial sector reforms (January, February 1994)
←—— Privatisation agency (February 1994)

2 Markets ←——————→ *Administrative processes*

←—— Elimination of restrictions on hiring agricultural workers and renting land (November 1991)*
←—— Investment code (May 1992)
←—— Increased NBE (National Bank of Ethiopia) allocation of foreign exchange to the private sector (October 1992, February 1993)
←—— Public enterprise proclamation (August 1992)
←—— Interest rate reform (October 1992)
←—— Liberalisation of the road transport sector (December 1992)
←—— Labour code (January 1993)
←—— Foreign exchange auctioning (May 1993)
←—— Liberalisation of product markets (mid-1993)
←—— Financial sector reforms (January, February 1994)
←—— Privatisation agency (February 1994)

3 Private ownership ←——————→ *Collective ownership*

←—— Investment code (May 1992)
←—— Public enterprise proclamation (August 1992)
←—— Increased NBE allocation of foreign exchange to the private sector (October 1992, February 1993)
←—— Liberalisation of the road transport sector (December 1992)
←—— Financial sector reforms (January, February 1994)
←—— Privatisation agency (February 1994)

(continued on next page)

116

4 Incentives ←————————→ *Orders*

←—— Security of land usership (November 1991)*
←—— Public enterprise proclamation (August 1992)
←—— Interest rate reform (October 1992)
←—— Liberalisation of product markets (mid-1993)
←—— Liberalisation of the road transport sector (December 1992)
←—— Privatisation agency (February 1994)
←—— Financial sector reforms (January, February 1994)

---

5 Competition ←——————→ *Non-competition*

←—— Liberalisation of franco-valuta imports (January 1992)
←—— Investment code (May 1992)
←—— Public enterprise proclamation (August 1992)
←—— Liberalisation of the road transport sector (December 1992)
←—— Labour code (January 1993)
←—— Foreign exchange auctioning (May 1993)
←—— Liberalisation of product markets (mid-1993)
←—— Harmonisation of customs duties and sales taxes (August 1993)
←—— Liberalisation of coffee trading and exports (August 1993)
←—— Financial sector reforms (January, February 1994)
←—— Privatisation agency (February 1994)
←—— Continued liberalisation of grain trade, inclusive of the elimination of the grain quota system
←—— Elimination of government monopoly power in some areas of production and trade

---

6 Internationalisation ←——————→ *Autarky*

←—— Liberalisation of franco-valuta imports (January 1992)
←—— Investment code (May 1992)
←—— Devaluation (October 1992)
←—— Increased NBE allocation of foreign exchange to the private sector (October 1992, February 1993)
←—— Reform of trade licensing procedures (December 1992)
←—— Elimination of taxes and duties on non-coffee exports (December 1992)
←—— Foreign exchange auctioning (May 1993)
←—— Liberalisation of coffee trading and exports (August 1993)
←—— Harmonisation of customs duties and sales taxes (August 1993)

Figure 7.3 Important transitional economic policy reforms in Ethiopia

Note: *To some extent these policies were announced by the Mengistu government in March 1990 (see Mengistu 1990)

117

As shown in Figure 7.3, the Ethiopian government has taken numerous measures and, as part of this, in 1992 the government agreed with the IMF, the World Bank, and the donors to adopt a structural adjustment programme. In September 1992 a *Policy Framework Paper for 1992/93–1994/95* (World Bank 1992b) was worked out and agreed upon with the World Bank and the IMF.

It should be noted that the reforms introduced by the transitional government mainly concern the non-agricultural sectors. This is natural since agriculture was already reformed through President Mengistu's reform announcement in March 1990. However, it is worth noting that in 1993 the government presented a development strategy paper emphasising Agricultural Development Led Industrialisation (ADLI). This strategy paper is based on the fact that the basic source of development and industrialisation in Ethiopia is the smallholder agricultural sector. Therefore it is important to strengthen this sector and to improve its economic performance, thus paving the way for generating an agricultural surplus that can be used in industrial activities, both directly by producing inputs for further industrial processing and indirectly by producing for exports that can be exchanged for imports of inputs and capital equipment. The strategy also aims at increasing incomes in the agricultural sector, thereby increasing the demand for industrial products. The ADLI strategy to improve peasant agriculture can be divided into stages:

- Stage 1 involves measures to improve agricultural practices and increase the use of better seeds.
- Stage 2 involves measures to develop agricultural infrastructure, for instance small-scale irrigation, and to improve rural banking.
- Stage 3 involves measures to increase farm sizes and to stimulate commercial large-scale farming by bringing unused land into use and by improving infrastructure.

It is too early to see the results of the above strategy. However, considering the dominant role of agriculture and the potential of this sector in Ethiopia, the further development and implementation of the ADLI strategy should be followed and analysed closely by the various aid organisations working in Ethiopia so that foreign assistance can be designed with due consideration to the new strategy.

PRIVATISATION IN ETHIOPIA – A REMAINING ISSUE OF DEBATE

One of the most critical and difficult issues in the process of transforming a former socialist, centrally planned economy to a market economy with private actors is that of privatisation. This is also the case in Ethiopia where, following the nationalisations in 1975, State-owned industrial enterprises dominated the industrial sector.

Table 7.2 State-owned establishments in Ethiopian industry, 1990

Industry	Establishments		Employment	
	Total no. *(public +* *private)*	*Public* *(%)*	*Total no.* *(public +* *private)*	*Public* *(%)*
Food	136	50.7	18 298	91.3
Beverage	29	75.9	8 863	97.0
Tobacco	2	100.0	925	100.0
Textiles	49	49.0	37 406	98.3
Wearing apparel (except footwear)	111	45.5	3 457	91.7
Tanneries and leather finish	10	80.0	3 142	97.0
Footwear	18	27.8	3 215	80.8
Wood and cork products	14	50.0	1 565	88.7
Furniture and fixture	18	22.2	1 429	54.9
Paper and paper products	7	42.9	1 453	92.0
Printing, publishing and allied	21	38.1	3 333	85.7
Chemical except fertilisers	3	100.0	319	100.0
Other chemical products	13	69.2	2 133	93.7
Petroleum refinery	1	100.0	1 433	100.0
Rubber products	5	40.0	1 904	92.6
Plastic products	9	44.4	1 671	90.9
Glass and glass products	2	100.0	675	100.0
Other non-metallic mineral products	32	43.7	3 851	82.5
Iron and steel	3	100.0	990	100.0
Fabricated metal (except machinery and equipment)	25	48.0	2 000	79.7
Electrical machinery	3	33.3	109	68.8
Assembly of motor vehicles	3	66.7	502	48.4
Total	414	50.2	98 673	93.2

Source: *Census of Manufacturing Industries in Ethiopia, 1990*, here calculated from Mishra 1991

The *Census of Manufacturing Industries in Ethiopia, 1990* shows that half of all industrial establishments were State-owned (Table 7.2). However, these establishments were quite large and employed over 90 per cent of all industrial employees. Thus, in Ethiopia privatisation of industrial establishments is a reform that affects nearly everyone in the industrial sector. Employment effects of privatisation and the consequences for industrial production must therefore be given due consideration by the government when deciding upon the strategy of privatisation.

The fact that privatisation, as a rule, is a complicated issue of reform and thus takes quite a time to implement is noted by Gelb (1993: 19) who concludes, from empirical and theoretical evidence, that 'the process and ownership restructuring is likely to be relatively slow'. One reason is that there is still much to be learnt from the experience of countries that have implemented ownership reforms even if it must be remembered that every country and sector has its own characteristics and problems in this respect also.

Ramamurti (1991: 23) concludes that the literature about State-owned enterprises is not 'sufficient to serve the needs of policy makers who must act in the face of incomplete understanding and information, and must develop solutions that reflect the unique circumstances in individual countries or industries'. Furthermore, he concludes: 'To be sure, policy makers may not look on their reform programs as experiments, but at the present state that is what they really are. Out of those experiments may come a better understanding of how elements of the public and private sectors can be fruitfully combined.' It is with this comment in mind, that we will discuss the privatisation problems and efforts in Ethiopia. First, we present some economic reasons behind public ownership and how these motives have changed since the transitional government of Ethiopia came into power and launched its economic reform programme. Then we will analyse the various principal stages in the process of increasing the role of the private sector in the economy and analyse how far in this process Ethiopia has moved so far.

Pros and cons of State-owned enterprises

Are there any economic efficiency motives that can be advanced in favour of having State-owned enterprises (SOEs)? Yes, there are. One such motive is that the actors within the private sector tend to be risk-averse compared to decision-makers in the public sector. This is not only natural, it is also rational from the point of view of economic efficiency. Risk calculations are due to the existence of uncertainty. Every decision-maker tries to reduce the uncertainty in order to reduce the risk related to the actual project. Since political development and economic policy lie to a large extent outside the direct control of the market, in particular in dictatorial or one-party States, the potential political constraints for economic activities are, as a rule, quite uncertain from the point of view of private actors. Thus, public sector or State involvement is needed if investments and economic activities are not to be too low in some sectors where political decisions and attitudes are of crucial importance for economic profitability.

In the case of socialist Ethiopia this aspect was of special relevance since the country was at civil war during the whole period from 1974 up to 1991. Naturally, the civil war introduced many uncertainties and thus made savings and investments in private property a high-risk activity both because of the direct risk of the property being destroyed or expropriated and also because of the indirect risks of changes in economic policy, such as various types of taxation (for an analysis of this type of uncertainties, see Azam *et al.* 1993).

Macroeconomic problems in terms of fiscal deficits and their inflationary consequences also tend to create uncertainty about future macroeconomic policy, inflation, exchange rates, etc. Thus, private sector activities also tend to become risky and thus tend to be reduced. In order to keep economic activities at a reasonable level, public sector involvement in commercial activities may be needed even if this is seldom the first best policy from an efficiency point of view. During the last decade of the Mengistu government the macroeconomic situation deteriorated dramatically, contributing to increased economic–political uncertainty for the private sector.

In addition to the above motives, many governments in less developed countries motivate public involvement and ownership in the business sector by ideological arguments and by making reference to the objective of reducing the concentration of economic power in the hands of large private enterprises and limited groups of capital owners. In the case of socialist Ethiopia, the ideological arguments played a central role in the far-reaching nationalisation of private enterprises in 1975 when the foundations of the socialist economic system were introduced.

The arguments *against* public ownership emphasise the problems of efficient management of public enterprises. These problems are mainly due to lack of a direct link between effort and reward, the distance between management and owners and the frequent existence of soft budget constraints, that is the availability of money from the government if the business operations result in losses. As a result, the profitability of public enterprises often becomes very low and even negative, which in turn means a burden on the fiscal balance at the national level.

As a consequence of the problems of efficiency in many public enterprises in less developed countries, a more or less complete reorientation of the economic system away from socialism to a market economy is under way in many of them. This is also the case in Ethiopia. In November 1991 the new government declared: 'One major hindrance to economic development in the past was the restrictive policies imposed on the activities of the private sector' (TGE 1991: 18). Thus, from the very beginning of its rule the transitional government made clear that the private sector should be encouraged and stimulated with the objective that it should come to play a dominant role in the economy.

How to increase the role of the private sector

When discussing the process of transition towards an increased role for markets and private ownership, it is important to distinguish three steps and their internal sequencing:

- deregulation of markets, i.e. making markets competitive;
- changed management guidelines for SOEs towards market-oriented

management; and
- denationalisation of SOEs, i.e. changes in ownership of the SOEs.

In addition to these three steps, the private sector can be increased by stimulating and attracting new private domestic and foreign investments, for instance through the introduction of various market liberalisations and strengthening of property rights.

In the implementation of structural adjustment reforms and economic system reform programmes the issue of denationalisation or privatisation of SOEs is one of the most critical components and also one of the most difficult from the point of view of both politics and economics. As a rule, too much emphasis seems to be placed on the issue of denationalisation in the early stages of reform. Even if, as in the case of transitional Ethiopia, it has been declared clearly that the private sector should increase and come to dominate the economy, and even if a number of changes have been introduced in order to stimulate such a development, a frequent criticism of the transitional government of Ethiopia during 1993/94 has been that the process of transferring ownership of SOEs to the private sector moves too slowly. However, even if one objective of privatisation is to increase efficiency in production and to improve allocative efficiency, it is important to stress that denationalisation or privatisation *per se* does not necessarily lead to an achievement of these objectives. It is as important, or even more important, to eliminate monopoly power and thus increase competition based on free entry and exit.

The fact that the issue of privatisation is not easy even from a strictly methodological point of view stands out clearly in a study by Vuylsteke (1988), where various alternative methods of denationalisation and experience are analysed. According to this study, the most frequent methods are:

- Public offering of shares
- Private sales of shares
- New private investment in a SOE
- Sale of government or SOE assets
- Reorganization (or break-up) into component parts
- Management/employee buyout, and
- Lease and management contract.

(Vuylsteke 1988: 8)

Public offering of shares has the positive characteristic of creating a widespread ownership of the denationalised enterprise. Furthermore, by definition the sale is characterised by openness and transparency. However, in the context of less developed countries with a socialist legacy and depleted enterprises this option is neither straightforward nor easy. The requirements for a successful implementation of sales to the general public as defined by Vuylsteke (1988: 13ff) are as follows:

122

- the enterprise should have a reasonable profitability record or potential;
- information about the financial situation should be available to the potential buyers;
- discernible liquidity should be available; and
- there should be a developed equity market or some other institutional set-up that can fulfil the functions of an equity market so that the buyers can avoid excessive financial risks.

The second alternative, private sale of shares, means that the government sells the enterprise that is to be privatised to a pre-identified buyer or group of buyers, through a competitive process or direct negotiations with the potential buyers. One problem with this alternative is the lack of openness and transparency that often characterises the process of pre-identification of buyers. Another risk with this alternative is that it merely transfers a state monopoly over to a private monopoly with a narrow ownership structure.

An advantage, on the other hand, is that this process makes it possible to select and engage buyers that can contribute relevant industrial and managerial knowledge and experience. Furthermore, this alternative, more easily than the previous one, can be used for privatisation of unprofitable or weak enterprises. The process of privatisation along this line is also less complicated from administrative or legal points of view.

Management/employee buy-outs can be seen as a special case of the above alternative. This alternative requires extensive information and education so that the workers can learn about the potential of a buy-out, since this alternative demands a competent management and a committed workforce. One positive characteristic of this alternative is that it constitutes a strong incentive to increase productivity and can thus be used as an alternative to liquidation when there is potential to make the company viable. A problem in less developed countries with far from perfect financial institutions is that financial institutions and techniques have to be developed so that the workers can borrow the required amounts of money and thus have the option of participating in the buy-outs.

Instead of selling shares in a going concern or privatising through management/employee buy-outs, the government can privatise an enterprise by selling assets to an existing or new company. Sometimes this means that the enterprise has to be dissolved and liquidated and that viable assets in the enterprise can be sold and can continue to be used in other enterprises while other parts of the enterprise remain government property. This relates to one problem with this alternative, namely that the government has to take the responsibility for the liabilities that exist in the enterprise prior to the privatisation.

Closely related to the asset-selling alternative is that of reorganising the enterprise into component parts with the government retaining some parts.

This alternative can be used to break up monopolies and thus increase competition.

An alternative to selling out whole or parts of State enterprises is to invite investors to joint ventures with the State, that is to invite the private sector to purchase new shares without reducing State equity in the enterprise. This alternative is particularly interesting when the main problem is under-capitalisation or when the objective is to reduce the degree of State ownership without selling out State property *per se*, thereby avoiding or reducing political problems related to the process of privatisation.

Increasing the role of the private sector in Ethiopia

The first, and also the most important issue to deal with in the process of increasing the role of the private sector is to introduce changes in the economic system so that markets become competitive. The transitional government of Ethiopia has introduced and begun to implement a number of deregulation proclamations. Thus, the first and perhaps most critical step towards a market economy and a more efficient allocation of resources has already been taken. There is, however, still need for changes in the commercial law to support the economic actors in the deregulated market.

The second step has also been taken and public enterprises are now headed by management boards that by and large have to act in line with the same principles they would have to follow if they were private companies. This second step was taken by the presentation of the *Public Enterprise Proclamation* on 27 August 1992 (*Negarit Gazeta* no. 25, 1992), the dissolution of State enterprises, and the subsequent creation of more market-oriented public enterprises in various sectors of the economy during the past year. In the new public enterprises, as a rule, soft budget constraints have been removed and managements operate largely on a free and decentralised basis in input and output markets and are supervised and responsible to their respective boards (see Teferra Demiss 1994 for a discussion). This means that both the decision-making and the responsibility for the operation of the enterprises have been decentralised. Furthermore, the removal of soft budget constraints implies that the enterprises can go bankrupt.

When it comes to the third step, denationalisation of SOEs, however, the process in Ethiopia has been slower. In February 1994 the government released the *Ethiopian Privatization Agency Establishment Proclamation*. The Ethiopian Privatization Agency is accountable to the Prime Minister's office. The objective of this agency is to 'carry out the process of privatizing public enterprises in an orderly and efficient manner' (*Negarit Gazeta* no. 67, 17 February 1994, p. 293). To achieve this objective the agency has been given a number of powers and duties in addition to handling the privatisation of SOEs *per se*. Among the most interesting are the powers and duties to:

- undertake detailed studies on the economic, technical, financial and price evaluation of public enterprises which the Government has decided to be privatized;
- create conditions which facilitate the successful completion of the privatization process;
- prepare detailed records of man power, assets, financial and legal affairs of public enterprises that are going to be privatized.

(*Negarit Gazeta* no. 67, 17 February 1994, p. 293, article 5, points 1, 6, and 7)

Considering the history of Ethiopia and the former government's attitude to private property and the socialist ideological background of the transitional government, the issue of denationalisation is politically quite sensitive and demands great confidence in the credibility of the transitional government and its policy.

Table 7.3 summarises the above brief discussion on privatisation and denationalisation.

Among the above alternatives it is clear that most requirements of the first alternative, selling to the general public, are not satisfied in the Ethiopian context. It is not always easy to make a historical judgement about the profitability or efficiency of Ethiopian industry (Alemu Mekonnen 1992: 38ff). The reason is that prices have been heavily distorted through the price-control system and the design of trade and exchange rate policies.

It is reasonable to assume that a great number, if not the majority, of the SOEs in Ethiopia, are unprofitable, at least when assessed in the new more market-oriented and liberalised environment. Furthermore, necessary information for potential buyers is not available, and there is no equity market or other institution that can substitute for such a market.

The other alternatives do not require profitability in the SOE before privatisation. As a rule, these alternatives have the advantage that they can be used to select buyers with managerial and industrial experience, for instance by selecting or inviting foreign owners. This may be of crucial importance in Ethiopia where, as a rule, the managements of the SOEs can be expected to lack experience from operations in a market-oriented economic system. On the other hand, to various degrees the alternatives that allow for a selective process in the search for new owners lack openness and transparency. Therefore, these alternatives can easily meet with criticism from opposition groups who can claim that the government is giving away property of the people to some specific privileged group in society.

In the current debate about privatisation in Ethiopia, the pricing problem seems to be central. This problem is present in all the above-mentioned alternatives of privatisation except the lease and management contract alternative. One important factor that worsens this problem in the case of Ethiopia is the lack of well-functioning financial institutions.

Table 7.3 Requirements and characteristics of various privatisation alternatives

	Requirements			Characteristics of the process and outcome			
	Profitable SOEs	Information demanding	Financial institutions/ equity market	Risk for monopoly	Widespread ownership	Openness/ transparency	Possibility of selecting buyers with managerial and industrial experience
Public offering of shares (SSA: 2.6%, LDCs: 13.7%)	Yes	Yes	Yes	Yes	Yes	Yes	No
Private sales of shares (SSA: 41.9%, LDCs: 49.2%)	No	No	No	Yes	No	No	Yes
New private investment in an SOE	No	No	No	Yes	–	–	Yes
Sale of government or SOE assets (SSA: 17.5%, LDCs: 10.3%)	No	Yes	No	–	No	No	Yes
Reorganisation (or break-up) into component parts	No	–	No	No	–	No	Yes
Management/employee buy-out	No	Yes	Yes	Yes	–	No	Yes
Lease and management contract (SSA: 29.9%, LDCs: 21.4%)	No	No	No	Yes	No	No	No
Others (SSA: 8.1%, LDCs: 5.4%)	–	–	–	–	–	–	–
Ethiopia	Mainly unprofitable SOEs	Problems of producing adequate information	Under-developed	Frequently SOEs are monopolies	–	–	–

Notes: SSA: sub-Saharan Africa; LDC: less developed country
Source: Compiled from the analysis in Vuylsteke 1988 and information gathered by the author

Another issue that is closely related to the pricing problem and that has been debated from the very start of the transition period is whether the public enterprises should be sold as they are or be reconstructed before they are privatised. Among the above alternatives of privatisation, only the first alternative, public offering of shares, requires that loss-making firms are to be reconstructed before being offered to the general public. In cases where the buyer can be selected this is, however, not necessary, since negotiations with the buyer can take the need for reconstruction into consideration when negotiating and deciding on the price for the SOE or the SOE assets.

There seems to exist a fear within the government that public enterprises will be sold at an all too low price. Since the public enterprises are the property of the Ethiopian people the opposition could easily criticise the government on the basis of the people's interest if it can be shown that the prices are too low. The present government's socialist background and rural peasant basis also imply a fear of giving away property to the capitalist class. This problem is one of the most important and politically sensitive problems for the privatisation agency to deal with.

However, it is important to remember that a market consists of two sides, sellers and buyers. Up to now the debate in Ethiopia seems to have been concentrated on the supply side. However, when discussing the 'correct price' it is important not to forget the demand side, that is the interest on the part of private individuals or enterprises in buying the public enterprises. The greater this interest the higher the price the government can obtain.

The interest of the private sector, in turn, is a function of the policy, stability, and credibility of the government. It is clear that policy changes in favour of the private sector have been made during the transition period. However, to create stability and credibility requires more time.

Finally, it is important not to sell out the existing State enterprises in cases where they have a monopoly position without making the actual market competitive through stimulating new investments and liberalising foreign trade. To have State monopolies turned into private monopolies does not necessarily improve efficiency. However, it certainly redistributes incomes and wealth, which can be expected to be a highly sensitive problem in a former socialist country such as Ethiopia. In particular this is true if foreign owners or companies step in and take over the State enterprises. All alternatives of privatisation, except the alternative to reorganise and break-up the SOEs into component parts, involve an obvious risk that State monopolies will merely be transferred to private monopolies.

This latter aspect relates to another important problem in contemporary Ethiopia, the issue of stimulating new private investments, both by Ethiopians and by foreigners. As noted above, a number of policy changes have been introduced that have meant liberalisation of markets, simplifying of licences for investments, introduction of a foreign exchange auction. To this should be added the fact that the government has established investment offices on a

127

regional level and also set up a national investment office in Addis Ababa, the latter dealing with investments from abroad and investments in regions without a regional investment office. It should be noted that these investment offices only deal with investments amounting to 250 000 birr (equivalent to US$40–50 000) or more. Furthermore, from 1 January 1994 the process for issuing licences for investments has been simplified by the introduction of a one-stop-shop procedure.

CONCLUSIONS

The termination of the war and the removal of the Mengistu government introduced a new period in Ethiopian political and economic history. In the field of economics the changes introduced by the transitional government have been impressive and quite far-reaching, and mean a more or less complete termination of the *Ethiopia Tikdem* period which was based on Ethiopian or scientific socialism (see Chapter 3). The next chapter analyses the expected and actual effects of this new policy. However, already at this stage it is possible to conclude that the economic reforms and policy changes introduced during the transitional period are quite positive from the point of view of most of the fourteen principles of good policy management. In particular we note the positive implications of the reforms of trade and exchange rate policies (principles 4, 5, 6, and 14), of the public enterprise reform (principles 12 and 13), and of the various measures that have liberalised both commodity and factor markets (principle 10).

In one particular field, however, namely privatisation of business, the transitional government has not progressed far enough to satisfy the demands from many foreign observers and donors. The problems are often discussed under the common heading of privatisation and, quite misleadingly, the debate often treats privatisation and denationalisation as synonyms. This study has argued that the process of privatisation can be split up into at least three steps, of which denationalisation or the transfer of ownership of State-owned enterprises is the last. Besides increasing the role of the private sector through the various steps in the process of privatisation, the government may also increase the role of the private sector by stimulating new private investments, by both domestic and foreign capital owners. This chapter has shown that the transitional government has introduced a series of measures that can serve this purpose.

8

EXPECTED AND ACTUAL EFFECTS OF THE TRANSITIONAL POLICY

INTRODUCTION

Following the change in government in 1991, completely new political, economic, and administrative policies and structures were introduced in Ethiopia. The previous chapter described how various economic systemic dimensions have been affected by the changes introduced. It may be argued that it is too early to see any major effects on economic performance from the new economic system. The reason is that it takes time to implement system changes and make economic actors aware of, and adjust to, the new rules of the game. Not all changes pay off in a short- and medium-term perspective. As most changes have been decided and implemented during 1993 and 1994, we should not expect drastic changes in economic performance yet. In particular, this applies to a country like Ethiopia, where civil war has destroyed infrastructure, where investments in human capital for long have had to stand back for security expenditure, where market economy traditions are lacking, and where the financial sector is still underdeveloped and largely owned by, and close to being completely controlled by, the government. However, by analysing the expected effects of the reform by using our institutional general equilibrium model and by analysing available statistical evidence for the first years of the transitional period, we argue that it is possible to draw some preliminary conclusions about the effects of the transitional economic policy programme. This is the objective of this chapter, which also includes a brief comparison of the Ethiopian experience and the experience in other sub-Saharan countries.

EXPECTED EFFECTS

In terms of our analytical framework the changes that have been introduced by the transitional government all go in the opposite direction compared to those of the *Ethiopia Tikdem* policy. According to both the two-sector dual model (see Figures 4.1 and 4.2) and the institutional four-sector model analysis in Chapter 4, this means that the effects can also be expected to go in the opposite direction if implemented efficiently.

Starting with our simple two-sector dual model, as with the March 1990 reform (see Chapter 6) the institutional changes that have actually been implemented by the transitional government (see Table 7.1) will shift the per capita agricultural production curve in Figure 4.1 upwards and thus create increased possibilities for increased imports of capital goods and other inputs, i.e. fuel and fertilisers, and consumer goods. Thereby, the per capita agricultural production can be expected to expand even more and this can also be expected to be the case for the modern sector.

The effects of the new government's trade liberalisation and the devaluation of the Ethiopian birr can also be analysed by means of our diagrammatic model. In terms of Figure 4.2 the effects will go in the opposite direction compared to the case analysed in Chapter 4. The starting point is c_0. As a consequence of trade liberalisation and devaluation, the relative prices will change. The per capita wage measured in non-agricultural goods will increase, *ceteris paribus*. The new consumption pattern will be given by c_i. Thus, the agricultural surplus will increase at a given agricultural labour force. However, the change in international prices also affects the MRP curve in non-agricultural production. Thus, the MRP curve will shift inwards and employment outside agriculture will decrease. As a result agricultural employment will increase and so will agricultural surplus production and thereby also the per capita export of agricultural produce, from X_0 to X_i. This means that per capita imports of capital and other inputs can increase from M_0 to M_i. Furthermore, the surplus from employment in non-agriculture will decrease. Thus, in short, the new policy can be expected to increase the relative share of foreign-produced capital goods in Ethiopian investments. This in turn can be expected to give rise to productivity gains both in agriculture and in non-agriculture and also improve the role of trade as an engine of growth in Ethiopian development.

Let us now turn to the more elaborate institutional four-sector general equilibrium model. Since the implementation of the new policy is taking place in various steps, both the expected and the actual effects during the first couple of years must also be analysed in a sequence, depending on when the various parts of the Transitional Economic Policy were first implemented.

Even though it was not an economic system change, the termination of the civil war has obviously affected the economy in various ways. The insecurity and risks directly related to the civil war have disappeared. This should be expected to have had a positive influence on all sectors but the defence sector, *ceteris paribus*. Furthermore, in terms of the institutional general equilibrium model, the termination of the civil war, and the concomitant lower priority (and smaller budget) given to the defence sector, can be represented as a reduction in the price of public sector production. According to Table 4.9, this reduction will leave all other sectors except the peasant sector unaffected. The total production in the peasant sector will be positively affected since the released labour from the defence sector will be employed in the peasant sector.

Turning to the economic system changes, the credibility of the new government is crucial to how the various economic actors respond to the changes introduced. It is important to note that, unlike the Mengistu government, the transitional government is a rural-based government. Therefore, there was no doubt that the transitional government should continue and strengthen the positive changes for agriculture that were introduced by the Mengistu government during its last year in power. Thus, in this field the new government did not have to work to create credibility for its policy. Therefore, the positive institutional changes for peasants from March 1990 were to continue. It is also realistic to assume that the peasants believed that this policy would be continued. From Table 4.3 it can be concluded that the peasant sector and thus the wage level or opportunity cost of working outside the peasant sector, will be positively affected by the changes. Furthermore, this higher wage level tends to reduce the use of labour outside the peasant sector, *ceteris paribus*. The total long-run effects on manufacturing and non-peasant agriculture depend on the relative factor intensities of these sectors. In Chapter 4 we argued that, in Ethiopia, non-peasant agriculture is more capital-intensive than the manufacturing sector. Then non-peasant agriculture tends to expand and manufacturing to decrease as a consequence of the positive institutional changes for the peasant sector, *ceteris paribus*.

As a consequence of the higher wage level, the public sector will contract, provided that the budget allocated to this sector does not increase.

The liberalisation of markets, including the trade liberalisation and the changes in the exchange rate policy, can be expected to give rise to important effects in the allocation of resources. In terms of our institutional dual economy model, these reforms can be represented by changes in the institutional variables I_M and I_C and in the price variable p_S. During the first year of the transition period, when the TEP was discussed and prepared, there was considerable and quite understandable uncertainty about the future political stability and economic policy. To various degrees these uncertainties still exist in Ethiopia. Therefore, the changes in the first two variables can be expected to need more time than the changes in prices before they result in changed behaviour in non-peasant agriculture and the manufacturing sector. As a consequence, besides the above effects on peasant production and the public sector, the first effects of the TEP would be expected to come from the liberalisation policies including trade liberalisation and changes in the exchange rate policy. The effects of these types of policy, $dp_S > 0$, are presented in Table 4.5. According to this we would expect increased peasant and non-peasant agricultural production, provided that, as argued in Chapter 4, non-peasant agriculture is more capital-intensive than manufacturing. Furthermore, we would expect a further reduction in the public sector and of

131

the manufacturing sector, *ceteris paribus.*

The changes in the institutional framework for non-peasant agriculture and manufacturing, that is dI_M and dI_C, are all positive and would be expected to stimulate these sectors. In a more complete perspective, according to Tables 4.1 and 4.2, taking one sector at a time, the improvements in institutional conditions that now have begun to be implemented would be expected to lead to increased production in the sector that has experienced improved institutional conditions and a contraction of the other sector. From Figure 7.1, which describes the economic reforms so far, it is reasonable to assume that the largest positive changes have taken place in manufacturing, while the positive changes for the remaining non-peasant agricultural sector have not been so far-reaching. Consequently, we would expect manufacturing to have been positively affected by the TEP, although the positive impact did not come until 1992/93 and 1993/94 when the policy was actually implemented.

Finally, as noted in the previous chapter, the major objective of the economic policy of the transitional government is relief and rehabilitation. Thus, the public sector would be expected to grow quite substantially after the initial drop when the civil war ended, as a consequence of the restructuring of the public sector and the decentralisation to regional administrations (see Chapter 9). In terms of our analytical model, these changes can be represented by an increase in the price of the output from the public sector, p_G. By the same line of reasoning as was presented above when resource allocation effects of the termination of the civil war were analysed, Table 4.9 shows that we should expect the expansion of the public sector to give rise to reduced employment and production in the peasant sector, leaving the other sectors of the economy unaffected. The reason is that in our model world the wage level has been assumed to be unaffected by changes in the public sector.

In conclusion, for the years of the transitional government, our analysis makes us expect an immediate reduction in the public sector after the termination of the civil war and then an increase in non-defence public sector activities. Furthermore, we would expect increased agricultural production, and, to begin with, a reduction of manufacturing production due to the higher wages that follow upon the improved incentives in the peasant sector. When the new government's economic system and policy intentions have been clarified and begun to be implemented, however, the manufacturing sector would be expected to react positively. According to our economic system analysis, for the Ethiopian economy as a whole, successful implementation of the changes now introduced by the transitional government should improve economic performance in Ethiopia. The extent to which this actually has been the case will be analysed in the following section.

ECONOMIC PERFORMANCE, 1991–1994

From the analysis of the expected effects of the intended transitional economic programme we concluded that efficient implementation should have a positive impact on economic performance. Even though, as mentioned above, it is at present not possible to assess the effects of most of the reforms, it may be of interest to analyse briefly the economic development during the past couple of years. First, we analyse the sectoral performance and growth in the Ethiopian economy. Then we turn to an analysis of how the macroeconomic stability has developed during the transitional period. Finally, the macroeconomic stance in Ethiopia is compared with the macroeconomic stance in some other reforming sub-Saharan countries.

Sectoral performance and growth

From Table 8.1 it can be concluded that during the transition period the economy has been positively affected. This is the result both of the peace and of the economic system changes that have been introduced.

Chapter 6 showed that the institutional framework for the peasant sector

Table 8.1 Sectoral and overall growth rates (1980 constant factor cost)

	1990/91	1991/92 (estimate)	1992/93 (estimate)	1993/94 (projected)*
Real GDP	−0.6	−7.4	7.6	3.0
Agricultural sector	8.0	−4.0	4.9	−1.5
Agriculture	8.4	−4.4	5.1	−1.7
Industry	−16.1	−4.9	12.5	10.5
Manufacturing	−26.8	−6.7	15.0	14.0
Handicrafts and small-scale industry	−2.0	3.0	10.0	7.0
Building and construction	−20.0	−11.1	7.1	10.0
Distribution services	−9.2	−4.1	9.3	6.0
Trade	−7.6	−6.0	9.8	5.3
Transport and communication	−11.8	−0.6	8.4	7.3
Other services	0.5	−18.1	9.2	5.4
Banking and insurance	−11.9	5.0	5.0	6.8
Public administration and defence	7.2	−48.3	16.2	4.5
Social services	−5.0	7.8	9.9	6.7

*Projections from December 1993, the text presents revised and less detailed estimates from June 1994
Source: National Bank of Ethiopia

133

underwent important changes during the last year of the Mengistu government. The March 1990 reform had a more or less immediate positive effect on the peasant sector, in particular the introduction of land usership security, liberalisation of the grain trade, and the relaxation of the emphasis on producer co-operatives. As a result, during 1990/91 the growth in output from the agricultural sector amounted to 8 per cent. This increase, which is in line with the expected effects derived in the previous section, cannot be explained by more favourable weather conditions, nor can it be explained by increased use of improved seeds or fertilisers. In fact, due to shortage of credit and foreign exchange, in particular during the last years of the Mengistu government, the use of improved seeds and fertilisers decreased (FAO 1991). Furthermore, the initial 27 per cent reduction in manufacturing production is in line with what we would expect from our model analysis where we emphasised the uncertainty factors about the future industrial policy and the increased opportunity costs of non-peasant employment. To this we could add the shortage of credit and foreign exchange when the transitional government came to power.

During 1991/92 the agricultural sector showed a decline of 4 per cent. This decline was mainly due to bad weather conditions and the restructuring of the State farms. The industrial sector continued to decrease as a consequence of lack of imported inputs and spare parts but also owing to uncertainties about the new industrial policies and the change of management and managers in many State-owned companies. The service sectors also decreased during the first year of the transitional government. That the civil war was over meant a reduction in the public administration and defence expenditures by close to 50 per cent, explaining part of the negative growth rate in GDP.

The available statistics for the fiscal year 1992/93, when quite a number of reforms were actually implemented, indicate drastic improvements in economic performance. GDP is expected to have grown by around 8 per cent. This growth is due to quite high growth rates in most sectors (around 4.9 per cent in agriculture, 12.5 per cent in manufacturing, 9.9 per cent in social services, and 16.2 per cent in public administration and defence). The relative distribution of the sectoral growth is largely in line with what we would expect from our model analysis.

For 1993/94, the projections made by the transitional government show a slight increase in GDP. Because of the drought, the output from the dominating agricultural sector decreased. In June 1994, officials within the government at an interview reported revised estimates that showed that the growth in GDP was just around 1 per cent, but that industry and services were growing at around 8 per cent. Thus, for both 1992/93 and 1993/94 the latter sectors have shown quite high growth rates. In particular it is interesting to note the positive response of entrepreneurs to the economic system reforms in Ethiopian industry, in particular in the manufacturing sector. It is interesting to note also that the government has invested a growing real amount of resources in the provision of social services.

It should be emphasised that the growth rates reported in Table 8.1 are preliminary and for 1993/94 are just projections and thus uncertain. However, the pattern of the sectoral distribution that is shown in the statistics is what we expect from our institutional general equilibrium model analysis. Thus, it does not seem too unrealistic to conclude that the information clearly indicates positive effects from the economic reforms and policy changes introduced by the transitional government.

It should be noted that the figures quoted above do not reflect the effects that can be expected to arise out of the recent new Ethiopian investment policy. The reason is of course the legacy of the Mengistu regime, the political uncertainty that still exists, and the fact that the new policy has been in place only since mid-1992.

As a consequence of the economic system changes introduced during the first years of the transition period, the private sector's share of total investments has increased from around 13 per cent in the late 1980s up to an estimate of just above 22 per cent in 1993 (World Bank 1994b).

In Table 8.2 the result of the activities in the field of investment policy from July 1992, when the changes were introduced, up to early June 1994 is presented. It can be seen that nearly 50 per cent of all investment certificates and of total capital costs concern the manufacturing sector. Furthermore, we

Table 8.2 Investment certificates issued by the Investment Office of Ethiopia and regional investment offices, July 1992–7 June 1994

Sector	No. of projects	Capital cost	
		Millions of birr (% own equity)	Foreign currency, millions of birr (%)
Industry/manufacturing	470 (44%)	3377 (39%)	2164 (64%)
Agriculture	188 (18%)	1171 (53%)	696 (59%)
Real estate	206 (19%)	1244 (46%)	88 (7%)
Hotel & tourism	94 (9%)	458 (62%)	175 (38%)
Social services	27 (3%)	103 (47%)	27 (26%)
Construction	15 (1%)	425 (73%)	309 (73%)
Trade	42 (4%)	180 (54%)	39 (22%)
Transport	23 (2%)	234 (51%)	154 (66%)
Mining	4 (0%)	185 (51%)	144 (78%)
Total	1069	7377 (47%)	3796 (51%)

Note: The total amount indicated for projects in the first four sectors is calculated on previous exchange rate US$1 = 2.07 birr. This means an underestimate since 5 birr per US dollar seems to be a more realistic exchange rate after the devaluation
Source: Unpublished data from Investment Office of Ethiopia, June 1994

Table 8.3 Foreign investments approved by the Investment Office of Ethiopia,
July 1992–7 June 1994

Type of project	No. of projects	Investment capital, millions of birr (% foreign)	Modality of investment
Construction	1	43 (80%)	Joint investment
Five star hotel	1	145 (96%)	Joint investment
Marble processing	1	44 (100%)	Foreign owned
Leather manufacturing	1	2 (80%)	Joint investment
Soap production	1	26 (66%)	Joint investment
Cattle fattening and meat processing	1	4 (100%)	Foreign owned
Cotton, corn, and groundnut production	1	404 (70%)	Joint investment
Special clinic	1	9 (100%)	Foreign owned
Total	8	598	

Source: Unpublished data from Investment Office of Ethiopia, June 1994

note that of the total capital cost of the investments 47 per cent is or will be financed by own equity. We also note that more than 50 per cent of the capital costs will be financed by foreign currency. Foreign currency can be mobilised either through foreign participation as owners in the investment activities or through the foreign exchange market of where the fortnightly foreign exchange auctioning has come to play an important role in financial Ethiopia (see above). Foreign direct investments still play a very minor role in Ethiopia. Table 8.3 shows that, for the period July 1992 to the beginning of June 1994, of the total 1069 investments that have been approved by the Investment Office of Ethiopia only 8 concern foreign investments. However, measured as the share of the total capital costs the foreign investments represent 9 per cent.

One problem in increasing private investments, and in particular foreign investments, is the economic–political environment in Ethiopia. It is clear that the economic reform achievements of the transitional government so far have produced increased interest from the private sector, also from abroad, in investing and setting up business in Ethiopia. Consequently, during the fiscal year 1993 commercial-bank lending to the private sector increased to 19 per cent of total commercial-bank lending, having lain round a more or less constant 10 per cent during 1990–1992 (World Bank 1994b). However, owing to remaining uncertainties, mainly in relation to the political situation but also in relation to land tenure, the interest for large-scale investments has mainly taken the form of applying for licences. Over a thousand certificates have been issued so far, of which only around 150 have resulted in actual investments. The final chapter of the present study will discuss how the government can reduce these uncertainties and thereby stimulate investors to turn the issued certificates into investments.

Macroeconomic situation

From the growth performance we now turn to the development of the macroeconomic situation in Ethiopia during the transition period. In the study, *Adjustment in Africa* (World Bank 1994a), the changes in macroeconomic policy and performance from the period 1981–1986 to the period 1987–1991 are analysed under three headings:

Fiscal policy:
    A. Change in overall fiscal balance excluding grants
    B. Change in total revenue
Monetary policy:
    C. Change in seigniorage
    D. Change in inflation
Exchange rate policy:
    E. Change in the real effective exchange rate
    F. Change in parallel market exchange rate premium.

Ethiopian reforms and adjustment do not go back more than to 1990 at the earliest. Therefore, it is not possible to make a direct comparison between the experience reported in the World Bank study (which ended in 1991) and the recent Ethiopian experience. Notwithstanding this circumstance, it is of some interest to make a preliminary evaluation of the recent development of the economic reforms in Ethiopia, using the same type of measures as the World Bank. However, in order to give a background and empirical basis for such an analysis and the comparison with other sub-Saharan countries, in Figures 8.1–8.3 we first give a brief description of the Ethiopian macroeconomic development from 1987 to 1994.

From Figure 8.1 it can be seen that the fiscal revenues decreased dramatically during the last years of the Mengistu government. This was due to a number of factors, among them decreasing trade taxes owing to lower agricultural production, lower industrial production, lower export volumes, and increased smuggling, both as regards exports and imports. Due to the ongoing and increasing civil unrest and alienation in the Ethiopian society, there was also a demoralisation in the public sector during these years. At the same time the civil war demanded increased resources and the various oppositionary regional groups increased in strength. As a consequence, the fiscal deficit increased. After the fall of the Mengistu government the public sector was reorganised and during 1992/93 and 1993/94 revenues started to increase again. However, the fiscal deficit increased even more. This is a natural consequence of the new policy, where reconstruction demands large

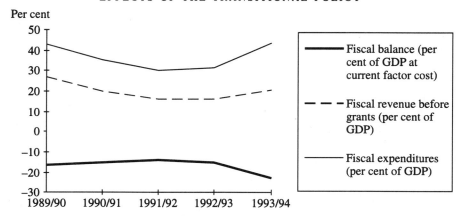

Figure 8.1 Fiscal balance, 1989/90–1993/94
Source: See Appendix C, Table C.1

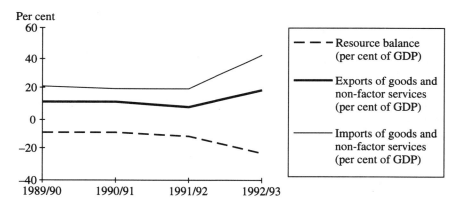

Figure 8.2 Foreign trade, 1989/90–1993/94
Source: See Appendix C, Table C.2

resources and the positive effects on economic activity and thus on revenue generation have not yet become apparent. This stands out clearly if a division is made between current and capital expenditures. In 1992/93 the fiscal gap between current expenditures and revenues was just around 5 per cent of GDP, as compared with the total fiscal gap of 17 per cent of GDP.

Figure 8.2 shows the development of Ethiopian foreign trade. Here it can be seen that the resource gap was more or less constant during the last years of the Mengistu government. As noted above, however, this is just the picture of official and registered trade. Estimates about unofficial trade or smuggling indicate that such activities were widespread; some estimates point to illegal exports amounting to as much as 40–45 per cent of official exports.

During the first year of the transition period, official imports increased whereas exports decreased. One explanation for the increase in imports is the increased demand for various commodities that were needed in the recon- struction and rehabilitation programme. Another explanation is the trade liberalisation and the fact that the customs had become more efficient. These latter factors reduce the incentives for smuggling and thus work towards a decreased share of illegal trade.

On the export side the Ethiopian economy was not able to adjust to the new policy of the transitional government. Because of the dominant role of coffee in Ethiopian exports, the collapse of the international coffee prices in the early 1990s hit Ethiopia particularly hard, a fact which, together with the Mengistu government's price and trade policy, contributed to lower coffee production in Ethiopia. However, during the past few years exports of coffee have increased again even if not to the maximum potential levels. Before these levels can be achieved new coffee bushes have to be planted on the destroyed coffee fields.

It is important also to note that the increase in the value of exports and in particular in the value of imports between 1991/92 and 1992/93 can largely be explained by the devaluation of the Ethiopian birr on 1 October 1992, when the official exchange rate changed from 2.07 to 5.0 birr per US dollar.

The trade liberalisation, together with the devaluation of the birr and the introduction of the foreign exchange auctioning in May 1993 all imply that the openness of the Ethiopian economy has increased significantly. Measured as the ratio of foreign trade (exports plus imports) to GDP, the openness increased from less than 30 per cent in 1990/91 and 1991/92 to around 50 per cent in 1992/93 (National Bank of Ethiopia).

Other important economic variables in an evaluation of macroeconomic policy are seigniorage and the rate of inflation. In this study seigniorage has been calculated as in World Bank (1994a: 59) and aims at measuring the impact of money creation on the rate of inflation. Figure 8.3 shows that seigniorage has decreased rapidly, that is the supply of money has been tightened, during the period. This is one reason why inflation also has decreased rapidly.

Then how can the reduced inflation be explained in a country that introduced such large devaluations? First, there seems to have been a more or less immediate supply response when the war ended. This is due both to increased production of goods (mainly agricultural goods) and improved efficiency in the distribution system as a consequence of less central control and the changes announced in the TEP. The credibility of the new policy has increased continuously through the government's issuing and implementation of various laws and proclamations, and through its tight monetary policy as indicated by the development of the seigniorage.

Another explanation for the price development during the last couple of years can be found in the international currency markets. In Figure 8.4 the development of the general retail price index for Addis Ababa since mid-1989

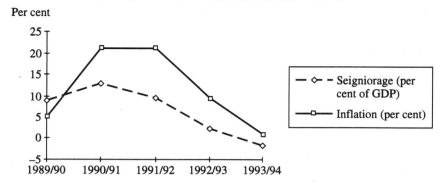

Figure 8.3 Seigniorage and inflation, 1989/90–1993/94
Source: See Appendix C, Table C.3

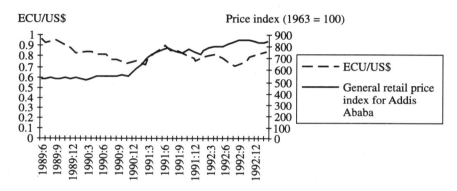

Figure 8.4 Exchange rates and prices
Source: See Appendix C, Table C.4

is compared to the development of the value of the US dollar measured in ECUs, which reflects the changes in the currencies of Ethiopia's major trading partners (see Chapters 3 and 5). Thus, the diagram shows how the Ethiopian birr would have developed relative to the US dollar if the birr had been pegged 100 per cent to the ECU instead of the US dollar.

After a more or less continuous increase in the price level up to May 1991, the price level began to fall when the US dollar depreciated. The figure indicates that in addition to the adjustment to the March 1990 reform, the Ethiopian economy outside the peasant sector had already almost adjusted to market economy realities when the formal decisions were made about the Transitional Economic Policy. This is not surprising considering the developments in Ethiopia.

Up to mid-1990, that is up to some months after the March 1990 reform announcement and the liberalisation of grain trading, changes in the general price level were relatively small and independent of the changes in the value of the US dollar. From mid-1990, however, the two curves begin to show the same development. In particular this is the case from February 1991 when the two curves show a more or less parallel development.

When the grain market was liberalised in March 1990, new traders entered the market. For other commodities the markets were also liberalised with price increases as a consequence of the shortage of commodities and the unrealistic and highly overvalued official exchange rate. When, during the last months of 1990 and early 1991, the government lost much of its control of foreign trade and currency exchange, black market or underground activities increased and the price level increased rapidly despite a fall of the US dollar. This can be explained by the large discrepancy that has long existed between the official exchange rate for the Ethiopian birr and the equilibrium exchange rate. When the transitional government came into power, the control of borders and currency exchange was further weakened. Smuggling or unofficial foreign trade increased very fast and by the end of 1991 currency exchange took place more or less everywhere at an exchange rate far above the official one.[1] Thus, one would expect the prices to adjust towards the prices that would have existed if foreign trade had been liberalised and the birr had been devalued to its equilibrium value and then been pegged to a basket of currencies with a heavy weight for the ECU. Figure 8.4 indicates that the market prices in Addis Ababa have largely developed in this way. The divergence of the two curves during 1992 was probably largely due to the negative growth in agriculture (see Table 8.1) and the concomitant reduced food supply. Since food has a heavy weight (49 per cent) in the price index, the fall in the ECU/US dollar exchange rate could not compensate for the domestically generated increases in food prices. Thus, we argue that through the underground market activities in foreign trade and in the currency market, the Ethiopian economy had already anticipated the devaluation of the birr. The devaluation of the birr to 5.00 birr per US dollar, effective from 1 October 1992, can be seen as an official adjustment towards the parallel market equilibrium exchange rate in Ethiopia. Therefore, it was not surprising that the price level did not increase as many politicians and observers feared when the government decided to devalue.

Macroeconomic policy stance in Ethiopia – a sub-Saharan comparison

As noted above, the World Bank recently published a study of macro-economic policy and performance in a number of sub-Saharan countries (World Bank 1994a). Ethiopia was not included in the study. Because of the extremely unstable situation in Ethiopia during the last years of the Mengistu government it is not possible to make a meaningful calculation, evaluation, and comparison of the macroeconomic policy during the pre-reform and post-reform periods along the same lines as those presented in World Bank (1994a)

Table 8.4 Macroeconomic policy stance in Ethiopia

	Mengistu government	*Transitional government*	
	1990/91	*1992/93*	*1993/94 (preliminary estimate)*
Fiscal policy			
Overall fiscal deficit after grants (% of GDP)	13.0 (4)*	10.9 (4)	9.3 (4)
Monetary policy			
Seigniorage (%)	13.2 (4)	2.4 (3)	−0.2 (1)
Inflation (%)	21.0 (2)	10.0 (1)	1.3 (1)
Nominal interest rate (%)	2–10	10–15	10–14
Real interest rate (%)	−19 to −11 (2–3)	0–5 (1–2)	8.7–12.7 (3)
Exchange rate policy			
Parallel market exchange rate premium (%)	250–300 (4)	around 40 (3)	10–20 (2)
Overall macroeconomic policy score	3.3	2.5	2.2

*Figures within parentheses are scores from 1 to 4. For the respective policy measures, the policy is considered adequate or good when the score is 1, fair when the score is 2, poor when the score is 3, and very poor when the score is 4. For the overall macroeconomic policy stance a score of 1.0–1.3 is considered adequate, 1.4–2.3 fair, 2.4–3.0 poor and a score of 3.1 or higher is considered very poor
Source: National Bank of Ethiopia, *Quarterly Bulletin* (various issues) and unpublished statistics from National Bank of Ethiopia

for other sub-Saharan countries. Instead we chose to limit our analysis by comparing the policy stance in 1990/91, that is the last year of the Mengistu government, and the most recent year of the transitional government for which data are available. In the latter case we use actual data from 1992/93 and preliminary estimates for 1993/94.

Table 8.4 presents the macroeconomic policy stance. In the calculations we have used the same principles for assessing the various components of macroeconomic policy as the World Bank (1994a: 266f and table B5).

From the table it can be concluded that the macroeconomic policy stance has improved during the transition period. From being very poor in 1990/91 it has changed to poor in 1992/93 and to fair in 1993/94 (estimate). What does this mean in a sub-Saharan adjustment perspective?

Table 8.5 compares the overall macroeconomic policy stance produced by the transitional government since July 1991 with the macroeconomic policy stance of other sub-Saharan countries in 1990/91 as reported in World Bank (1994a). It should be noted that the countries in Table 8.5 are all countries that implemented adjustment programmes during the period 1987–1991. From

Table 8.5 Macroeconomic policy stance in sub-Saharan Africa, 1990/91

Score*		*Number of sub-Saharan countries in the World Bank sample, 1990/91*
1.0–1.3 (adequate)	1	(Ghana)
1.4–2.3 (fair)	13	(Burundi, Burkina Faso, Gabon, The Gambia, Kenya, Madagascar, Malawai, Mali, Mauritania, Nigeria, Senegal, Togo, Uganda)
2.4–3.0 (poor)	6	(Benin, Central African Republic, Niger, Rwanda, Tanzania, Zimbabwe)
≥ 3.1 (very poor)	6	(Cameroon, Congo, Côte d'Ivoire, Mozambique, Sierra Leone, Zambia)

*See Table 8.4
Source: World Bank 1994: 269

this table, it can be seen that from a comparative sub-Saharan perspective, the recent adjustment process in Ethiopia has been successful. Going back to Table 8.4 it can be seen that the problematic policy areas in Ethiopia are the fiscal policy (very poor) and the interest rate policy (poor).

As mentioned before, the problems in terms of fiscal policy are natural in view of the ambitious reconstruction and rehabilitation programmes introduced after the end of the civil war and the fact that the economic activities that can generate fiscal revenues have not yet adjusted fully to the new more liberal and market-oriented economic system. The heavy weight of capital expenditure in the fiscal balance also means that the deficit is less inflationary than it might seem at first glance. Consequently, even though the government still has some problems with principle 2 of good policy management (see Chapter 1), the fiscal deficit should not be overstated as a problem since in the long run the capital expenditure, that is investments of various kinds, will contribute to increasing the productive capacity and production in the economy.

As far as the interest rate policy is concerned, the principles behind the scoring of the policy stance can be debated. According to the principles used by the World Bank (1994a) there has been a slight deterioration of the interest rate policy stance in Ethiopia. However, we would claim that there has been an improvement instead. When the Mengistu government was replaced, Ethiopia had negative real interest rates of around 10–20 per cent. With close to 20 per cent negative rate of interest on savings, it is not surprising that domestic savings were very low. Today, due to a change in the interest rate policy and low inflation, real interest rates have turned positive, around 10 per cent. Even if this may be rather high to stimulate investments, savings are definitely stimulated by this policy. It is too early to evaluate the effects of the new policy on domestic savings and investments. The result will depend on the privatisation policy, the outcome of which will depend on the credibility of the government, which in turn depends on the degree of political stability in the country.

CONCLUSIONS

As concluded in Chapter 7 the economic system changes introduced by the transitional government so far are impressive and far-reaching, and do mean a more or less complete termination of the *Ethiopia Tikdem* period which was based on Ethiopian or scientific socialism (see Chapter 3). Even though the reforms are recent and it is therefore premature to make a true evaluation of their long-run impact on the Ethiopian economy, the indications in place give support to the expectations that can be derived from our economic system and institutional general equilibrium model analysis. Thus, it seems reasonable to conclude that through its introduction and implementation of economic system reform and policy the transitional government of Ethiopia has succeeded in improving economic performance and growth. In particular this is the case for the peasant sector and the former State-dominated manufacturing sector. Furthermore, available statistics show that the macroeconomic situation in the country has improved during the transitional period.

Notwithstanding the fact that much remains to be done before the intended changes to the Ethiopian economic system are complete, it is important to stress that, considering the short time the reform programme has been under way, Ethiopia has made considerable progress on her way from socialism and towards more private-based economic activities where markets, rather than the government, play an increasingly central role in the determination of the allocation of resources. This is particularly so if comparisons are made with the experience (speed and magnitude of changes) in many other reforming sub-Saharan countries.

The future of the Ethiopian economy largely depends on the success of the government to create a climate for the private business sector so that both domestic and foreign private investors will find it interesting and attractive to make investments in Ethiopia. In particular this can be expected to be important in a country like Ethiopia with its legacy of seventeen years of extreme socialist rule. Political stability, transparency, and credibility of the government are all crucial components in an attractive climate for business. The final chapter of this study analyses some of the problems in creating such a situation in Ethiopia.

9

POST-*ETHIOPIA TIKDEM*
Possibilities and obstacles for
growth and development

INTRODUCTION

Following the change of government in 1991, not only a new economic system but also new political and administrative structures were planned to be introduced in Ethiopia. The declared objective was to transform the dictatorial, one-party State of Ethiopia, with its frequent violations of human rights and its socialist command economy, into a multi-party democratic society, where human rights are respected, where the regions benefit from a large degree of autonomy, and where private entrepreneurs and the operation of market forces are encouraged.

In short, the process of systemic transition that has been going on in Ethiopia since mid-1991 can be said to have three major aims:

- the creation of a market-oriented economic system;
- the creation of a democratic political system; and
- the decentralisation of administrative powers and functions to secure ethnic and regional autonomy.

As economics, politics, and institutional structures are closely related and interdependent, and as the previous chapters have focused on the economic system changes, the analysis in this final chapter will deal mainly with the other two components of the ongoing transition in Ethiopia. We start, in the next section, by commenting on the political changes under way in Ethiopia and their consequences for the implementation of economic reforms, and thus for economic performance. Then we turn to an analysis of the issue of decentralisation of power to local and regional authorities and its political and economic implications. Finally, the main conclusions of the chapter and the whole study are summarised and some recommendations for the future, both in relation to the principles of good domestic economic policymaking (see Chapter 1) and in relation to foreign assistance, are presented.

POLITICAL TRANSITION – IMPLICATIONS FOR DEMOCRACY AND THE ECONOMY

Even if our main interest is with the introduction and implementation of changes to the economic system, political conditions and changes in Ethiopia must also be considered. First, as noted by Hansson (1993a), the major problems for the new economic strategy in Ethiopia lie in the political risks. Among these risks, the issues of ethnic conflict, regional liberation, independence, and nation building are of particular concern. Second, as stressed throughout this study, economic performance is heavily dependent on political and institutional factors.[1] The political system defines both the rules and the institutional framework of the economy, and thereby has an important influence on economic performance.

An important link between the political system and economic performance and the possibility of carrying through economic reforms is the existence of rent-seeking, or other so-called directly unproductive profit (DUP)-seeking activities. This type of activity is introduced by economic actors in order to obtain advantages without adding to the production of goods and services. Examples of such activities are bribing and lobbying. As a rule this type of activity has a negative impact on economic performance and growth.[2]

The more pluralistic and democratic the society, the higher tends to be the transparency of the political decision-making and implementation. Furthermore, it is clear that the more transparent the political decision-making and the legal system, the higher the cost of efficient rent-seeking and DUP activities and the less attractive, and thereby less frequent, this type of activity tends to be. The reason is that in a pluralistic and transparent system with clearly defined laws that are efficiently supervised by democratic institutions, more people have to be subject to the rent-seekers' activities if rents really are to be obtained. This view is supported by a recent study by Scully who concludes that:

> Politically open societies, subscribing to the rule of law, private property, and the market allocation of resources, grow at three times the rate and are two and one-half times as efficient economically in transforming inputs into national output as societies in which these rights largely are proscribed.

> (Scully 1992: 12)

In most dimensions of liberty, political as well as economic, Ethiopia during the Mengistu period ranked at the very bottom in the world (Scully 1992: chapter 5). As noted above, the transitional government has introduced a great number of economic system changes that have definitely liberalised the Ethiopian economy. In the field of politics, the government has also introduced numerous changes, even if there is still an urgent need for reforms, not least reforms that can handle the important and sensitive issue of ethnicity.

This conclusion is in line with Otunnu (1992) who, in an analysis of the situation in Africa, discusses the paradox that exists whereby Africa is a continent that is particularly rich, with rich endowments of minerals, agricultural land, favourable climate, water resources, and 'very resilient people' (Otunnu 1992: 288), and yet it is also a continent whose inhabitants are the poorest on earth. Otunnu concludes that probably the major challenge of Africa today is 'how to transform the ethnic diversities inherited from colonial boundaries into national States' (Otunnu 1992: 288). The crisis of identity that characterises many African countries has in many cases resulted in wars. Up to May 1991 this was also the case in Ethiopia, inclusive of Eritrea. Even though ethnic diversity in Ethiopia is not the result of European colonialism, one of the most challenging and important issues for the future of Ethiopia is to find politically acceptable solutions for a peaceful coexistence of various ethnic groups.

War does not only lead to direct war victims but also occupies vast quantities of economic resources and gives rise to enormous material and infrastructural damage and great uncertainties. All these factors have both direct and indirect negative impacts on the economy (Azam *et al.* 1993). Obviously, war has directly and indirectly contributed to the recurrent famines that have hit several African countries, including Ethiopia, during the last few decades. According to Otunnu (1992: 290) 'these internecine conflicts have become a kind of political hemorrhage, steadily draining the collective strength of the African peoples.' Thus, it is concluded that 'the way out of this tragic quagmire involves two related steps: the fashioning of a new democratic space and the rediscovery of the art of political compromise' (Otunnu 1992: 290).

The art of political compromise is important for achieving political stability and strength, which in turn are of the utmost importance for the successful implementation of economic reforms in Ethiopia. In a democracy, the relationship between the elected parliament, the government and the State on the one hand, and the voters (or the public in general) on the other, is crucial for the stability and strength of the government.

The following quotations from the *Transitional Period Charter* of Ethiopia of 22 July 1991, describe the democratising objectives of the transitional government:

WHEREAS the overthrow of the military dictatorship that has ruled Ethiopia for seventeen years presents a historical moment, providing the Peoples of Ethiopia with the opportunity to rebuild the country and restructure the state democratically;

WHEREAS the military dictatorship was, in essence, a continuation of the previous regimes and its demise marks the end of an era of subjugation and oppression thus starting a new chapter in Ethiopian history in which freedom, equal rights and self-determination of all the peoples shall be the governing principles of political, economic and social life and thereby contributing to the welfare of the Ethiopian Peoples and rescuing them from centuries of subjugation and backwardness;

...

WHEREAS peace and stability, as essential conditions of development, require the end of all hostilities, the healing of wounds caused by conflicts and the establishment and maintenance of good neighbourliness and co-operation;

...

WHEREAS to this end, all institutions of repression installed by the previous regimes shall be dismantled, regional prejudices redressed and the rights and interests of the deprived citizens safeguarded by a democratic government elected by and accountable to the People.

(*Negarit Gazeta* no. 1, 22 July 1991: 1)

When working on transforming a former dictatorial system into a democratic one it is important to keep in mind that implementing political reforms of the magnitude aimed for in Ethiopia is an extremely difficult and complex project, in particular in a country that lacks democratic traditions and has a low level of education and literacy. Such a transformation demands a thorough revision of the constitution. Leaving aside the central issue of who is to have the right to decide upon the proposed constitution, we note that in Ethiopia a commission has worked out a new constitution that, among other things, is intended to govern the coming regular national elections. After the national elections in May 1995, the transitional government 'shall hand over the power to the party or parties that gain a majority in the National Assembly' (*Negarit Gazeta* no. 1, 22 July 1991: 4).

In political science a distinction is made between 'democracy *of* the people' and 'democracy *for* the people': the former requires knowledge about the will of the people, unlike the latter, in which the interest and the liberties of the individual are less important than equality, for example. Many of the African countries that claim to be democracies, up to now, have been democracies *for* rather than *of* the people. Thus, elections of the type we are used to in the Western democracies have not been regarded as necessary or even important.[3]

According to the Transitional Charter, 'the rights and interests of the deprived citizens [should be] safeguarded by a democratic government elected by and accountable to the People' (*Negarit Gazeta* no. 1, 22 July 1991: 1). Thus, the intended form of democracy in Ethiopia is democracy *of* rather than *for* the people.

To make 'democracy of the people' work, some basic liberties, such as freedom of expression, assembly, organisation, and publication are needed. In Ethiopia these rights or liberties are guaranteed by the Charter. To pave the way for the democratisation process, the July 1991 conference proclaimed that the United Nations' Universal Declaration on Human Rights from 1948 shall be respected fully. Thus, every individual shall have:

- The freedom of conscience, expression, association and peaceable assembly;
- The right to engage in unrestricted political activity and to organise political parties, provided the exercise of such right does not infringe upon the rights of others.

(Negarit Gazeta no. 1, 22 July 1991: 2)

It should be noted that there are several opposition groups, i.e. parties and other organisations, that now are active and work openly in Ethiopia. Even if there are abuses reported by some of these groups, the main impression seems to be that the transitional government has taken a leap towards a system in which basic human rights are respected. In a critical assessment of the first year of the transitional government, Africa Watch concluded that even if there is still much to be criticised:

Africa Watch applauds the Transitional Government's commitments to basic human rights, democratic governance and the rule of law, and recognizes the very real progress that has been made in all of these areas.

(Africa Watch 1992: 17)

The electoral system – general comments

In liberal democracies people should feel that political participation is possible for them and that their concerns and interests are represented in the elected parliament and government. Therefore, the design of the electoral system is of crucial importance and an important factor that determines the interest among the ordinary men and women in voting and engaging in active political work.

Among the most important – and, arguably, *the* most important – of all constitutional choices that have to be made in democracies is the choice of electoral system, especially majoritarian election methods vs proportional representation (PR), and the choice of relationship between the executive and the legislature, in particular presidential vs parliamentary government.

(Lijphart 1992: 207)

Since it is clear from the Charter that the intended political system in Ethiopia is a parliamentary system, in this study we will focus on the remaining, but equally important, choice between a plurality/majority electoral system and a proportional system.[4]

Table 9.1 Characteristics of the two electoral systems

	Plurality/majority elections	Proportional elections
1. Manipulation of the division of the country into voting districts	+	−
2. Two-party system	+	−
3. Multi-party system	−	+
4. Consensus democracy	−	+
5. One-party cabinet	+	−
6. Coalition cabinet	−	+
7. Executive vs. legislature	Executive dominates	Balance
8. Ethnic/minority representation	−	+
9. People's access to legislature	−	+
10. Accountability	+	−
11. Capacity to govern	+	−
12. Unity and peace in divided societies	−	+
13. Strong leadership	+	−
14. Stability and continuity in leadership	−	+
15. Speed in decision-making	+	−

Note: + (−) denotes stronger (weaker) tendency compared to the other type of electoral system
Source: Compiled from the discussion in Lijphart 1991

It falls outside the scope of this study to make an extensive analysis of the concept of democracy and different electoral systems. However, it is important to keep in mind that, depending on the electoral system, the same distribution of votes among the population can give rise to completely different representation in the National Assembly. The electoral system is also of crucial importance for the creation of legitimacy, credibility, and governance of the economic reforms to be introduced and implemented in the near future.

In Table 9.1 various characteristics or dimensions of democracies are listed and for each one the plurality/majority electoral system is compared to the proportional electoral system. It should be noted that the table should be read as describing *tendencies* of the respective system for the various variables rather than clear-cut unique differences. Depending on the relative values attached to the various variables or characteristics of democracy, the choice will fall on one or the other system.

Table 9.1 suggests that in a proportional electoral system the minorities tend to be better protected or represented than in a plurality/majority system. This is due to the fact that in the former system, the districts' representation in the parliament will be proportional to the actual votes in the respective districts, whereas in a plurality (majority) system the candidate or party obtaining most (majority of the) votes in the district will take all seats for the district in the parliament. Thus, in a country aiming at democracy *of* the people we should expect a preference for a proportional electoral system, *ceteris paribus*. Furthermore, in comparison with a plurality/majority system, a proportional electoral system leaves less room for manipulation of the division of the country into voting districts.

On the other hand, in a country where there is a high preference for strong governments, we should expect a preference for a plurality/majority system. In such a system, there is a relatively strong tendency for a two-party system and a government with an absolute majority in the parliament. With a plurality/majority system there is a greater potential to carry through difficult policy programmes, for example various types of economic or structural adjustment programmes, *ceteris paribus*. This is an important aspect, in particular in countries that face deep economic crisis and where far-reaching structural reforms are needed.

The choice of electoral system – the case of Ethiopia

The choice of electoral system is an important instrument of politics, or as Sartori has classified it 'the most specific manipulative instrument of politics' (quoted from Lijphart 1991: 73). Therefore, it is surprising and quite problematic that there has been so little debate and so few investigations on this issue in Ethiopia.[5]

At a first glance, in the case of present-day Ethiopia, with its economic crisis and a need for successful implementation of economic reform and thus a need for a strong government, there seems to be an obvious case for choosing a plurality/majority electoral system. However, this conclusion should be subject to closer inspection.

Capacity to govern has a time dimension. In the short run, it is obvious that centralised and heavily concentrated power, in its extreme form a dictatorship, is more efficient in terms of governance. In a longer-term perspective, however, governance is not just a question of strength of the executive and the speed of the decision-making process but also of the credibility, stability, and continuity of government. This is particularly important in societies like Ethiopia where structural changes must take place, changes that require a long period of implementation before they have become well-established in legislation and attitudes among the population.

Furthermore, in Ethiopia there are a large number of ethnic or regional groups with political ambitions. This makes the situation quite complex in terms of stability and continuity.

Majority rule is central in democratic decision-making. It is important, however, to note that in the doctrine of liberal democracy, decision-making is preceded by discussion and a search for compromise so that the opinion of the minorities can be taken into explicit consideration. This should be particularly important in multi-ethnic societies like Ethiopia.

It should be noted that the EPRDF has formed its own ethnic and regional groups that compete with the 'original' groups, something that tends to weaken these latter groups. In the local and regional elections in 1992, the EPRDF and its direct associate ethnic and regional parties obtained more than 90 per cent of all votes. These elections and the result have been criticised by other groups, in particular the Oromo Liberation Front, who think that they were not given a fair chance to prepare and organise themselves for the elections.[6]

Due to the lack of democratic tradition, and thus of well-organised parties and well-functioning information channels in the country, together with the low level of education and literacy, it will take considerable time to build a basis for democratic elections of the type we are used to in the Western world. Coalitions between various parties in the electoral processes will be difficult to establish on a national level. It should also be noted that at present there are great differences in the resources available for political work; naturally the parties in the transitional government, in particular EPRDF, have a better position than most other organisations. It is likely that for quite a long time the EPRDF and its associate parties will obtain a clear majority of the votes and a majority of the seats in the National Assembly. Therefore, in the short- and medium-term perspective the electoral system *per se* will probably not be a critical factor in the governance of the country and the possibility of implementing economic reforms. However, with a plurality/majority system, the EPRDF and its associate ethnic and regional groups will probably obtain a clear majority of the votes and the resulting National Assembly will be close to a one-party assembly. This was what happened in the 5 June 1994 national elections to the constitutional National Assembly where the EPRDF and its associate regional parties obtained 484 (88 per cent) out of the total 547 seats. If this becomes the case also in the coming regular elections for the National Assembly and the result can be traced back to the electoral system, there is a risk that political democracy will be seen as something unattainable among groups in opposition. As a consequence, there is a risk that any enthusiasm for political work will disappear and the democratisation project declared in the Charter will fail. Regional opposition against the national government may also arise, and could easily develop into a series of regional conflicts and eventually into a civil war.

Looking at the history of democracy, according to Rokkan 'it was no accident that the earliest moves toward proportional representation (PR) came in the ethnically most heterogeneous countries' (quoted from Lijphart 1991: 75). In the case of a highly complex country like Ethiopia, which has just embarked on the road to liberal democracy, it is important to attain a high degree of political participation among the very large number of ethnic and regional groups, and to create a constitutional framework of peaceful coexistence among these groups. According to Lijphart (1991: 81) 'such power sharing can be arranged much more easily in parliamentary and PR [proportional representation] systems than in presidential and plurality systems'. The conclusion of the above discussion is that there seems to be a case for a proportional electoral system in Ethiopia.

In late August 1993, a proclamation on electoral law was released which stated that the coming Ethiopian national elections will take place in a parliamentary plurality/majority electoral system, with single-member districts normally comprising 100 000 persons each (*Negarit Gazeta* no. 64, 23 August 1993). In each district, probably equal to Woredas (the lowest administrative unit), only 12 candidates (parties) will be allowed. Every candidate will have to find support from at least 500 voters in order to be registered as a candidate. If more than 12 candidates (parties) qualify, only the 12 candidates with the most signatures will be registered. The candidate obtaining the most votes will take the seat for the district in the National Assembly. According to the Charter, the party or coalition of parties that holds a majority of seats in the National Assembly will form the government of the country.

One important reason behind the choice of a plurality/majority electoral system is probably the emphasis on the capacity to govern the country. However, as noted above, from a long-term perspective, stability and continuity are crucial prerequisites for introducing and implementing substantial and thus time-consuming economic changes of the kind now under way in Ethiopia. Stability and continuity in a democracy are dependent on the situation of minority groups. Even if the electoral law contains some brief and imprecise declarations about minority groups, the electoral system, and thus the political system in Ethiopia, is not satisfactory from the perspective of the

Table 9.2 Characteristics of the intended Ethiopian electoral system

1. *Manipulation of the division of the country into voting districts*	+
2. Two-party system	+
3. Multi-party system	−
4. *Consensus democracy*	−
5. One-party cabinet	+
6. Coalition cabinet	−
7. *Executive vs. legislature*	*Executive dominates*
8. *Ethnic/minority representation*	−
9. People's access to legislature	−
10. Accountability	+
11. Capacity to govern	+
12. *Unity and peace in divided societies*	−
13. Strong leadership	+
14. *Stability and continuity in leadership*	−
15. Speed in decision-making	+

Note: + (−) denotes stronger (weaker) tendency compared to the other type of electoral system minority groups, whose interests tend to be better protected in a proportional electoral system.

In terms of the various characteristics in Table 9.1, Ethiopian democracy can be described as in Table 9.2 where the most problematic characteristics have been italicised.

With the intended electoral system there will be an obvious risk of manipulation of the geographical division of voting districts and there will be few incentives for creating a consensus democracy. Furthermore, minority interests will find it difficult to become represented in the National Assembly and thus to influence the national policy. This constitutes a risk to unity and peace in the country which in turn will threaten stability and continuity in the State leadership, at least in a medium- and long-term perspective.

Considering the lessons from the political history of other multi-ethnic societies, the lack of political democratic tradition in Ethiopia, the severe regional resource imbalances (see below for some examples), and the current economic problems and challenges, Ethiopia should reconsider the choice of a pluralistic/majority electoral system by closely investigating the more complete and long-term consequences of the various options at hand.

DECENTRALISATION THROUGH REGIONALISATION

In the previous section the problems of ethnic diversity and strife were emphasised, as was the importance of considering these problems when designing the model of democracy, in particular in relation to the choice of electoral system. In Ethiopia the ethnic problems are exemplified by the Ethiopian–Eritrean conflict that came to an end in May 1991.

By giving the people of Eritrea the right to decide their future status, the new leadership made a clear break with the history of Ethiopia. In imperial as well as in socialist Ethiopia national unity was heavily stressed. In the latter case national unity was one of the major points included in the political slogan *Ethiopia Tikdem*. In the ten-point programme the military government issued on 20 December 1974 it was stated that: 'Ethiopia shall remain a united country, without ethnic, religious, linguistic and cultural differences.'

Even if in the fourth point of the ten-point programme it was stated that 'every regional administration and every village shall manage its own resources and be self-sufficient', it is obvious that the policy of the transitional government as declared in the Charter means a clear break with the past government's policy about the status of various groups in the Ethiopian society. In the second article of the Transitional Charter it is declared:

The right of nations, nationalities and peoples to self-determination is affirmed. To this end, each nation, nationality and people is guaranteed the right to:

154

a/ Preserve its identity and have it respected, promote its culture and history and use and develop its language;

b/ Administer its own affairs within its own defined territory and effectively participate in the central government on the basis of freedom, and fair and proper representation;

c/ Exercise its right to self-determination of independence, when the concerned, nation/nationality and people is convinced that the above rights are denied, abridged or abrogated.

(Negarit Gazeta no. 1, 22 July 1991: 2)

The transitional government has changed the regional division of Ethiopia and thereby reduced the number of regions from 30 to 14.[7] The new division

Table 9.3 Agricultural production by region, 1989/90

Region	Total production (million quintals)	%	Per capita production (quintals)
Arssi	6.7	12	3.5
Bale	1.3	2	1.4
North Omo	1.6	3	0.6
South Omo	0.1	0	0.6
East Gojjam	3.3	6	2.2
West Gojjam	4.0	7	2.0
Metekel	0.6	1	1.7
North Gonder	1.6	3	0.9
South Gonder	1.7	3	1.0
Dire Dawa	0.0	0	0.1
East Hararghe	1.9	3	0.8
West Hararghe	1.9	3	1.4
Gambella	0.1	0	0.6
Illubabor	4.5	8	1.6
Keffa	1.6	3	1.5
Addis Ababa	1.4	2	0.6
East Shoa	2.2	4	2.4
North Shoa	3.7	6	1.6
South Shoa	5.8	10	1.9
West Shoa	4.1	7	1.6
Borena	0.3	1	0.4
Sidamo	2.0	3	0.8
Assosa	0.6	1	1.1
Wellega	3.1	5	1.3
North Wello	1.4	2	1.0
South Wello	2.2	4	0.9
Total	57.5	99	1.2

Note: Eritrea, Tigray, Assab, and Ogaden autonomous regions are not included
Source: CSA, Statistical Abstract 1988 and CSA 'Crop Production Forecast 1990/91', 1990

Table 9.4 Some social indicators by region, 1987/88

Region	Enrolment in primary and academic secondary school (% of population)	No. of people/ hospital bed (1000s)	Malnourished (% of total number of malnourished)
Arssi	12.6	7.9	4
Bale	11.3	7.6	2
Eritrea	7.1	1.1	7
Gamogoffa	7.7	7.5	3
Gojjam	7.4	9.6	7
Gonder	3.9	5.7	8
Harerghe	5.3	4.4	9
Illubabor	14.6	3.6	2
Keffa	8.7	11.1	5
Shewa	8.8	9.4	22
Sidamo	8.2	9.1	10
Tigray	3.5	4.6	6
Wellega	11.3	5.8	5
Wello	5.8	7.9	9
Addis Ababa	26.9	0.4	
Asseb adm.	8.6	0.4	
Total	8.3	3.8	99

Source: Calculated from CSA Statistical Abstract 1986 and 1988. Here from Mishra 1991

is based on nationality and ethnicity. A majority of these regions consist of between 5 and 13 nationalities each. Only three consist of just one nationality and another two were largely one-nationality regions. Thus, also within regions there exists a danger of ethnic tension and conflicts.

Another problem in contemporary Ethiopia is that there are very large differences between the regions in terms of, for instance, agricultural production, schools, health facilities, and roads (Tables 9.3 and 9.4). There are various reasons for this. In the Transitional Period Charter and Transitional Economic Policy Programme it is stated that areas that have suffered from the previous civil war and droughts shall be guaranteed relief assistance (TGE 1991: 45f, *Negarit Gazeta* no. 1, 22 July 1991: 4), but that special attention shall also be given to those groups of the Ethiopian population that have suffered from the villagisation and resettlement programmes of the former government and to 'hitherto neglected and forgotten areas' (*Negarit Gazeta* no. 1, 22 July 1991: 5). It is also stated that the government 'shall make special efforts to dispel ethnic mistrust and eradicate the ethnic hatred that have been fostered by the previous regime' (ibid.). These statements can be interpreted as an announcement of a redistribution strategy with the aim of reducing regional differences and leading to greater equality among regions.

The Transitional Charter declares that the regions shall have a far-reaching degree of self-determination. In the proclamation on national/regional self-government from January 1992, it is stated that:

National/Regional Transitional Self-Governments shall have legislative, executive and judicial powers in respect of all matters within their geographical areas except such matters as defence, foreign affairs, economic policy, conferring of citizenship, declaration of a state of emergency, deployment of army where situations beyond the capacity of National/Regional Transitional Self-Governments arise, printing of currency, establishing and administering major development establishments, building and administering major communications networks and the like, which are specifically reserved for the Central Transitional Government because of their nature.

(Negarit Gazeta no. 2, 14 January 1992: 10)

Accordingly, the same proclamation includes an extensive list of the powers and duties of the national/regional transitional self-governments. Among these powers and duties are the following:

* To borrow from domestic lending sources and to levy dues and taxes.
* To prepare, approve and implement their own budgets.
* To administer, develop and protect the natural resources of the region in accordance with the relevant general policy and law of the central transitional government.

Furthermore, it is stated that 'National/Regional Transitional Self-Governments are, in every respect, entities subordinate to the Central Transitional Government' *(Negarit Gazeta* no. 2, 14 January 1992: 8). Thus, it is not possible yet to know the degree of freedom that the national/regional transitional self-governments really will have. However, since spring 1993 the transitional government has begun to move parts of the administration, for example in the Ministries of Agriculture and Education, out to the various regions, in line with the above-mentioned objective of decentralising power.

The decentralisation of power and the regionalisation of administration have both positive and negative implications for the governance and efficient performance of the economy. In general it is positive to follow the principle of subsidiarity, i.e. to try to delegate functions to as low a level as possible, given that efficiency and consistency on the national level can be preserved. There are, however, policy areas that should be kept on a central national level. Areas that fall into this category are monetary and fiscal policy, which are necessary to achieve macroeconomic balance in the economy. The dissolution and privatisation of State enterprises falls into this category also. The same is true for the provision of public and semi-public goods, such as the institutions that are necessary supports to the intended market-oriented economic system, but also public and semi-public goods that are characterised by indivisibility and high fixed costs, such as some parts of the physical infrastructure.

Environmental policy also risks becoming inefficient when determined and implemented on a local or regional level. Bourdet (1992: 81) points to the experience of the forest sector in Laos where there is a conflict between the interests of the provinces, who tend to overexploit the forest resources, and the central government's objective of environmental protection. The experience of Laos in this respect should be of great interest for other less developed countries, such as Ethiopia, which are transferring executive and legislative power from the national to the regional and local authorities. In Laos, which seems to be ahead of most sub-Saharan African countries in the implementation of economic reforms, and clearly is so compared to Ethiopia, the central government in 1990 started to implement a recentralisation process as a response to the experience of the earlier decentralisation policy (Bourdet 1992: 82).

In view of the ongoing economic changes and the lack of competent personnel to design and administer the new economic system at the central national ministerial level, it is a problematic task to decentralise powers and functions at the speed and on the scale that is now being introduced in Ethiopia. By moving the employees that are available out to the regional administrations, the national objectives risk having to stand back, rendering the implementation of policies inconsistent and inefficient. Here it is important to make a close investigation of the experience of other countries and make a long-term plan for the decentralisation process in which the building up of competence is given due consideration.

CONCLUDING REMARKS AND FOREIGN AID IMPLICATIONS

When the Mengistu government was defeated in May 1991 a new era in the history of Ethiopia began. The former dictatorial and centralised war-ridden country with its frequent violations of human rights was to be transformed into a democratic country based on the United Nations' Universal Declaration on Human Rights and a market-oriented and increasingly privately owned economy.

This study has shown that during the years when *Ethiopia Tikdem* was the governing political slogan the economic development and performance were deteriorating. This was the case both in absolute terms and in an international perspective. As a consequence of the poor economic development and performance, Ethiopia experienced a poor development of many social dimensions of development. Table 9.5 presents some social indicators and their trends during the last 15–25 years and compares them with the situation in the average less developed country and in the group of sub-Saharan African countries.

158

Table 9.5 Social indicators in Ethiopia and in some groups of developing countries

	Ethiopia		All LDCs	Least developed countries	Sub-Saharan Africa
	15–20 years ago	*1990*	*1990*	*1990*	*1990*
Education (gross enrolment rates, % of school-age group)					
Primary	24	39	99	67	69
Male	32				
Female	15				
Secondary (% of school-age population)	6	12	41	16	18
Female	4	11	34	12	15
Illiteracy (% of population, age 15+)	na	50	31	54	49
Infant mortality (per 1000 live births)*	151	123	69	112	101
Life expectancy (years)*	44	46.4	63.0	50.1	51.1
Total fertility rate (births per woman)*	5.9	7.0	3.8	6.1	6.5
Access to health care (%)†	na	46	81	54	59
Population per physician (persons)	86 100	33 330	6 670	19 110	35 680
Population per nurse (persons)	na	13 890	3 390	7 430	8 190
Access to safe water (% of population)†	8	28	70	45	45
Urban	58	91	85	60	74
Rural	1	19	62	30	31
Newspaper circulation (per 1000 population)	2	1	44	6	12

*1992
†1988–91
Sources: World Bank 1993, UNDP 1994

The negative development during the *Ethiopia Tikdem* period was, of course, a huge challenge for the transitional government of Ethiopia when it took power in 1991. One important condition for making social improvements is that there exist economic resources for improvements. This, in turn, is dependent on the performance of the Ethiopian economy and on the possibilities for the government to mobilise foreign aid.

Chapter 7 has shown that during the years that have passed since the change of government, the new government has introduced an impressive number of reforms in the economy. However, it has also been concluded that there are still some important fields (e.g. exchange rate policy, trade policy, financial sector, and the issue of ownership of both land and other productive resources) where further changes are needed before the full gains of the measures introduced so far can be realised.

In the field of politics, the process of democratisation has been set in motion. Local/regional elections took place in 1992 with a great victory for the EPRDF and its associated local parties. A constitutional commission has been working on the preparations for regular national elections. In 1993, a decision was taken to introduce a plurality/majority electoral system. This choice was probably prompted by the need to have a strong government able to implement the far-reaching economic changes that have already been introduced or are about to be introduced. However, by looking a little closer at the relative merits of a plurality/majority electoral system and a proportional system, it can be shown that from the point of view of democracy, stability, and efficient long-term implementation of the economic changes, there seem to be strong arguments in favour of a proportional electoral system. Further analyses of the implications of various electoral systems are needed in Ethiopia to come to a more definite answer.

Analyses of the decentralisation of powers and functions to the local and regional level in Ethiopia are also required. The reason is that there is an obvious risk that conflicting interests between local/regional and national levels will result in problems of efficiency and national stability. The overall shortage of competent personnel for the implementation of the new economic policy and legislation also makes it a risky task to implement the rapid decentralisation of powers and personnel, i.e. before sufficient competent staff are available to efficiently co-ordinate and supervise policies at the national level.

This relates to the first principle of good economic policy management (see Chapter 1) 'avoid poor technicians in policymaking'. In the previous government it was clear that the recruitment of civil servants for policy design did not always take place on the basis of professional qualifications even if there seemed to be more of this than expected. Thus, for the present Ethiopian government and successive governments, it is important to guarantee availability of good technicians in the central ministries and not to delegate out functions and powers at a speed that is beyond the qualifications of the staff at various levels of the bureaucracy.

One closely related issue that really will be demanding for the government in the coming years is the second principle of good economic policy management, i.e. to 'keep budgets under adequate control'. As should be clear from the above analysis, the previous government fell short on this principle and left a high fiscal deficit to the new government. The situation becomes even more problematic when the enormous need for investments both in physical and human capital is considered. At the same time, the tax basis is very limited.

Even though improving the tax system and the tax administration in Ethiopia is imperative, there is also an obvious risk of introducing severe distortions through the tax system and of setting taxes at a level that destroy the incentives structure (principle 7). This was clearly what happened during the *Ethiopia Tikdem* period with the taxation of the peasants through the tax system but also through the quota delivery system and the price system *per se*.

For the foreseeable future, therefore, there seems to be a strong case for trying to close the resource gap through foreign assistance. If such external resource mobilisation does not happen, the government will run a heavy risk of facing problems with the third principle of good policy management, i.e. to 'keep inflationary pressures under reasonable control'. We saw in Chapters 6 and 8 that during the last years of the Mengistu government, when foreign assistance from the former East European countries fell drastically, the government relied on money creation to finance the fiscal deficit. As a result inflation rose to levels which were high by Ethiopian standards.

This study has underlined the role of the external sector in getting the economy on a track of sustainable growth and development. Trade must be given the potential to work as an 'engine of growth'. This is in fact the fourth principle of good policymaking.

Closely related to this is knowledge about the relative merits of various trade policy measures (principles 5 and 6). It is clear that the former government did not take full or even reasonable advantage of the potentials of international trade. Furthermore, when they restricted trade, it often took the form of quotas, which are well known to have a greater tendency to distort than other types of trade policy measures (see also principle 11 in Chapter 1).

We noted in Chapter 7 that the transitional government has introduced far-reaching trade liberalisation. This is a clear positive change, not least for potential investors in Ethiopia, but will it remain? This is still an open issue, in particular since Ethiopia is not a member of GATT nor one of the countries that have announced that they would like to become members of the new World Trade Organization (WTO). An Ethiopian application for membership in this organisation would definitely be a positive signal to potential investors and businessmen that the new more liberal policy will remain. The reason is of course that an international agreement like the one on international trade disciplines the participating countries and makes their policy more predictable. Since the WTO contains great potential benefits for less developed countries in general and for very poor countries like Ethiopia in particular (see e.g. Hansson 1994 and references therein), the issue of WTO membership should be relatively easy to decide upon without strong internal opposition.

In the new market-oriented Ethiopian economic system it is also important to keep to the new strategy about the role of the State in business life. Here the twelfth and thirteenth principles of good economic policymaking should be kept in mind, i.e. to 'take a technical rather than ideological view of the problems associated with public sector enterprises' and to 'make the borderlines between public and private sector activity clear and well defined'.

One area where there continues to be misunderstandings and a risk of running into bad management is the exchange rate policy. As noted in Chapter 6, the transitional government devalued the exchange rate as from 1 October 1992. However, there is still a risk of running into conflict with the fourteenth principle of good policymaking, 'don't overvalue the exchange rate' because the present government in its official exchange rate policy works with a 100 per cent pegging of the Ethiopian birr to the US dollar.

Finally, let us say something about the issue of foreign assistance and how the donors can assist Ethiopia in her transition from a centralised, command type of dictatorial country to a democratic, decentralised and market-oriented society.

It falls outside the scope of this study to give a detailed answer to the issue of appropriate foreign assistance to Ethiopia, but it is obvious that there are few areas where Ethiopia does not need foreign assistance to build her future after the decades of dictatorship, war, droughts, and economic policy failures. However, one of the most urgently needed areas of foreign assistance concerns investments in human development, in particular education. In comparison with other less developed countries, Ethiopia has a very low educational and literacy standard among its population. This applies to women in particular. If democracy is to have a chance to succeed, people must be able to read and understand the documents, e.g. papers and programmes, from the various political parties.

The low level of education among the Ethiopian population also causes a problem in the implementation of the economic reforms. In a market-oriented system of the kind that has now been opted for in Ethiopia, the economic performance of individuals, as well as of the economy at large, will be heavily dependent on the abilities, and thus on the qualifications, of the individual entrepreneurs, i.e. farmers, traders, manufacturers, etc. Thus, if the Ethiopian government is to achieve its objectives of democratising Ethiopia and decentralising power from the ministries out to the regions, and to realise its goal of transforming the economy into a market-oriented private-dominated economy, there is an obvious and urgent need for support in the field of education. This type of aid can also be motivated from a gender perspective. Today, Ethiopian women have a severe lack of education. This gives them a handicap not only in their working lives but also in their role as citizens in a democratic society.

Another area in which foreign assistance has an important, not to say crucial, role to play is in assisting Ethiopia in building new or reforming existing institutions to satisfy the needs of the new political and economic system. Examples of urgently needed institutions are the whole legislative system, in particular commercial law, which is crucial in the definition and protection of property rights. A reform of the financial sector is also urgently needed if the objective of encouraging the private sector is to be realised. To this should be added the need to reform and improve the governmental or public institutions, such as the various ministries and the tax authorities. Finally, to provide a basis for economic policy decision-making and evaluation, statistical data are of the utmost importance. Foreign assistance in this area should also be given high priority.

In conclusion, besides the reconstruction and emergency programme, which is already heavily involved with rebuilding the physical infrastructure, the role of foreign assistance is particularly important in the area of public administration, i.e. support in building institutions and providing education. It is particularly important to support these activities in rural areas where the vast majority of the population live and from where the economic growth and development must come. However, direct support to individual productive sectors, such as industry and agriculture, should be limited so as to avoid foreign assistance running into conflict with the overall objective of efficiency in the new economic system. From the point of view of economic efficiency, the major role of foreign assistance, besides emergency or catastrophe relief, should be to pave the way for the creation of a well-functioning economy, i.e. by assisting Ethiopia in the provision of education and appropriate market institutions.

APPENDIX A

Statistical tables relating to Figures 5.1–5.17

Table A.1 GDP per capita and domestic savings,
1966–1987

	GDP/capita (factor cost 1980 birr)	Domestic savings (% of GDP)
1966	199	10.6
1967	202	11.7
1968	200	12.1
1969	202	11.3
1970	208	11.2
1971	211	9.9
1972	215	10.8
1973	215	13.4
1974	212	13.3
1975	206	7.5
1976	206	8.7
1977	201	5.7
1978	193	1.9
1979	198	3.4
1980	204	3.7
1981	204	3.1
1982	200	2.2
1983	206	2.7
1984	193	2.4
1985	180	−1.8
1986	191	2.7
1987	183	3.0

Source: National Bank of Ethiopia

Table A.2 GDP by industrial origin, 1974/75–1993/94
(constant 1980/81 factor cost, millions of birr)

	Agricultural sector*	Other commodity sectors†	Services‡	GDP
1974/75	3640.1	1029.2	2258.4	6927.7
1975/76	3750.3	973.8	2324.2	7048.3
1976/77	3753.2	1001.6	2368.1	7122.9
1977/78	3698.5	968.8	2364.7	7032.0
1978/79	3789.1	1110.6	2552.5	7452.2
1979/80	3969.8	1217.2	2667.6	7854.6
1980/81	4071.5	1258.3	2766.8	8096.6
1981/82	3807.7	1312.5	2850.8	7971.0
1982/83	4204.2	1376.1	3030.1	8610.4
1983/84	3685.7	1460.1	3039.3	8185.1
1984/85	3125.3	1473.5	3105.1	7703.9
1985/86	3480.6	1516.0	3240.2	8236.8
1986/87	4008.7	1588.6	3426.9	9024.2
1987/88	3923.7	1604.9	3664.2	9192.8
1988/89	4011.4	1611.6	3718.8	9341.8
1989/90	4020.5	1537.9	3742.6	9301.0
1990/91	4042.7	1301.7	3635.0	8979.4
1991/92	3965.7	1226.4	3083.7	8275.8
1992/93§	4375.3	1379.4	3367.7	9122.4
1993/94§§	4311.7	1524.3	3559.2	9395.2

*Agricultural sector = agriculture + forestry + hunting and fishing

†Other commodity sectors = mining and quarrying + manufacturing + handicraft and small industry + building and construction + electricity and water

‡Services = wholesale and retail trade + transport and communication + financial services + public administration and defence + social services + dwellings and domestic services + others

§Estimated. Based on unpublished statistics from the Ethiopian authorities

§§Projected. Based on unpublished statistics from the Ethiopian authorities

Sources: 1974/75–1980/81: World Bank 1990, Annex: table 2.2

Table A.3 Agricultural production and food availability,
1979/80–1988/89 (volumes)

	Agricultural production per capita (1979/80 = 100)	*Per capita food availability (1979/80 = 100)*	*Agricultural food production per capita (1979/80 = 100)*
1979/80	100	100	100
1980/81	99	86	86
1981/82	95	80	81
1982/83	97	94	95
1983/84	84	79	77
1984/85	67	64	54
1985/86	72	72	59
1986/87	81	82	76
1987/88	78	79	71
1988/89	80	83	78

Source World Bank 1990, Annex

Table A.4 Expenditure on GDP, 1974/75–1992/93
(current market prices, millions of birr)

	Private consumption	*Public consumption*	*Gross fixed investments*	*Resource gap (negative)*
1974/75	4 405	730	580	164
1975/76	4 678	866	510	58
1976/77	5 542	968	561	217
1977/78	5 915	1240	545	405
1978/79	6 551	1168	699	425
1979/80	6 798	1293	854	440
1980/81	7 185	1400	922	603
1981/82	7 499	1487	1082	900
1982/83	7 371	1997	1240	849
1983/84	7 431	1879	1570	1044
1984/85	7 529	1957	1541	1103
1985/86	8 376	2103	1563	1137
1986/87	8 623	2230	1797	1251
1987/88	8 421	2846	1873	1239
1988/89	8 768	3040	1661	1098
1989/90	8 856	3386	1535	1244
1990/91	9 321	3753	1421	1163
1991/92	11 706	2165	1215	1578
1992/93	13 951	3208	3502	3853

Sources: 1974/75–1981/82 World Bank 1990, Annex: table 2.3
1982/83–1992/93: National Bank of Ethiopia

Table A.5 Resource gap and fiscal balance,
1974/75–1987/88 (% of GDP)

	Resource gap	Fiscal balance
1974/75	−3.00	−6.40
1975/76	−0.90	−7.10
1976/77	−3.10	−5.00
1977/78	−5.50	−7.10
1978/79	−5.30	−5.90
1979/80	−6.30	−6.80
1980/81	−7.20	−6.20
1981/82	−9.40	−8.50
1982/83	−8.50	−16.50
1983/84	−10.40	−9.20
1984/85	−11.20	−16.80
1985/86	−10.50	−12.80
1986/87	−11.10	−11.30
1987/88	−11.90	−11.40

Source: National Bank of Ethiopia

Table A.6 Central government expenditure, 1974/75–1992/93
(millions of birr)

	Capital expenditures	Current expenditures	Total government expenditures
1974/75	237.6	815.4	1053.0
1975/76	282.8	932.9	1215.7
1976/77	324.6	1043.8	1368.4
1977/78	329.4	1399.8	1729.2
1978/79	368.8	1520.8	1889.6
1979/80	443.2	1742.5	2185.7
1980/81	505.1	1854.1	2359.2
1981/82	715.0	1998.5	2713.5
1982/83	1245.3	2632.1	3877.4
1983/84	961.6	2236.7	3198.3
1984/85	944.5	2696.4	3640.9
1985/86	1471.9	2593.1	4065.0
1986/87	1219.3	2507.9	3727.2
1987/88	1226.2	2889.4	4115.6
1988/89	1499.4	3589.3	5088.7
1989/90	1144.9	3831.4	4976.3
1990/91	1217.1	3419.2	4636.3
1991/92	878.6	2867.5	3746.1
1992/93	1800.2	3309.8	5110.0

Sources: 1974/75–1982/83: World Bank 1990, Annex: tables 5.3 and 5.5
1983/84–1992/93: National Bank of Ethiopia, *Quarterly Bulletin*, various
issues

Table A.7 Central government current expenditure, 1974/75–1992/93
(millions of birr)

	General services	Economic services	Social services	Pensions	Interest and charges	Unallocated expenditures
1974/75	358.8	69.2	201.6	44.4	20.1	121.3
1975/76	496.4	80.9	198.4	48.6	32.9	75.7
1976/77	588.9	82.4	212.9	52.9	42.4	64.3
1977/78	916.3	90.4	227.2	57.2	48.3	60.4
1978/79	839.8	86.5	256.4	66.0	58.5	213.6
1979/80	917.3	100.1	286.1	68.1	63.5	307.4
1980/81	951.6	98.8	337.7	90.4	77.7	297.9
1981/82	1101.7	124.1	358.6	87.7	83.8	242.6
1982/83	1346.3	150.0	415.7	92.2	91.3	536.6
1983/84	1259.9	134.6	444.2	100.8	147.4	149.8
1984/85	1242.1	138.8	536.4	108.5	225.4	445.2
1985/86	1257.0	141.5	550.5	116.4	191.1	336.6
1986/87	1394.9	148.0	580.4	123.2	204.1	57.3
1987/88	1729.6	191.3	529.0	130.4	237.1	72.0
1988/89	2077.2	202.6	625.8	139.6	255.4	288.7
1989/90	2414.9	207.5	633.3	157.3	228.3	190.1
1990/91	2078.3	202.7	628.2	154.2	264.6	91.2
1991/92*	1133.6	234.8	705.8	197.4	345.4	250.5
1992/93*	1173.1	333.3	882.9	233.4	554.8	132.3

*Preliminary
Sources: 1974/75–1982/83: World Bank 1990, Annex: table 5.3
1983/84–1992/93: National Bank of Ethiopia, *Quarterly Bulletin*, various issues

Table A.8 Central government capital expenditure, 1974/75–1992/93
(millions of birr)

	Total capital expenditures	Economic development	Social development	Others
1974/75	237.6	194.0	39.2	4.4
1975/76	282.8	231.9	51.0	−0.1
1976/77	324.6	280.1	44.6	−0.1
1977/78	329.4	294.8	32.6	2.0
1978/79	368.8	320.7	45.7	2.4
1979/80	443.2	382.3	56.0	4.9
1980/81	505.1	431.9	68.5	4.7
1981/82	715.0	607.9	105.1	2.0
1982/83	1245.3	1144.1	88.9	12.3
1983/84	961.6	802.7	137.9	21.0
1984/85	944.5	852.7	79.4	12.4
1985/86	1471.9	1327.8	109.0	35.1
1986/87	1219.3	1058.2	121.6	39.5
1987/88	1226.2	1096.7	109.1	20.4
1988/89	1499.4	1307.7	146.9	44.8
1989/90	1144.9	1061.8	57.2	25.9
1990/91	1217.1	941.9	57.2	218.0
1991/92	878.6	807.9	55.2	15.5
1992/93	1800.2	1508.8	267.9	23.5

Sources: 1974/75–1982/83: World Bank 1990, Annex: table 5.5
1983/84–1992/93: National Bank of Ethiopia, *Quarterly Bulletin*, various issues

Table A.9 Central government revenue by source, 1974/75–1992/93 (millions of birr)

	Income and profit taxes	Rural land use fee	Domestic indirect tax	Import taxes	Export taxes	Non-tax revenue
1974/75	168.6	8.2	200.8	172.6	42.5	118.7
1975/76	160.8	13.4	183.6	171.4	86.1	165.6
1976/77	191.6	17.4	188.2	243.5	218.7	151.9
1977/78	206.5	19.3	188.7	238.3	281.8	252.5
1978/79	268.4	47.2	282.5	322.7	229.0	232.3
1979/80	332.0	48.3	385.5	239.4	297.3	265.0
1980/81	439.4	50.2	399.1	285.4	188.2	394.6
1981/82	515.3	48.8	403.8	277.1	190.4	441.3
1982/83	545.9	51.3	447.3	302.2	199.4	637.7
1983/84	601.3	151.5	501.3	314.2	253.7	524.4
1984/85	655.0	42.0	524.2	285.4	172.6	582.5
1985/86	722.0	44.0	556.0	291.3	263.0	929.8
1986/87	858.6	46.0	623.7	433.3	146.8	750.1
1987/88	1038.9	46.7	516.5	479.0	143.7	961.5
1988/89	1391.2	45.2	785.0	371.5	163.2	982.2
1989/90	972.9	35.9	764.9	425.9	56.8	837.0
1990/91	760.1	28.9	754.0	541.6	24.6	581.4
1991/92	614.1	3.9	531.7	425.4	8.2	540.8
1992/93	670.5	37.9	711.2	697.0	18.7	956.0

Sources: 1974/75–1982/83: World Bank 1990, Annex: table 5.2
1983/84–1992/93: National Bank, *Quarterly Bulletin*, various issues

Table A.10 Private international capital flows, 1965–1976
(millions of birr)

	Direct investments	Long-term loans (net)
1965	27.4	–0.5
1966	27.4	–1.1
1967	7.8	3.3
1968	13.2	5.7
1969	6.7	3.7
1970	9.6	3.7
1971	14.2	5.5
1972	22.3	6.8
1973	65.0	–0.8
1974	60.3	0.0
1975	39.6	–4.3
1976	8.7	–1.8

Source: National Bank of Ethiopia, no. 4, 1983

Table A.11 Rate of inflation, 1974–1991
(percentage change in Addis Ababa retail price index)

	General price index	Food price index
1974	8.6	8.6
1975	6.4	4.5
1976	28.6	41.9
1977	16.6	16.8
1978	14.3	17.0
1979	16.0	18.0
1980	4.5	5.2
1981	6.1	4.6
1982	5.6	6.0
1983	−0.4	0.7
1984	8.4	11.0
1985	19.1	25.2
1986	−9.8	−15.2
1987	−2.4	−6.1
1988	7.1	7.9
1989	7.8	6.5
1990	5.1	5.2
1991	35.7	41.3

Source: National Bank of Ethiopia

Table A.12 Import composition, 1974/75–1987/88 (millions of birr)

	Foods and live animals	Petroleum and petroleum products	Chemicals	Metal and metal manu-factures	Machinery including aircraft	Road motor vehicles	Other	Total
1974/75	18.7	112.8	93.0	52.8	90.0	68.3	253.2	688.8
1975/76	24.2	130.2	79.3	37.7	114.9	80.7	222.4	689.4
1976/77	33.9	164.4	65.6	42.3	90.0	110.5	403.7	910.4
1977/78	45.3	158.3	63.0	48.3	102.0	127.9	581.1	1125.9
1978/79	60.2	227.4	151.3	93.6	140.9	184.6	362.1	1220.1
1979/80	72.3	339.4	113.2	104.2	202.2	135.8	465.5	1432.6
1980/81	88.9	345.4	85.5	100.1	213.4	165.3	541.0	1539.6
1981/82	135.5	361.4	89.5	76.9	227.6	259.4	606.3	1756.6
1982/83	174.5	397.0	136.6	146.0	234.4	164.8	519.6	1772.9
1983/84	168.5	378.4	107.2	162.9	519.8	210.6	577.6	2125.0
1984/85	345.0	318.0	76.7	143.3	225.1	179.6	730.3	2018.0
1985/86	530.6	252.6	87.9	166.9	274.7	287.1	651.1	2250.9
1986/87	390.4	225.8	115.0	156.4	327.7	339.3	682.4	2237.0
1987/88	246.6	216.5	110.8	159.6	477.0	369.9	694.2	2274.6

Sources: Customs Office and National Bank of Ethiopia

Table A.13 Net barter terms of trade,
1974–1988 (1980 = 100)

	Terms of trade
1974	87.5
1975	82.4
1976	142.2
1977	198.8
1978	131.8
1979	132.2
1980	100.0
1981	84.0
1982	89.6
1983	91.0
1984	101.2
1985	99.1
1986	110.1
1987	83.5
1988	94.5

Source: World Bank 1990, Annex: table 3.13

Table A.14 Real effective exchange rates and resource balance,
1975–1988

	Resource gap (negative) (1980 = 100)	*Trade-weighted real effective exchange rate (1980 = 100)*
1975	15	80.7
1976	47	102.6
1977	82	109.4
1978	78	109.0
1979	76	110.2
1980	100	100.0
1981	144	110.3
1982	125	119.8
1983	153	125.8
1984	165	140.9
1985	154	168.6
1986	163	129.1
1987	165	113.6
1988	144	116.0

Sources: Real effective exchange rate: World Bank 1990, Annex: table 3.12
Resource gap: National Bank of Ethiopia

Table A.15 Export composition, 1974/75–1987/88
(millions of birr)

	Coffee	Pulses	Oilseeds	Hides and skins	Live animals	Petroleum	Other	Total
1974/75	117.5	73.5	89.1	37.2	16.9	7.4	134.6	476.2
1975/76	297.7	52.8	35.4	42.7	31.4	12.7	66.4	539.1
1976/77	408.9	48.6	26.9	52.3	3.6	26.0	80.0	646.3
1977/78	512.5	30.8	11.9	58.0	1.5	25.3	30.7	670.7
1978/79	541.6	17.9	9.6	107.1	1.5	28.2	39.0	744.9
1979/80	631.7	24.8	13.6	138.7	8.3	54.2	79.4	950.7
1980/81	524.3	23.7	28.4	92.7	9.8	76.1	96.5	851.5
1981/82	480.3	30.9	19.5	98.3	8.3	52.2	88.6	778.1
1982/83	495.9	28.8	15.3	77.3	16.3	68.8	108.1	810.5
1983/84	590.4	20.3	27.9	93.4	13.6	74.2	110.3	930.1
1984/85	466.3	16.9	15.6	95.4	19.7	67.3	62.1	743.3
1985/86	664.8	12.6	7.9	119.5	18.2	44.2	56.6	923.8
1986/87	524.3	8.5	9.8	108.3	15.6	27.3	101.0	794.8
1987/88	439.2	16.1	22.0	133.0	32.4	36.0	94.9	773.6

Sources: Customs Office and National Bank of Ethiopia

Table A.16 Per capita exports of major export commodities, 1974/75–1987/88
(volume index)

	Coffee	Pulses	Oilseeds	Hides and skins	Live animals
1974/75	64	456	1450	75	1950
1975/76	100	344	750	75	3800
1976/77	54	289	550	75	400
1977/78	71	178	250	100	150
1978/79	100	100	100	100	100
New series					
1979/80	100	100	100	100	100
1980/81	105	67	133	67	100
1981/82	91	100	100	100	100
1982/83	100	100	100	67	130
1983/84	105	78	266	67	110
1984/85	77	56	100	67	150
1985/86	73	33	33	100	170
1986/87	82	11	67	67	110
1987/88	68	33	133	67	310

Note: 1978/79 = 100 for 1974/75–1978/79; 1979/80 = 100 for 1979/80–1987/88
Source: World Bank 1990, Annex: table 3.3

Table A.17 Debt service ratio and international reserves

	Debt service ratio (a) (% of exports)	Debt service ratio (b) (% of exports)	Net international reserves (months of import cover)
1975			11.8
1976			13.3
1977			8.1
1978			5.8
1979/80	5.8		4.4
1980/81	8.6		3.1
1981/82	10.5		1.9
1982/83	12.3		2.5
1983/84	13.8	21.3	1.5
1984/85	21.5	30.9	0.8
1985/86	27.3	31.2	1.4
1986/87	28.4	40.6	3.1
1987/88	39.1	45.7	2.9
1988/89	39.5	45.6	0.7
1989/90		47.4	1.0

Sources: Debt service ratios: (a) Ministry of Finance, TGE 1991: 8, (b) World Bank 1987: 5, 1989: table 21, 1990: 4, IMF 1988: iv
International reserves: National Bank of Ethiopia

APPENDIX B

Statistical tables relating to Figures 7.1 and 7.2

Table B.1 Foreign exchange auctions, 1 May 1993–5 February 1994

	Marginal rate	Highest bid	Amount of US dollars actually sold (millions)
1 May 1993	5.00	7.00	3.55335
15 May 1993	5.00	6.50	5.04701
29 May 1993	5.00	7.05	6.30600
12 June 1993	5.00	6.50	9.97492
26 June 1993	5.10	6.56	6.04708
10 July 1993	5.20	6.10	6.00000
24 July 1993	5.35	5.76	6.25153
7 August 1993	5.56	6.50	6.03887
21 August 1993	5.90	6.51	6.57044
4 September 1993	5.90	6.75	10.29104
18 September 1993	5.10	6.40	8.90927
2 October 1993	5.01	6.10	6.87269
16 October 1993	5.18	6.05	5.53278
30 October 1993	5.41	5.75	5.51566
13 November 1993	5.61	6.05	6.15717
27 November 1993	5.61	6.51	7.01546
11 December 1993	5.80	6.10	8.05103
25 December 1993	5.86	6.20	8.42023
8 January 1994	5.77	6.12	8.06796
22 January 1994	5.82	6.01	7.99689
5 February 1994	5.92	6.06	8.22557

Source: Unpublished memo from IMF, Addis Ababa

175

Table B.2 Development of the composition and the number of items on the National
Bank's negative list, 1 May 1993–1 March 1994

	Original list as of 1 May 1993	Negative list as of 5 September 1993	Negative list as of 1 March 1994
0 Food and live animals	27	22	12
1 Beverages and tobacco	3	3	3
2 Crude materials, inedible	16	10	4
4 Animal oils and fats	5	4	0
5 Chemicals	1	1	1
6 Manufactured goods	27	11	7
7 Machinery and transport	4	4	4
8 Miscellaneous manufactured goods	17	16	10
9 Unclassified commodities	2	2	2
Total number of items	102	73	43

Source: National Bank of Ethiopia

APPENDIX C

Statistical tables relating to Figures 8.1–8.4

Table C.1 Fiscal policy, 1989/90–1993/94

	Fiscal balance (% of GDP at current factor cost)	*Fiscal revenue before grants (% of GDP)*	*Fiscal expenditures (% of GDP)*
1989/90	−16.47	27.04	43.51
1990/91	−15.80	19.80	35.60
1991/92	−14.00	16.30	30.30
1992/93	−15.40	16.10	31.50
1993/94	−22.80	20.50	43.30

Source: National Bank of Ethiopia

Table C.2 Foreign trade, 1989/90–1992/93

	Exports of goods and non-factor services		*Imports of goods and non-factor services*		*Resource balance*	
	Millions of birr	*(% of GDP)*	*Millions of birr*	*(% of GDP)*	*Millions of birr*	*(% of GDP)*
1989/90	1369	10.92	2613	20.85	−1244	−9.93
1990/91	1450	10.88	2613	19.6	−1163	−8.72
1991/92	1039	7.69	2617	19.37	−1578	−11.68
1992/93	3165	18.83	7018	41.75	−3853	−22.92

Source: National Bank of Ethiopia

Table C.3 Seigniorage and inflation, 1989/90–1993/94

	Seigniorage (% of GDP)	Inflation (%)
1989/90	8.6404	5.2
1990/91	13.1938	20.9
1991/92	9.7274	21.0
1992/93	2.4036	10.0
1993/94	−1.6350	1.3

Source: National Bank of Ethiopia

Table C.4 Exchange rates and prices

	ECU/US$	*General retail price index for Addis Ababa*
1989:6	0.9552	521.5
1989:7	0.9137	524.4
1989:8	0.9278	527.5
1989:9	0.9406	514.1
1989:10	0.9066	522.5
1989:11	0.8939	533.1
1989:12	0.8562	524.8
1990:1	0.8318	533.6
1990:2	0.8208	522.4
1990:3	0.8352	512.6
1990:4	0.8254	525.8
1990:5	0.8110	544.0
1990:6	0.8177	547.6
1990:7	0.7926	540.1
1990:8	0.7598	546.4
1990:9	0.7614	555.3
1990:10	0.7395	555.8
1990:11	0.7243	553.2
1990:12	0.7394	593.8
1991:1	0.7364	625.5
1991:2	0.7224	661.4
1991:3	0.7809	722.2
1991:4	0.8264	744.8
1991:5	0.8341	761.4
1991:6	0.8686	794.0
1991:7	0.8695	772.5
1991:8	0.8501	765.1
1991:9	0.8269	754.9
1991:10	0.8255	747.5
1991:11	0.7950	773.4
1991:12	0.7690	740.8
1992:1	0.7724	731.5
1992:2	0.7918	783.3
1992:3	0.8127	781.2
1992:4	0.8049	803.7
1992:5	0.7886	798.5
1992:6	0.7673	810.3
1992:7	0.7297	824.4
1992:8	0.7133	854.5
1992:9	0.7225	857.0
1992:10	0.7544	863.2
1992:11	0.8070	852.6
1992:12	0.8071	836.4
1993:1	0.8254	834.8
1993:2	0.8458	836.0

Sources: IMF, International Financial Statistics, National Bank of Ethiopia

NOTES

2 ANALYTICAL FRAMEWORK

1 The economic literature contains a number of, in general largely overlapping, definitions of the concept *economic system*. See, for example, Prybyla (1969), Lindbeck (1973: 3), and Eidem and Viotti (1978: 1).

3 *ETHIOPIA TIKDEM*: THE CREATION OF THE SOCIALIST ECONOMY

1 For a more complete description of the process that led up to the 20 December programme, see, for instance, Clapham (1990: 42ff), Schwab (1985: 24ff), and in particular Tiruneh (1993: 86ff).
2 For a politically oriented analysis, see, for example, Clapham (1990) and Schwab (1985).
3 For a closer analysis of the nationalisation of urban lands and extra houses, see, for instance, Schwab (1985: 31f) and Tiruneh (1993: 115f). The following analysis does not deal with urban land reform, since this had mainly a political and household income and wealth effect. A much more limited influence of this reform is likely on the functioning of the productive sectors, and thereby on the overall functioning of the Ethiopian economy, in which the main interests of this study lie.
4 See Dessalegn Rahmato (1984: chapter 3) and Pausewang (1990b) for an analysis of Ethiopian land reform. For a background to the reform, see Cohen and Weintraub (1975: chapter 2) and Dessalegn Rahmato (1984: chapter 2).
5 For a background to and closer description of the villagisation programme see Africa Watch (1991: chapter 13) and Clapham (1990: 174ff).
6 On agrarian socialism see Cohen (1987: 161ff), Cohen and Isaksson (1987), Clapham (1990: chapter 7), Alemayehu Lirenso (1990), Brüne (1990: 27ff), Dessalegn Rahmato (1990), Alemneh Dejene (1987: chapter 4, 1990), Pankhurst (1990), Pausewang (1990b), and Ståhl (1989). On agricultural surplus extraction see, for instance, Befekadu Degefe and Tesfaye Tafesse (1990) and Eshetu Chole (1990).

4 EXPECTED ECONOMIC EFFECTS OF THE
ETHIOPIA TIKDEM PERIOD

1 If, however, manufacturing is capital-intensive relative to non-peasant agri-culture, $k_M > k_C$, the tendency for a negative outcome for non-peasant employment depends on (i) the magnitude of the difference in capital intensities between the two capital-using sectors (the smaller the difference, the stronger the tendency for a negative effect on non-peasant employment), (ii) the supply response in the capital market to the institutional changes in manufacturing (the greater K_r and K_{IM} the stronger the tendency for a negative effect on non-peasant employment), (iii) the land–labour ratio (R_C/L_C) and finally on (iv) the complementarity of labour and land (C_{LR}) in non-peasant agriculture (the greater the land–labour ratio and the higher the complementarity between land and labour, the stronger the tendency for a negative effect on non-peasant employ-ment), *ceteris paribus*.

6 *ETHIOPIA TIKDEM* REVISED: PRESIDENT
MENGISTU'S REFORM ANNOUNCEMENTS

1 See Stewart (1987: 43). For a discussion and analysis of the World Bank and IMF policy in Africa, see also Loxley (1987), Svendsen (1987), and UNECA (1989, 1991).
2 For a more complete description of the steps taken after the 1988 resolutions up to March 1990, see Eshetu Chole and Makonnen Manyazewal (1992: 35).
3 The following description of the reform of March 1990 is based on Mengistu (1990) and the *Ethiopian Herald* from 8 March 1990.
4 See Dornbusch (1989) and Dornbusch and Kuenzler (1993).

7 *ETHIOPIA TIKDEM* FAREWELL: THE
TRANSITIONAL ECONOMIC POLICY

1 Having discussed the draft policy paper at the EMI Workshop for Cabinet Members on the Future of the Ethiopian Economic System and Macroeconomic Management, November 1991, and at the Inter-Africa Group Symposium on Rehabilitating the Ethiopian Economy, January 1992, it is my view that the reasons behind this problem were and to some extent still are based on a natural scepticism towards the potentials of the market mechanism and a lack of knowledge of the functioning of a market economy after seventeen years of socialist rule. In particular the scepticism relates to the short-term effects of economic reforms where there is an obvious risk of running into rapid unemployment problems and price increases and thus increased poverty before there is a supply response. To some extent the scepticism is also based on the experiences of nearby countries that have introduced economic reform pro-grammes (see UNECA 1989, 1991: 2f).
2 The higher figures are from Africa Confidential 1991 and the lower figures are from interviews by the author in Addis Ababa in March 1991.
3 The negative list was eliminated in February 1995.

8 EXPECTED AND ACTUAL EFFECTS OF THE TRANSITIONAL POLICY

1 The parallel and quite openly offered exchange rate varied around 6–7 birr per US dollar in January 1992.

9 POST-*ETHIOPIA TIKDEM*: POSSIBILITIES AND OBSTACLES FOR GROWTH AND DEVELOPMENT

1 For the experience from different less developed countries, see Hansson (1993d).
2 For a general economic-theoretical analysis of DUP activities, see Bhagwati (1982). For an analysis of rent-seeking and economic growth in Africa, see Gallagher (1991).
3 For a description and analysis of African democracy, see Diamond *et al.* (1988).
4 For an analysis of the choice between a presidential and a parliamentary system, see Linz (1990), Horowitz (1990), and Hyden (1993).
5 In May 1993, however, there was a conference on constitutionalism arranged by the Inter-Africa Group (see Inter-Africa Group 1993).
6 Oromo Liberation Front (1993: 3f). For the history of the Oromo issue, see Sisai Ibssa (1990).
7 The Southern Peoples' region was formed in late 1992 by the elected representatives of five of the south-west regions. This means that the number of regions in Ethiopia was reduced to ten.

REFERENCES

Adelman, I. (1991) 'Institutional change, economic development, and the environment', paper presented at the Holger Crafoord Lectures 1991, Lund University.

Africa Confidential (1991) 'Ethiopia: the market effect', *Africa Confidential* 32 (2): 3–4.

Africa Watch (1991) *Evil Days: 30 Years of War and Famine in Ethiopia*, New York, Washington, Los Angeles and London: Human Rights Watch.

Africa Watch (1992) *News from Africa Watch, May 8*, Washington, D.C.: Africa Watch.

Alemayehu Lirenso (1990) 'Villagization: policies and prospects', in Pausewang, S., Fantu Cheru, S. Brüne, and Eshetu Chole (eds), *Ethiopia: Rural Development Options*, London and New Jersey: Zed Books.

Alemneh Dejene (1987) *Peasants, Agrarian Socialism, and Rural Development in Ethiopia*, Boulder and London: Westview Press.

Alemneh Dejene (1990) 'Peasants, environment, resettlement', in Pausewang, S., Fantu Cheru, S. Brüne, and Eshetu Chole (eds), *Ethiopia: Rural Development Options*, London and New Jersey: Zed Books.

Alemu Mekonnen (1992) 'Efficiency of Ethiopian manufacturing enterprises and the policy environment', *Ethiopian Journal of Economics* 1 (2): 38–52.

Azam, J-P., D. Bevan, P. Collier, S. Dercon, and J. Gunning (1993) *Some Economic Consequences of the Transition from Civil War to Peace*, Oxford: Centre for the Study of African Economies.

Befekadu Degefe and Tesfaye Tafesse (1990) 'The marketing and pricing of agricultural products', in Pausewang, S., Fantu Cheru, S. Brüne, and Eshetu Chole (eds), *Ethiopia: Rural Development Options*, London and New Jersey: Zed Books.

Berhanu Abegaz (ed.) (1994) *Essays on Ethiopian Economic Development*, Aldershot, UK and Brookfield, Missouri: Avebury.

Bhagwati, J. (1982) 'Directly unproductive profit-seeking (DUP) activities', *Journal of Political Economy* 90: 988–1002.

Bourdet, Y. (1992) 'Reforming Laos' economic system', *Economic Systems* 16: 63–88.

Brüne, S. (1990) 'The agricultural sector', in Pausewang, S., Fantu Cheru, S. Brüne, and Eshetu Chole (eds), *Ethiopia: Rural Development Options*, London and New Jersey: Zed Books.

Bulti Terfassa (1990) 'Recent trends in the development of manufacturing industries in Ethiopia', in Pausewang, S., Fantu Cheru, S. Brüne, and Eshetu Chole (eds), *Ethiopia: Rural Development Options*, London and New Jersey: Zed Books.

Bulti Terfassa (1992) 'Recent trends in the development of manufacturing industries in Ethiopia', in Mekonen Taddesse (ed.), *The Ethiopian Economy: Structure,*

Problems and Policy Issues, Addis Ababa: Addis Ababa University.

Census of Manufacturing Industries in Ethiopia, 1990, Addis Ababa: Central Statistics Office.

Clapham, C. (1989) 'The state and revolution in Ethiopia', *Review of African Political Economy* 44: 5–17.

Clapham, C. (1990) *Transformation and Continuity in Revolutionary Ethiopia*, African Studies Series no. 61, Cambridge: Cambridge University Press.

Cohen, J.M. (1987) *Integrated Rural Development: The Ethiopian Experience and the Debate*, Uppsala: Scandinavian Institute of African Studies.

Cohen, J.M. and N.-I. Isaksson (1987) *Villagization in the Arsi Region of Ethiopia*, Swedish Rural Development Studies no. 19, Uppsala: University of Agricultural Sciences, International Rural Development Centre.

Cohen, J.M. and D. Weintraub (1975) *Land and Peasants in Imperial Ethiopia: The Social Background to a Revolution*, Assen, The Netherlands: Van Gorcum and Comp. B.V.

Considerations on the Economic Policy of Ethiopia for the Next Few Years (1985) Report prepared by the team of Soviet consulting advisers attached to the NCCP of Socialist Ethiopia, Addis Ababa.

Dawit Woldi Giorgis (1989) *Red Tears: War, Famine and Revolution in Ethiopia*, Trenton, New Jersey: The Red Sea Press.

DEP (1975) *The Declaration on Economic Policy of Socialist Ethiopia*, Addis Ababa, 7 February.

Dessalegn Rahmato (1984) *Agrarian Reform in Ethiopia*, Uppsala: Scandinavian Institute of African Studies.

Dessalegn Rahmato (1990) 'Cooperatives, state farms and smallholder production', in Pausewang, S., Fantu Cheru, S. Brüne, and Eshetu Chole (eds), *Ethiopia: Rural Development Options*, London and New Jersey: Zed Books.

Diamond, L., J.J. Linz, and S.M. Lipset (eds) (1988) *Democracy in Developing Countries: Africa*, Boulder, Colorado and London: Lynne Rienner Publisher and Adamantine Press.

Dornbusch, R. (1989) 'Overvaluation and trade balance', in Dornbusch, R., F. Leslie, and C.H. Helmers (eds), *The Open Economy: Tools for Policymakers in Developing Countries*, New York: Oxford University Press.

Dornbusch, R. (1993) 'Introduction', in Dornbusch, R. (ed.), *Policymaking in the Open Economy: Concepts and Case Studies in Economic Performance*, New York: Oxford University Press.

Dornbusch, R. and L.T. Kuenzler (1993) 'Exchange rate policy: options and issues', in Dornbusch, R. (ed.), *Policymaking in the Open Economy: Concepts and Case Studies in Economic Performance*, New York: Oxford University Press.

Draft Policy Paper (1991) *Draft Economic Policy of Ethiopia During the Transition* (unofficial translation), Addis Ababa, August.

Eidem, R. and S. Viotti (1978) *Economic Systems*, Oxford: Martin Robertson.

Eshetu Chole (1990) 'Agriculture and surplus extraction', in Pausewang, S., Fantu Cheru, S. Brüne, and Eshetu Chole (eds), *Ethiopia: Rural Development Options*, London and New Jersey: Zed Books.

Eshetu Chole and Makonnen Manyazewal (1992) 'The macroeconomic performance of the Ethiopian economy', in Mekonen Taddesse (ed.), *The Ethiopian Economy: Structure, Problems and Policy Issues*, Addis Ababa: Addis Ababa University.

Ethiopian Herald (1988) 8–12 November, Addis Ababa.

Ethiopian Herald (1989) 17 June, Addis Ababa.

FAO (1991) *FAO Crop Assessment Mission Report, Ethiopia, October–December 1990*, Rome: FAO.

184

Fischer, S. (1987) 'Economic growth and economic policy', in Corbo, V., M. Goldstein, and M. Khan (eds), *Growth-Oriented Adjustment Programs*, Washington, D.C.: IMF and World Bank.

Gallagher, M. (1991) *Rent-Seeking and Economic Growth in Africa*, Boulder, San Francisco and Oxford: Westview Press.

Gelb, A. (1993) 'Socialist transformations: some lessons and implications for assistance', in SIDA, *Redefining the Roles of the State and Market in the Development Process*, Stockholm: SIDA.

Goyder, H. and C. Goyder (1988) 'Case studies of famine: Ethiopia', in Curtis, D., M. Hubbard, and A. Shepherd (eds), *Preventing Famine: Policies and Prospects for Africa*, London: Routledge.

Griffin, K. (ed.) (1992) *The Economy of Ethiopia*, Basingstoke, London and New York: Macmillan Press and St. Martin's Press.

Hansson, G. (1989) *Ethiopia: Macroeconomic Performance, Economic Policy and Swedish Aid*, Macroeconomic Studies no. 1/89, Stockholm: The Planning Secretariat, SIDA.

Hansson, G. (1990) *Ethiopia 1990: A Change of Economic System? A Critical Assessment of the Economic Reform Programme of March 5th, 1990*, Macroeconomic Studies no. 9/1990, Stockholm: The Planning Secretariat, SIDA.

Hansson, G. (1993a) 'Ethiopia away from socialism', in Blomström, M. and M. Lundahl (eds), *Responses to the Economic Crisis in Africa*, London and New York: Routledge.

Hansson, G. (1993b) 'International trade and economic growth – the experience of Ethiopia', in Hansson, G. (ed.), *Trade, Growth and Development*, London and New York: Routledge.

Hansson, G. (1993c) 'Ethiopia: towards the year 2000 – prospects for economic development', in *Changing Realities in the Horn of Africa: The Challenges of Political Pluralism and Economic Reconstruction, Proceedings, 7th International Conference on the Horn of Africa, May 23–24, 1992*, New York: Center for the Study of the Horn of Africa, City College of CUNY.

Hansson, G. (ed.) (1993d) *Trade, Growth and Development – The Role of Politics and Institutions*, London and New York: Routledge.

Hansson, G. (1993e) *Transition in Ethiopia 1991–1993*, Macroeconomic Studies no. 45/93, Stockholm: The Planning Secretariat, SIDA.

Hansson, G. (1994) *From GATT to WTO – A Potential for or a Threat to Economic Development*, Stockholm: The Planning Secretariat, SIDA.

Hansson, G. (1995) *Ethiopia 1994: Economic Achievements and Reform Problems*, Macroeconomic Studies no.61/95, Stockholm: The Planning Secretariat, SIDA.

Harberger, A.C. (1984) 'Economic growth and economic policy', in Harberger, A.C. (ed.), *World Economic Growth*, San Francisco: Institute for Contemporary Studies.

Horowitz, D.L. (1990) 'Comparing democratic systems', *Journal of Democracy* 1: 73–79.

Hyden, G. (1993) 'Electoral systems and political reform', in Inter-Africa Group, *Constitutionalism: Reflections and Recommendations*, Addis Ababa: Inter-Africa Group.

IMF (1988) *Ethiopia – Recent Economic Developments*, SM/88/239, Washington, D.C.: IMF.

IMF. *Direction of Trade Statistics Yearbook, 1982, 1988, 1989.*

Inter-Africa Group (1992) *Final Report of the Symposium on Rehabilitating the Ethiopian Economy, 15–18 January 1992, Africa Hall, Addis Ababa*, Addis Ababa: Inter-Africa Group.

185

REFERENCES

Inter-Africa Group (1993) *Constitutionalism: Reflections and Recommendations*, Addis Ababa: Inter-Africa Group.
Kidane Mengisteab (1990) *Ethiopia: Failure of Land Reform and Agricultural Crisis*, New York, Westport, Connecticut, and London: Greenwood Press.
Kirsch, O.C., F.V. Göricke and J.F.G. Wörz (1989) *Agricultural Revolution and Peasant Emancipation in Ethiopia: A Missed Opportunity*, Saarbrüchen, Fort Lauderdale: Verlag breitenbach.
Koopmans, T. and J. Montias (1971) 'Description and comparison of economic systems', in Eckstein, A. (ed.), *Comparison of Economic Systems*, Berkeley: University of California Press.
Korn, D.A. (1986) *Ethiopia, The United States and The Soviet Union*, Carbondale and Edwardsville: Southern Illinois University Press.
Krueger, A. (1990) 'Government failures in development', *Journal of Economic Perspective* 4 (3): 9–23.
Lefort, R. (1983) (translated by A.M. Berrett) *Ethiopia: An Heretical Revolution?*, London: Zed Press.
Lewis, A.W. (1954) 'Economic development with unlimited supplies of labour', *The Manchester School of Economics and Social Studies* 22: 139–191.
Lijphart, A. (1991) 'Constitutional choices for new democracies', *Journal of Democracy* 2: 72–84.
Lijphart, A. (1992) 'Democratization and constitutional choices in Czecho-Slovakia, Hungary and Poland 1989–91', *Journal of Theoretical Politics* 4: 207–223.
Lindbeck, A. (1973) 'Ekonomiska system – ett mångdimensionellt fenomen', *Ekonomisk Debatt* 1: 3–18.
Linz, J.J. (1990) 'The perils of presidentialism', *Journal of Democracy* 1: 51–69.
Loxley, J. (1987) 'The IMF, the World Bank, and sub-Saharan Africa: policies and politics', in Havnevik, K.J. (ed.), *The IMF and the World Bank in Africa*, Uppsala: Scandinavian Institute of African Studies.
Mekonen Taddesse (ed.) (1992) *The Ethiopian Economy: Structure, Problems and Policy Issues, Proceedings of the First Annual Conference on the Ethiopian Economy*, Addis Ababa: Addis Ababa University.
Mengistu, H.M. (1988) *Interview Granted to the New York Times, November 26, 1988*, Addis Ababa: Ministry of Information Press Department.
Mengistu, H.M. (1990) *Report by Mengistu Haile Mariam, Resolutions Adopted by the Plenum*, Documents of the 11th Plenum of the CC WPE, Addis Ababa, March.
Mishra, S. (1991) 'The identification and management of critical economic inter-linkages in the Ethiopian economy', paper presented at the Ethiopian Management Institute's Executive Workshop for Ministerial Cabinet Members, 7–10 November, Addis Ababa and Debre-Zeit.
Morris, C.T. and I. Adelman (1989) 'Nineteenth-century development experience and lessons for today', *World Development* 17 (9): 1417–1432.
National Bank of Ethiopia. *Quarterly Bulletin of Statistics*, various issues, Addis Ababa: National Bank of Ethiopia.
Negarit Gazeta (1991) 'Peaceful and democratic transitional conference of Ethiopia', 50th Year, no. 1, 22 July, Addis Ababa.
Negarit Gazeta (various issues) Addis Ababa.
North, D. (1990) *Institutions, Institutional Change and Economic Performance*, Cambridge: Cambridge University Press.
Oberai, A.S. (1992) 'An overview of settlement policies and programs', in Dieci, P. and C. Viezzoli (eds), *Resettlement and Rural Development in Ethiopia*, Milano: Franco Angeli.
Oromo Liberation Front, Central Committee (1993) *Statement of the Secretary*

REFERENCES

General on the State of the Oromo People's Struggle, Addis Ababa, 1 March.
Oshima, H.T. (1991) 'Impacts of economic development on labour markets, education and population in Asia', paper presented at the Holger Crafoord Lectures 1991, Lund University, Lund.
Ottaway, M. (ed.) (1990) *The Political Economy of Ethiopia*, New York: Praeger.
Otunnu, O.A. (1992) 'Africa: between uncertainties and hope', in *Change: Threat or Opportunity? Political Change*, New York: United Nations.
Pankhurst, A. (1990) 'Resettlement: policy and practice', in Pausewang, S., Fantu Cheru, S. Brüne, and Eshetu Chole (eds), *Ethiopia: Rural Development Options*, London and New Jersey, Zed Books.
Pausewang, S. (1990a) 'The peasant perspective', in Pausewang, S., Fantu Cheru, S. Brüne, and Eshetu Chole (eds), *Ethiopia: Rural Development Options*, London and New Jersey: Zed Books.
Pausewang, S. (1990b) 'Meret Le Arrashu', in Pausewang, S., Fantu Cheru, S. Brüne, and Eshetu Chole (eds), *Ethiopia: Rural Development Options*, London and New Jersey: Zed Books.
Pickett, J. (1991) *Economic Development in Ethiopia: Agriculture, the Market and the State*, Paris: OECD.
Polyakov, G. (1990) 'Soviet–Ethiopian cooperation in agriculture', in Pausewang, S., Fantu Cheru, S. Brüne, and Eshetu Chole (eds), *Ethiopia: Rural Development Options*, London and New Jersey: Zed Books.
Prybyla, J.S. (1969) 'Meaning and classification of economic systems: An outline', in Prybyla, J.S. (ed.), *Comparative Economic Systems*, New York: Appleton-Century-Crofts.
Ramamurti, R. (1991) 'The search for remedies', in Ramamurti, R. and R. Vernon (eds), *Privatization and Control of State-Owned Enterprises*, Washington, D.C.: Economic Development Institute of the World Bank.
Ranis, G. (1988) 'Analytics of development: dualism', in Chenery, H. and T.N. Srinivasan (eds), *Handbook of Development Economics, Volume 1*, Amsterdam: North-Holland.
Schwab, P. (1981) 'Socialist Ethiopia', in Szajkowski, B. (ed.), *Marxist Governments, A World Survey*, vol. 2, London: Macmillan.
Schwab, P. (1985) *Ethiopia: Politics, Economics and Society*, London: Frances Pinter.
Scully, G.W. (1992) *Constitutional Environments and Economic Growth*, Princeton, New Jersey: Princeton University Press.
Sisai Ibssa (1990) 'The question of colonialism in the Horn of Africa: the Oromo case', in *Conditions for the Possibility of Peace in the Horn of Africa, Proceedings 4th International Conference on the Horn of Africa, May 26–28, 1989*, New York: Center for the Study of the Horn of Africa, City College of CUNY.
Stewart, F. (1987) 'Should conditionality change?', in Havnevik, K.J. (ed.), *The IMF and the World Bank in Africa*, Uppsala: Scandinavian Institute of African Studies.
Ståhl, M. (1989) 'Capturing the peasants through cooperatives: the case of Ethiopia', *Review of African Political Economy* 44.
Ståhl, M. (1990) *Ethiopia: A Macro-Political Survey*, Stockholm: SIDA.
Svendsen, K.E. (1987) 'The Nordic countries and the IMF/World Bank', in Havnevik, K.J. (ed.), *The IMF and the World Bank in Africa*, Uppsala: Scandinavian Institute of African Studies.
Teferra Demiss (1994) 'Allocation of management and supervisory responsibilities in State-owned enterprises in comparative perspective: a cursory review', *Birritu* no. 55, May.
Tegegne Teka (1988) 'The State and rural cooperatives in Ethiopia', in Hedlund, H.

REFERENCES

(ed.), *Cooperatives Revisited*, Uppsala: Scandinavian Institute of African Studies.

TGE (1991) *Ethiopia's Economic Policy During the Transition Period* (official translation), November, Addis Ababa.

Tiruneh, A. (1993) *The Ethiopian Revolution 1974–1987: A Transformation from an Aristocratic to a Totalitarian Autocracy*, Cambridge and New York: Cambridge University Press.

UNDP. *Human Development Report*, various issues, New York and Oxford: Oxford University Press.

UNECA (1989) *African Alternative Framework to Structural Adjustment Programmes for Socio-Economic Recovery and Transformation*, Addis Ababa: United Nations Economic Commission for Africa.

UNECA (1991) *African Alternative Framework to Structural Adjustment Programmes for Socio-Economic Recovery and Transformation: Selected Policy Instruments*, Addis Ababa: United Nations Economic Commission for Africa.

Vuylsteke, C. (1988) *Techniques of Privatization of State-Owned Enterprises, Volume I, Methods and Implementation*, Washington, D.C.: The World Bank.

World Bank (1987a) *Ethiopia: Recent Economic Developments and Prospects for Recovery and Growth*, Report no. 5929-ET, Washington, D.C.: The World Bank.

World Bank (1987b) *Ethiopia: Agriculture – A Strategy for Growth, A Sector Review*, Report no. 6512-ET, Washington, D.C.: The World Bank.

World Bank (1989) *Sub-Saharan Africa: From Crisis to Sustainable Growth*, Washington, D.C.: The World Bank.

World Bank (1990) *Ethiopia's Economy in the 1980s and Framework for Accelerated Growth*, Report no. 8062-ET, Washington, D.C.: The World Bank.

World Bank (1992a) *Towards Poverty Alleviation and a Social Action Program, Preliminary Mission Conclusions*, Addis Ababa, 7 May: The World Bank.

World Bank (1992b) *Ethiopia: Policy Framework Paper, 1992/93–1994/95*, 5 October, Washington, D.C.: The World Bank.

World Bank (1994a) *Adjustment in Africa – Reforms, Results, and the Road Ahead*, New York: Oxford University Press.

World Bank (1994b) *Public Expenditure Review – Data*, Addis Ababa: World Bank Resident Mission in Ethiopia.

World Development Report, various issues, New York: The World Bank and Oxford University Press.

INDEX

administrative processes/markets dimension: economic system approach 10, 11

administration, public: need for foreign aid 163; regionalisation 157–8

Afars 28

Africa Watch 149

Agricultural Development Led Industrialisation (ADLI) 118

Agricultural Marketing Corporation (AMC) 31–2, 50

agriculture: in dual economy model 12–14; in *Ethiopia Tikdem* period 23, 25, 26–33; expected effects of *Ethiopia Tikdem* 44–5, 46–52, 55–66; expected effects of transitional policy 130–2; in institutional dual economy model 15–18; private sector 85, 106; production 59–62, 130, 155, 165, 166; transitional policy 105–7, 118, 133–4

arms imports 71, 92, 100

assets, company: sale of 123

auctions: foreign exchange 114–15, 136, 175

autarky/internationalisation dimension: economic systems approach 10–11

Bourdet, Y. 158

budgets, government: *Ethiopia Tikdem* period 62–5; transitional period 111

buy-outs: management/employee 123

capital 170; expected effects of *Ethiopia Tikdem* 43–6; in institutional dual economy model 15–18

capital accumulation 81–2

Census of Manufacturing Industries in Ethiopia 1990 118–19

central planning 83, 85, 100

centralisation/decentralisation dimension: economic systems approach 9–10

civil war: costs of 5, 22, 58–9, 73, 92; demoralisation in 53–5, 94, 100–1; economic uncertainty in 120; effect on foreign aid 99; imports 71, 92, 100; termination 130, 132

cleansing campaigns 2–3; *see also* human rights violation

co-operatives 29–31, 77–8; *see also* producer co-operatives; service co-operatives

Cohen, J.M. 33–4

collective ownership/private ownership dimension: economic systems approach 10

collectivisation 61, 105; *Ethiopia Tikdem* period 23–4, 29–33; expected effects of *Ethiopia Tikdem* 40–1, 48; *see also* producer co-operatives; service co-operatives

commercial agriculture 85, 106; in institutional dual economy model 15–18; nationalised 25, 28–9

commercial law 162–3

commercial-bank lending 136

communist countries: support from 36, 71, 89; *see also* Soviet Union

competition/non-competition dimension: economic systems approach 10–11

compromise, political 147

Confederation of Ethiopian Labour Unions (CELU) 2

consumer goods 81

Coordinating Committee of the Armed Forces, Police and the Territorial Army (Derg) 1–3, 20–3; nationalisation 24–6; *see also Ethiopia Tikdem*

coup d'état: against *Ethiopia Tikdem* 92

debt, foreign 90, 91, 174; *Ethiopia Tikdem* period 63, 71–2, 73

decentralisation 160; through regionalisation 154–8

decentralisation/centralisation dimension: economic systems approach 9–10

Declaration on Economic Policy of Socialist Ethiopia (DEP) 2, 3, 20–1, 22

defence resources: *Ethiopia Tikdem* period 53–5, 63–4, 86, 92, 100–1; transitional period 130

democracy: transitional policy 3–4, 146–54, 160

denationalisation: State-owned enterprises 122, 124–5; *see also* privatisation

deregulation 93, 124

devaluation 93, 96; transitional policy 111, 114, 130, 139, 141

directly unproductive profit (DUP) 146

domestic savings *see* savings

Draft Economic Policy of Ethiopia During the Transition 103–12

droughts *see* famines

dual economy model 12–14; expected effects of *Ethiopia Tikdem* 39–42; March reforms 94;

189

DATE